RAILROADED

FRAMED FOR MURDER, FIGHTING FOR JUSTICE

SAMUEL L. SOMMER
CHRISTOPHER JOSSART

WildBluePress.com

RAILROADED published by:

WILDBLUE PRESS
P.O. Box 102440
Denver, Colorado 80250

Publisher Disclaimer: Any opinions, statements of fact or fiction, descriptions, dialogue, and citations found in this book were provided by the author, and are solely those of the author. The publisher makes no claim as to their veracity or accuracy, and assumes no liability for the content.

Copyright 2019 by Samuel L. Sommer and Christopher Jossart

All rights reserved. No part of this book may be reproduced in any form or by any means without the prior written consent of the Publisher, excepting brief quotes used in reviews.

WILDBLUE PRESS is registered at the U.S. Patent and Trademark Offices.

ISBN 978-1-948239-07-3   Trade Paperback
ISBN 978-1-948239-06-6   eBook

Interior Formatting/Book Cover Design by Elijah Toten
www.totencreative.com

RAILROADED

FRAMED FOR MURDER, FIGHTING FOR JUSTICE

RAILROADED

DEDICATION

To my late wife, Elaine, who has been my partner through everything. There are no words that can express how I feel.

I'll always thank you for our time together and for memories of unconditional love.

You were my breath of life and gave me the drive to tell this story.

I miss you.

Sam

SPECIAL THANKS

Phil and the late Susan Cirrone for their unwavering friendship

Kelly DuBray for providing the Introduction, poem, and behind-the-scenes research

Kim Jossart for her research and editorial leadership

Benee Knauer for her literary direction and mentorship

The Sommer Children for their bravery and love

The Father, Son, and Holy Spirit

A TIP OF OUR HATS:
Deana Dor
Debra Dor
Ann Marie Ganizier
Jill Goldstein
Jane Kepoghen
Corey Kilgannon
The Honorable Robert Levy
Andrew Metz
Frank Morano
Karen Oesterle

Joe Scibilia
Joe Scibilia, Jr.
Leonard Sparks
Calvary Chapel, Appleton, Wisconsin
City Bar Justice Center, New York City
St. John's Law Library
WildBlue Press Team

Sam and Chris

TABLE OF CONTENTS

INTRODUCTION 11

1. Stolen in Suffolk 19
2. Career Kid 38
3. Full Plates 51
4. Deep Waters 69
5. Avalanche on Long Island 80
6. Ghostly Gavel 91
7. Off the Rails 103
8. A Haunted Prelude 115
9. True Colors 125
10. Knee Jerks 137
11. A Rivalry and a Rock Star 152
12. Back Peddling 165
13. Hatred 182
14. Boxes in Time 188
15. Short of a Whisper 192
16. Game Faces 209
17. Lifetime 220

18.	A Sticky Note from the Seventies	227
19.	Citizen Lawman	235
20.	1982	240
21.	Home Stretch?	249
22.	Court Crusader, Cuomo, and Commissioner	259
23.	Outside, In	269
24.	Turntables	277

ACKNOWLEDGEMENTS	287
ILLUSTRATIONS AND DOCUMENTS	291

INTRODUCTION

This is the real life story of how an innocent family was destroyed by members of society with power. As Jews we have been targets of hate and oppression for generations, but this story takes that discrimination to a new level.

It speaks volumes when you consider my great grandfather escaped Nazi-occupied Europe at the age of nine after his parents and siblings were all killed. As poor kids who grew up in the Bronx, no one expected our grandparents, or any of us for that matter, to make anything out of life for ourselves. If the Series of Unfortunate Events didn't already exist, it could serve as the title of our family story.

This book is a story of police brutality, corruption, discrimination, abuse of power, and the effects it put on an innocent family. My grandfather, Mr. Samuel Sommer, was an innocent man who lost over half his life incarcerated on false pretenses. I've grown up my whole life being judged and told it was because my grandfather was a "murderer." My mother, aunts, uncles, cousins, even my grandmother, Elaine Sommer, all went through the same experiences—some worse than others.

To some he was Mr. Sommer, to others he was Sam, to his wife, Elaine, he was Beb, to his seven loving children he was dad, and to me, my two siblings, and my seventeen cousins he was grandpa. The New York State Department of Corrections had a different name for him. To them he was inmate #71A0141.

This is America, land of the free, home of the brave, where every citizen is deemed innocent until proven guilty. Well that's what the politicians, judges, police, and fellow civilians want you to think. As of recent, DNA testing has aided in overturning many guilty convictions. After three decades of imprisonment and slander against an honest business man's name, he is still disallowed the use of DNA testing. All the evidence against him has been "lost" by the same people who placed him behind bars, the Suffolk County Fourth Precinct Homicide Department.

My grandfather wasn't the only one who got shafted by being pinned with this murder charge. My grandmother needed to find a way to survive and raise seven children completely on her own. My mother, aunts, and uncles never had a father around to help them maneuver their day-to-day lives, teach them to ride a bike, to fish, not a thing that couldn't be explained during a prison visit.

We grandkids didn't have a normal grandfather experience either. I do not believe that my grandpa ever had the pleasure of meeting any of his grandchildren for the first time outside of a prison visiting room until at least 1998 when he was around sixty-two.

Most of us are claustrophobic and suffer from paranoia (especially towards authority figures), high anxiety, and Post Traumatic Stress Disorder. Loud noises will forever make us jumpy. Our first loud noises were the prison gates closing behind us at the beginning of every visit. The loud noises meant 'yes' because we get to finally see grandpa! They also meant we were trapped in a maximum security facility with bad men and no escape.

Mr. Samuel Sommer, the person who identified the victim in the morgue for police, has been the one convicted of murdering Mr. Irving Silver. You may wonder while page turning through this story why my grandfather was asked to identify the victim. First, Mr. Silver was my grandfather's business partner, but that's not all he was. Mr. Silver was a part of our family. He was my grandmother Elaine's uncle.

Mr. Silver was a good business partner and a wonderful family member. That said, I'm sure everyone can relate to the fact that most families have their own idiosyncrasies. Mr. Silver had an addiction; he loved to gamble. Unfortunately for him he wasn't a very lucky man. He dabbled in various gambling rings and owed thousands of dollars to many people.

During the 1960s the Italian Mafia ran many parts of New York City. They put police officers, judges, and politicians on their payroll with personal interests in mind. The mobsters also ran a number of other underground and aboveground activities including racketeering, illegal gambling rings, cat houses, and trying to create a labor union for garbage collectors. Their full influential reach has still to this day never been determined.

My grandpa was an honest businessman who didn't partake in any such activity. Since he was Mr. Silver's business partner, the police just assumed my grandfather had him killed to keep his own business interests intact. They weren't interested in using any more manpower to solve the case.

The State denied our family a husband, a father, a father-in-law, and a grandpa for all of our entire childhood lives and part of our adulthood as well. Even after being released from prison, he had an unreasonable amount of time on parole. This prevented him from doing things like joining family members for dinner at certain times, attending concerts and athletic events, and many other opportunities to bond with his family because of a parole curfew. I'll never forget the day my grandpa was "FREED."

I was twenty-four years old when my grandfather happily handed me a legal paper. I gazed down and read the entire document before I looked back up.

"Grandpa," I paused cautiously. "I don't understand what this means."

He smiled even brighter. He pointed to a sentence and read it aloud. Then he glanced at me to gage my reaction, which was still bewilderment and confusion.

"Kel, this is the paper I've waited for what seems like forever," he said with a dose of emotion. "I am finally free! No more suffering, no more parole, no more visits. I am finally free to live my life as I should have been able to for the last forty-two years."

Little did he know the falsity behind that statement. If within ninety-nine years after his original incarceration date if for some reason the cops ever felt that he so much as stepped one toe out of line, they would just toss him back "where he belongs" with little or no proof just like the last time. Welcome to America where innocent until **proven guilty** has never been put into play for Samuel Sommer or the rest of his family.

Tears of happiness flooded tears down our cheeks. We embraced in celebration for his freedom. A freedom that had long been denied to him by so many other greed-driven forces.

All my grandpa wanted to accomplish since the day he was accused of killing his uncle-in-law was to prove his innocence. When courtrooms continually beat him down, just as the Suffolk County Police did with phonebooks to coerce a confession, he seemed to realize that perhaps the only way to prove his innocence was to devote time to complete this book.

At age eighty-two, this one desire has not been derailed. We hope this book helps avenge the wrong doings of our legal system by certain power hungry individuals. More importantly, this literary work is poised to prove through all opposition that Samuel Sommer is truly free in every aspect of the word.

The Men of Authority

First they came for my Pop
They didn't get him to stop
But all his siblings and his parents
Hitler unleashed an onslaught.

Then they came for my Grandpa
They framed him for murder he did not commit
And kept him in a cell to rot
Hoping he would forever "Take the Hit."

Then they came for my uncles
Slandering their names
In situations they were tricked
Into being engaged.

Then they came for the grandkids
Red-flagged since the day we were born
So throughout eternity
These men take our name in scorn.

Now we come for them
The power has now changed hands
To right the scales of justice.
To help our fellow man.

Introduction and Poem by Kelly DuBray

Authors' Disclaimer: *Any opinions, statements of fact, descriptions, dialogue, and citations found in this literary work were provided by the authors and are solely those of the authors. The publisher makes no claim as to their veracity of accuracy, and assumes no liability for the content.*

The authors' recollections of some material may be subjective based on the extensive duration of the subject matter. The authors' content was supported by as much documentation still accessible over the span of fifty-plus years. The authors are not liable for any claims that may be subjectively argumentative in the literary work due to the nature of how difficult it was to obtain evidence.

Since some parts of the content used to tell this story were withheld by people in positions of authority over the course of six decades, the narrative by any means is not intended to mislead readers.

Some individuals involved in this case were contacted in 2018 and refused to comment on their involvement in the subject's demise. They were offered a voice in collaboration with the project, yet remain silent to this day.

Copyright 2018 Samuel L. Sommer and Christopher Jossart

1.

STOLEN IN SUFFOLK

Three men in sharp suits briskly walked toward Sam Sommer's car. Sam looked down at the D on his automatic transmission console inside his Chevy station wagon, grabbed the door handle with his left hand, and poised his right hand atop the horn. His vehicle slowly coasted with one foot on the brake. He wasn't sure whether to squeal out, park and run, lay on the horn, or just keep coasting and jittering.

For someone who made a living making decisions that affected dozens of people each day, Sam couldn't decide what to do in a flash for his own good. His 150-pound furry backseat driver did a better job on demonstrating some damn decisiveness than he did. Sam figured the hell with indecision; it felt better to freeze and hope they would go away. He parked the car—stopping just inside a driveway from a well-travelled street. The unorthodox position of the vehicle appeared foreign to structured rows of parking stalls that filled the lot.

One of the men shouted, "Sommer!" This was all business whomever these good ole' boys were, and the unfolding encounter made Sam realize it included a one-sided agenda. One guy looked familiar from a recent civil, yet macho-style encounter he experienced with a member of Suffolk County law enforcement almost a week ago.

Sam quickly caught a glimpse of an unmarked car parked on the other side of the lot near Walter Court, which runs next to Long Island's busy Jericho Turnpike. The observation of the car parked away from everything else made Sam's already sweaty predicament even more of a salty horror.

He pulled into a Dunkin' Donuts parking lot adjacent to the freeway in Commack, New York, with his big St. Bernard dog. The 2073 Jericho Turnpike establishment opened in 1964 and was a favorite destination for a blossoming community. It was within blocks of Sam's house. The donut shop still stands today near the long-running Mayfair Shopping Center.

Sargent started barking wildly at the sight of oncoming strangers. Sam squinted out the window in an attempt to muster some last-second negotiation to slow the men's collective pace. The way the men marched spelled trouble.

"Who are you and what do you want?" Sam contended. Nothing but steps for an answer, now a few feet from his car.

The pleasant distraction of sweet dough aroma in the air moments earlier was now history. It was replaced with the stench of something dirty going down around 8:10 p.m. on Wednesday, May 22, 1968.

Sargent's momentous fit temporarily distracted the three intruders from their pursuit. The hiccup in an imminent showdown of three-against-one (plus canine) gave Sam an attempt to slide across the seat and exit the passenger side. It was too late for man and best friend. One of the three men had already swung around that side of the car to guard the passenger door.

The man who was shouting "Sommer" identified himself as Detective Thomas Gill with Suffolk County Homicide. The officer, a bit older than Sam, commanded him to join his men in going to the homicide division fourth precinct in nearby Smithtown.

The guy that Sam believed he met days earlier was another detective, Thomas Mansel, who piggybacked Gill's command. "You heard him, Sommer, let's go." Mansel was with the County's Homicide Squad as well.

Sam boldly said he wasn't going anywhere until he learned why.

"Let's go, Sommer," Gill said. He and another man opened the door before Sam could roll up the window and lock his vehicle. They clutched him by the shoulders.

Two men yanked Sam out of his idling station wagon head first in waning daylight at Dunkin' Donuts. Sam thought for a second that the orchestrated grab-and-go was a bad joke somehow tied to a call he received around dinner time to meet someone at the donut shop. He winced in pain from the deep grabs that latched into his sunburned skin. The men rolled Sam to his side on the concrete and cuffed him.

"What the fuck?" cried the thirty-one-year-old family man and business pro in feeble resistance to a kidnapping. Sam's five foot, eight inch frame fell prey to two taller kidnappers. "Stop!" A chorus line of pleas continued during the out-of-the-blue confrontation. While resisting he received a kick in the back of his knee from one of the detectives while being prone on his side for the wide open target. The men quickly dragged Sam across the parking lot toward the unmarked car.

"All right, all right," Sam yelped. Mansel and the other detective following Gill let go of Sam. They lifted him up and let him walk on his own toward their vehicle after a hard shove from Mansel. Sam resumed the journey to the police car voluntarily.

It was still bright enough to notice a man being dragged against his will. Some teenagers had been hanging out in the store for quite some time. Less than a minute before the men left their car from across the lot, Sam entered the

Dunkin' Donuts property to meet another man for a meeting concerning one of his business associates, a family relative. The man had not yet arrived, but Sam arrived expecting to wait for him.

Sam slowed his pace toward the car and glanced at the men, expressing concern for Sargent. The dog was left alone in a running car with the driver's side door partially opened. A response came in the form of another shove forward. Sam looked back again toward his station wagon without breaking his stride to catch a glimpse of Sargent. The car bounced like a modern-day pimp mobile from Sargent's display of protection toward his master.

Within feet from the unmarked vehicle, Sam switched his cadence from a defensive tone to one of cooperation. "What's this all about? Please, stop."

Gill opened the back seat door and the other men chucked Sam into the car. After avoiding a brush with his head against the far side door, Sam tried to roll on his back. He was instantly lifted up to a sitting position and buckled. While vehicles zoomed next to one of New York's busiest thoroughfares, a group of men allegedly sworn to serve and protect were stealing a man's freedom amidst the roaring engines.

The door closed to the back seat while Sam realized there were no inside handles. His capturers were in a hurry. The car instantly hit the turnpike and in no time it merged with traffic.

Sam was shaking too much to play eye games with Mansel and Gill, who were seated on each side of him. He just closed his eyes and prayed for the best—whatever that meant. The car quickly exited the turnpike and within a few blocks ended up parked in what seemed like a bumpy lot right next to a main road. That made Sam breathe a little better knowing he wasn't going somewhere far—a self-fulfilling means of fabricating hope.

The driver got out, and Sam asked Gill what this ordeal was about. Gill said he'd find out soon enough and told him to shut up. The driver came back and in less than five minutes the journey to purgatory resumed. No more freeway. Sam arrived in what appeared to be an alley by the narrowing of a street between two lit buildings. He then realized he was at the police station in Hauppauge, a suburb of Smithtown to the south.

It was dusk when the three men placed Sam to his feet in the parking lot of the back entrance to the Suffolk County Fourth Precinct. The whole thing about being around cops suddenly didn't feel right. Sam was supposed to find comfort at a police station; yet, he felt increasingly scared while the three men assertively escorted him toward the back entrance. Once inside, they led Sam down a long hallway to a room on the right.

The average-sized room, about twelve by twelve, was filled with some office equipment, a stool, a couple of chairs, and a square table. It resembled an interrogation room but with a more office-like feel to it. The men immediately shoved Sam against the table and then dropped his fumbling body onto a hard wooden stool and removed his cuffs. They seemed to be setting a tone of play along or it's gonna get physical. The three men convened with a fourth badge from the station outside the room while the door remained open. Sam mulled the connection of a few dots.

How in the world does one go from hooking up with someone in a parking lot to finding a home in a Suffolk County police station in the snap of a finger?

He tried to link learning about the sudden death of his business partner and relative, Irving Silver, to the current madness. Sam flew home last Wednesday, May 15, from

Florida by himself while his family remained vacationing with both sets of in-laws. Sam had to deal with a dilemma Silver was having with Sommer's businesses, in particular a man named Harold Goberman.

Goberman was the one who called Sam around dinner time to meet at Dunkin' Donuts regarding Silver's death. Sam recently hired Goberman, who went with an alias of a Harold Masterson, to do some work at his deli in Commack, the Deli-Queen. His hiring was the result of a recommendation from Silver to help Goberman get reacclimated into society. He retained a vast criminal record and was out of prison on parole. Sam wanted to give the man another chance at life.

Detective Mansel rather forcefully asked Sam to help Suffolk County police identify Silver's body on the afternoon of Friday, May 17. Silver was apparently killed during the early morning on the same day. His body was found on Wheatley Road, a rather unfrequented rural artery off the Jericho Turnpike southeast of Commack.

"You're going to confess, Sommer, right now," instructed Gill in the interrogation room. No identification given of the other men. No reading of any rights concerning a kidnapping called an arrest. The door slammed from the hallway and the same two men who nabbed him plus another stood behind Gill in the crowded room.

"About what?" Sam inquired, still cuffed.

The new man on the scene from the precinct grabbed Sam under his arms and lifted him off of the stool. Gill then pushed Sam head first into the wall and proceeded to shove him onto the floor. Still cuffed, Sam was then harshly seated and punched across the left eye by another officer. His sunburned skin absorbed the beating with needlelike pain.

Another greeting with the concrete floor. Picked up again and placed on the stool, Gill got in Sam's face.

"Want a lawyer, Sommer, or you gonna fess up?"

"For what?" Sam shouted.

"Killing your business buddy," Mansel shouted. "We know you wacked him with a lead pipe and then ran him over. Son of a bitch."

Stunned by what he heard, Sam offered a left-to-right head nod that suggested a nonverbal "No" in reply to the men's accusations. Bewildered with the name Harold Goberman taking over his mind as the centerpiece part of a jigsaw puzzle, Sam started to describe his phone call to Gill tied to a meeting at Dunkin' Donuts.

"A Harold Goberman is behind this" … stars—a galaxy of pain. A thump on the head by an undetected detective from behind with a telephone book while Sam was held down on the stool blurred his vision. Another whack on the neck from the phone directory ensued in what seemed to be a one-sided conversation. The Goberman mention obviously set off the detectives.

More pounds from the phone book behind Sam's head continued until his ability to sit upright in the stool gave way to the hard floor. Sam laid with his hands over his head and shook enough to trip a Richter scale. His fear couldn't muster any words.

The persuasive techniques used in the basement of Suffolk County's Homicide Unit didn't stop. The men of the badge kicked and yelled at Sam while he curled up on the floor. Realizing there was no other choice but to possibly die, Sam begged to tell the officers about the Goberman phone call. They would have nothing to do with the Goberman thing.

The four men huddled together as if it was fourth-and-goal on the one-yard line and Sam was on defense all by himself. Too pissed off to think about a lawyer, Sam wanted to fight the assholes head on. It was evident there was no more hope for textbook interrogation procedures; it was now all about survival—in a damn police station.

Further beating might have killed Sam. Why didn't they just kill him? That question is still debated today by people who know and love him. God's grace allowed for his story to be told for the benefit of others in the name of justice, Sam offered in retrospect.

"Think about what comes out of your mouth before we come back, Sommer," asserted Gill. The men then left the smoke-filled whipping chamber to the hallway with the door still open. In a cloud of chaos sat a man who a couple of hours earlier left home to learn something to aid in the case of a loved one.

The origination of Sam Sommer's fateful trip to Dunkin' Donuts came with risks and uncertainties in dealing with Goberman. The disgruntled Goberman set Sam up, or so it appeared.

To this day, dear friends Phil and Susan Cirrone from Long Island remember that day more than fifty years later. Philly, as Sam coined the nickname of his close friend, detailed the circumstances leading up to the kidnapping and subsequent aftermath.

> **A personal recount of horror:**
>
> *I got a call around 8:00 from Elaine Sommer to come over earlier than planned the evening of the twenty-second of May. We were going to leave shortly anyway to see Elaine's parents visiting from Florida, but Elaine said it was important. We heard earlier in the week that a family member died unexpectedly.*
>
> *Susan and I are the type of friends to Sammy and Elaine that wouldn't question them in a time of*

need. We got a babysitter in light of the urgent development and headed to their house.

Upon arrival, Elaine greeted us by the front door. We could tell something was up. She told us that Sam didn't return yet from a meeting at Dunkin' Donuts near the freeway. Elaine didn't have time to go into detail. All she said was that Sam had been involved in trying to find out what happened to her uncle, Irving Silver. She was beside herself; Susan and I were barely inside the door.

Sam was going to meet some guy who had information about Silver at a donut shop. She said Sam drove the station wagon to Dunkin' Donuts with their dog and that something felt wrong.

We didn't know Irving Silver, but Elaine quickly filled us in about his connection to her family and that he was dead. Regardless, friends are friends, and there was no need to pry at the moment about what happened to him. Shocked and saddened by the news, we kept listening. Her parents hugged us and just remained silent the whole time.

Elaine asked me to kindly take her to check on Sammy at Dunkin' Donuts. Of course Susan and I agreed, but first I told Elaine to call the store. She did so and learned Sam wasn't inside the establishment. We then left, determined to find out where he was. Her parents remained at the house for the kids.

The three of us arrived at a nearby Dunkin' Donuts off the turnpike and immediately saw the Sommer's vehicle barely inside the lot from the road. We cautiously circled the car to get a pulse on the situation and noticed their dog going berserk in the back seat.

Creepy shit, yet we remained calm for a horrified Elaine. The lot was well lit and a couple of cars were parked near the store's entrance. Elaine jumped out of our car and yelled to us that Sam's vehicle was still running. We could see, too, that the driver's side door wasn't closed all the way either.

Unquestionably, this was a spine-chilling scene. The dog increased its barking likely from recognizing Elaine. Susan and I both hesitated to go near the car. We advised Elaine not to touch anything and told her that we were going inside the donut shop to see if anyone knew anything. Susan and I sped to the entrance of the donut shop and ran inside for answers.

Inside the store we couldn't find Sammy, but we found the sight of curiosity all over the joint from the way a couple of workers and a group of kids looked at us. They all appeared dazed.

I was working as a corrections officer at the time and learned a few things when it came to reading people. Susan kept an eye on Elaine while I asked the manager what was going on. Sweat drenched my shirt. Where in the hell was Sammy?

A few teenagers congregated around the counter in front of the manager. He said the person in the car who parked weirdly in his lot was taken by some guys. One of the teens chimed in and said the man he thinks we were talking about was dragged out of his car and taken away (pointing in the direction of the turnpike). Another teen described the dog in *the back seat running around so wildly that the car bounced.*

Susan and I grabbed hold of one another. "What?" we collectively bellowed. "Like kidnapped?" I piggybacked the disbelief with a question to continue the inquisition. We froze with jaws on the floor. The first kid said they were like gangsters and asked if we knew the guy who was taken.

The store manager indicated that the men, unable to recall how many for sure—a few he proclaimed, looked like a bunch of wise guys. Another teen said that they looked like bad asses and one of them carried a gun. The same youngster believed there were three men working together against one victim.

I asked the manager if he called the cops. He said no. I got the impression he wanted to look the other way, so to speak. The kids were kind enough to wish us well and they split, too, likely not wanting to stick around much longer. The described mobster-type men had everyone on edge.

On the verge of calling the police, I noticed a cop car pull into the lot. It felt comforting, yet odd. If no one called the police how would they know what was going on? Maybe someone else around the neighborhood or store called, I thought. Anyway, Susan went outside toward Elaine, who quickly grabbed the officer's attention for obvious reasons. I made a quick call to a lawyer friend of mine to explain what was going down and then joined the commotion outside.

The front driver's side door was part way open. A slimy mist, like dew, covered most of the windows, probably from the dog's cries. It didn't look like Sammy was around. All eyes fixated on the cop for answers. Car running. Dog freaking out. No Sammy. The officer then did a quick search of the car.

Elaine then left with the officer to go across the way a short distance to the Mayfair Shopping Center to use a phone. We just stood by the car trying to comfort the dog without being able to touch anything. The biggest thing we couldn't touch was reality. We were scared and more so for Sammy.

The officer said that he and Elaine would be back in a matter of minutes. Their poor dog's barks grew hoarser. I told Susan that I called Joe Scibilia, and that he might be able to help Sammy from a legal standpoint, if needed.

Like the officer promised, he returned with Elaine. She looked as mad as she did worried a few moments ago. I asked what was going on. The officer informed us that he called the station to see if there was anything on Mr. Sommer. I could tell Elaine was pissed. She then insisted that her husband was kidnapped. Just hearing that word sent shivers through my body.

The officer said that she would need to fill out a Missing Persons Report at the police station in Hauppauge. He told Elaine that she could take the car home (for perceived concern about the dog). The cop's intention appeared heartfelt toward the dog; yet, I found it strange that he would release the car back to its owner so quickly. Theoretically, this location and the vehicle itself could still be considered a potential crime scene, I thought.

Here's what else seemed screwed up. The officer didn't write anything down up until this point. From my years in corrections, documentation means everything. Writing something down gave an impression of importance and focus. How do you dismiss a running car with the driver's side door left open and a dog going nuts in the back seat as anything not related to foul play?

Nonchalantly like another day at the office, the officer reminded us of the Missing Persons Report and departed the scene. His calmness drove me nuts. No urgency. It was going to be a long night.

Susan skillfully excelled in the field of empathy. She was a gentle offset to my dealing with hard asses all the time. I thanked her for comforting Elaine. I trusted her more than myself to handle Elaine the best way possible given the circumstance. I was too upset at this farce of an investigation.

We both agreed to bring the vehicle and dog back to Sam's home. It might buffer the heart-stopping news a bit for Elaine about her husband, and frankly, the dog was pretty messed up. Susan and I followed Elaine back to her house where she parked the car and took the dog inside. A neighbor was watching the Sommer kids, and the three of us proceeded to the fourth precinct.

Susan guided a tear-drenched Elaine into the back seat of our car, and in a flash we took off to get this report done. Maybe then we could start to get somewhere concerning Sammy. There we went...

into the waning abyss of hell known as May 22, 1968.

***

Gill and his men quickly returned to Sam's abuse chamber from just outside the room at the Suffolk County Fourth Precinct Homicide Division. A day etched in lawlessness against a hardworking young man, husband, and father of seven came close to an end—at least based on the time of day. Sam didn't know if these sworn men of honor were just getting warmed up for an all-nighter or maybe an amateur form of execution.

Sitting with his head resting on a small table, Sam fielded a command from Gill to get up and pay attention. He gingerly rose and hunched over in a state of pain and stood as attentive as possible. A slap to the back of Sam's head and neck with a phone book now serving as a weapon staggered him from wall-to-wall in another round of late night captivity. He felt like dying. Gill felt impatient, like he didn't want to be there and would rather have the whole thing over with.

Lowered back in the chair, Sam's head tilted toward God in prayer of something to happen—heaven or home. Surrounded by folded arms and smoky drags around the table, Gill leaned into his helpless prey. "Fess up, Sommer."

The verbal onslaughts that previously followed with a physical bashing took a different turn this time. Two men behind Sam rather gently lifted him upright. What should have felt comforting seemed creepy to Sam. After he was lifted, the stool beneath him was removed and the detectives laid him on the ground. The men ripped his t-shirt and removed his clothes. Sam curled into a ball on a cold floor, stark naked.

"Gonna speak now, Sommer," one of the detectives asked pompously in a new twist of torture. The room succumbed to silence. Suffolk County's interrogation techniques were building in stunning infamy. "Come on, Sommer," insisted Gill or Mansel based on Sam's aged recollection. "Fess up."

"Florida," Sam uttered from his shell. No response. No punches. No accusations. He prayed for even a belch in the room. The stillness defined a level of fear that Sam never fathomed. He believed the next phase in this scheme was death. He knew that protecting himself was even more of a fairy tale since he wasn't wearing any clothes.

Sam lifted his head a smidgeon to see that the men walked away from the table. In the first act of a humane tone since getting seized from a donut shop parking lot, Gill calmly inquired, "Tell us more, Sommer, about Florida. What the hell does that mean?"

Sam as a suspect suddenly had a voice in this assumed interrogation proceeding going down in the final hours of May 22. The interrogators welcomed his voice for the first time outside the realm of being toyed with to make a false confession. "Took my family to Florida… came back early to help Silver deal with a matter about the business," murmured a drained Sam.

"You told me last week you were going to meet Silver, and that was around the time he was wacked," Mansel reminded Sam.

"We were working together on some bad shit with Goberman—you need to talk to Harold Goberman," uttered the helpless suspect.

No reply. Sam heard some shuffling of feet and a whisper or two. He could sense growing frustration in the room among the badges. He predicted that these guys weren't going to leave him alone until they got what they sought—a confession to the murder of Irving Silver. His prediction materialized. In so many testy words, Gill told him that he needed to give them what they wanted so they could wrap up the investigation.

At one point the detectives moved Sam into a basement room for a few minutes. His state of confusion disallowed him to really make heads or tails of what was going on. Since Sam was so weak, he kind of went with the flow during this peculiar little tour of the precinct's lower level. The detectives didn't say much—it seemed like they were hiding him. Within moments, they returned Sam upstairs to his original interrogation room.

The smell of judicial corruption took over. Whoever was orchestrating the targeting of Sam Sommer was friends with the devil. 'What the…?' Sam internalized while wincing in pain moving his exposed body to the floor. 'This is serious shit. First, a dead relative. Then a phone call from a guy we were trying to help get his life together, followed by getting nabbed from my own damn car to having the shit kicked out of me and stripped. Why ask me about Florida and then disregard it?'

***

Phil Cirrone and the two ladies arrived at the same Suffolk County precinct near Smithtown where Sam was getting tortured. Unaware of that coincidence upon arrival, Philly tried to work over the officers by way of influence as a member of the New York City Department of Corrections. He started to flex his relational muscle for the Sommers to get some real answers.

Bingo, but not on Philly's card. No more than a couple of minutes after the three entered the station, Susan recognized a friend of her brother, an FBI special agent. He was there conducting some business related to a case on Long Island.

"Remember me?" asked Susan. "I'm Marvin's sister."

"Yes," replied the agent. "You're"...

"Susan, Susan Cirrone."

She briefly small talked about her brother after shaking hands with the agent. She then reintroduced her husband, recalling their paths crossed before through her brother. Phil was consumed in watching over Elaine so Susan could converse with her brother's friend. Elaine wanted to speak to someone in charge, ASAP.

"What brings you here? Is everything OK?" the agent asked Susan.

Phil introduced Elaine to the agent, and she explained the situation to him with reference to Sam's name. Expecting support related to the process of reporting a missing person, the three instead hear an Orson Wells-caliber revelation.

"I think he's down the hall, locked up."

Paled and going through her own version of abuse from yet another bomb dropped, Elaine darted toward a long hallway, the direction in which the agent glanced when he made the claim. Phil grabbed Elaine's arm and slowed her enough to allow Susan to thank the agent and apologize for the trouble. The three citizen investigators of Sam heard the word "locked," and an aura of injustice dismissed the conversation.

The agent embarrassingly gathered that he shouldn't have disclosed Sam's whereabouts. He added out of desperation to deflect the situation elsewhere, "They've moved him to another precinct. It's common to rotate someone... uh." The agent stopped talking and left abruptly.

Whether he was lying or inferred "elsewhere" as being a hospital remains unsettled today. The agent could not later testify to such a claim for obvious reasons of conflict of interest. Incidentally, Sam was moved from his first-floor

RAILROADED | 35

interrogation room to a similar room in the basement at some point between 10:00 and 11:00 that night. He believes to this day the move was made out of fear by the police that three people were there looking for him.

After the agent split, Phil's gut told him that Sam was still down the hall. He led the ladies past the front desk on a mission. *Authorized Personnel Only* signs warned of their against-the-grain gamble to another part of the building. One officer emerged from another room past the desk and thwarted their journey. He sandwiched the Sam-seekers. Right out of a movie.

Elaine was in no mood to be trapped by the very people who may have something to do with her husband's quandary. The officers instructed the organic search party to leave the unauthorized location. Elaine wasn't accepting such orders. She demanded to know where her husband was.

The front desk officer said he would make a call for her. After a few attempts, the officer verified that her husband was taken into custody. He told her that he was relocated to another part of the multiple-facility complex. This was a far cry difference than what she heard a few minutes earlier that there was no Sam Sommer on site for sake of interviewing or lodging. The officer insisted that Elaine go home and that her husband would call her.

A salty and red-faced Elaine Sommer slowly made her way out of the station under the care of Phil and Susan. She wondered where Sam was—the rock in her world, loving husband, lover of the Lord Jesus Christ, and devoted father who'd been building American Dreams for so many people. Elaine felt empty without the strength to take another step toward the Cirrone's car. Sam wouldn't be coming home tonight was all her mind held.

It was late. Wednesday, May 22, 1968, was winding down into a day of sobering consequences to whatever Suffolk County, New York wants, it supposedly gets.

***

Sam did not confess to killing Irving Silver from his holding cell or anytime afterward. On a note pad, Sam recalled Thomas Gill recording that he did confess. The "official" form of documentation resembled a third-grader pulling out a piece of paper from his desk to draw a picture at will.

Finally, the brutality ended. The detectives escorted Sam across a parking lot to a different building where he was photographed, fingerprinted, and processed for arrest and lodging purposes. They then transported him to a hospital in Riverhead, New York, to be treated for injuries. He then slept a few winks in a cell at the Suffolk County Riverhead Police Station.

2.

CAREER KID

A hug between the two young men drained air from their lungs. It was the first time the two blood rivals ever genuinely and openly hugged one another. The suffocation expressed an untold story.

Hard to let go, but time to go. Big brother was heading off to serve at the onset of the Korean War in early summer of 1950, a year out of high school. Fourteen-year-old Sam Sommer and his parents didn't know when they'd see Morris again, so the hug felt valid for a lifetime.

Tears did the talking before Morris grabbed his suitcase. He then headed out the front door without looking back. Sam and his parents each dispersed to their own window to watch Morris get into an important-looking car and travel away down the crowded streets of South Bronx toward the unknown. One war just ended and another began.

Goodbye family unit of nearly twenty years. Two decades of witnessing the effects of war, ethnic cleansing, economic suppression, and learning to grow in faith and family opened another chapter for these pursuers of the American Dream.

***

Most of Sam's and Morris' Jewish-American 1940s upbringing in a South Bronx lower-to-middle-class neighborhood came with baggage. There was enough competition between the boys to make ringside alive and well anywhere in their two-bedroom, fourth-floor tenement at 1125 Evergreen Avenue. These units in the Bronx's southern neighborhoods mostly all mirrored one another for several blocks.

If Sam lost a fight to Morris in his parents' eyes, he would take his defeat to a rusty view of humanity known as a fire escape. He accessed the getaway to solitude from his bedroom window, and from there he would watch the world go by in catlike curiosity. Sam may have lost a brotherly dispute or two like most all kids, but he gained a good release from that metal perch. It also provided a snapshot of a neighborhood trying to find an identity.

Morris Sommer's reserved character became easily annoyed by Sam's extroverted dabbles in people and projects. Morris waited for the right moves; Sam made moves. Cultural affiliations and turf wars slowly started to define the New York City streets, and the two boys seemed to handle the inner city influences and cultural growing pains differently.

Despite their distinctions and five-year separation, the two Sommer lads bonded in standing tall together. The boys grew strong and critical in thought from hearing about the persecution of Jews during World War II. Regular showers of propaganda made the act of living in the 1940s under a big city umbrella a distrustful walk around the block. By the latter part of the decade, television entered the mecca of journalism. The technology launched a visual springboard of opinion, bias, and emotional tugs into the world of assimilating news.

Television created images of an unsettled New York City predicated on robust immigration. Sons of a father who emigrated from Austria, the boys were exposed to a strong work ethic and commitment to family from a steady diet of their elders' spiritual faith in Yahweh, the God of Israel.

Maximillian Sommer left Austria after studying to be a rabbi for an American version of similar understudy in New York City. He felt a hub in the United States would give him both an education as a rabbi and the surroundings to put his preaching into practice faster than overseas. Then a woman entered the scene.

In 1930, Max married Anna, a local gal who worked feverishly to finish junior high school despite expectations during the Great Depression that meant finding work and nothing more. Anna looked beyond the bare trees to know that one day an orchard would bless her family in the shape of a high school education for her future kids.

The couple welcomed Morris Sommer into the world in 1931. Max worked long days in a men's garment factory while Anna tended to the apartment and child. Rare family time was spent practicing faith and planning for the future—one that would bring a sibling to Morris.

Anna gave birth to Samuel L. Sommer on June 9, 1936, near the end of the Depression but at the beginning of world conflict and Nazi Germany. Looking ahead, the couple was happy with two children—an unusual level of contentment in this regard for traditional Jewish families.

Max glorified God in gratitude for his factory job. He could provide for a young family while some folks didn't see a paycheck during times of strife. Whenever he could, however, Max would nurture the spirits of others in faith as kind of an ad hoc rabbi. His spiritual volunteering for other families served as occasional capstones to long hours at the factory. It was therapeutic.

Growing up, the two boys sensed the stress on their parents from trying to provide for a Jewish family in wartime. Even though World War II wasn't fought on American soil, racism was evident in New York. The introverted Morris kept to himself for the most part during high school. Conversely, Sam showed his personality hand often as early as middle school. That hand revealed an ace in the hole: charm.

***

While eighth grade came to an end in 1950 for Sam Sommer, life under the same roof with his only sibling reached culmination, too. Morris Sommer left for the unknown of battle. Sam eventually succumbed to enjoying the house to himself at the start of high school, but he worried often about his brother. His short-lived role as the sole child king of the house quickly faded.

Sam could barely get his stuff spread across state lines in the once-shared bedroom when he heard that Morris was returning home. He was scheduled to come home the following spring from serving in Korea due to the Marine Corps reassigning his duties. Mixed emotions for the younger Sam.

Sam's charm and athleticism directed his acclimation to high school. Natural grit grabbed the attention of coaches in the fall of 1950. He turned a few heads on the football field and in gym class with an uncanny balance of agility and toughness for a smaller frame.

James Monroe High School in the South Bronx functioned more like a discipline station than a place where apples sat on teachers' desks in symbolism of harmony. Its climate protruded activities designed to get a handle on a heavy influx of cultural diversity in the Big Apple. Getting along superseded getting good grades.

A spotlight continued to shine on Sam his freshman year. Spring 1951 meant baseball, and the diamond sparkled when Sam skillfully consumed base paths. He let go of the attention he felt at school when Morris returned home later that spring. His presence humbled Sam. The two started a different relationship together predicated on Sam's maturation. Chasing grounders on baseball fields held nothing to what his brother went through on minefields.

The brotherly bond opened a new synergy in the Sommer household. The family grew spiritually before the plug was pulled on graceful memories when Morris departed again in a couple of months. He was going to learn sonar technology with the Marines. The Corps was impressed with his ability to work controls and read radar images while in Korea, and the military branch wanted to train him further on related applications.

Morris left home in early fall of 1951 to master a craft in digital technology that would bring him around the world. He did not return to New York other than a holiday here and there for several years. Sam and Morris grew apart over time from simple logistics, yet their childhood trials together would lead to a foundation of mutual success.

The summer gel of '51 between Sam and Morris drove the younger Sommer to begin his sophomore year with budding confidence. Watching his older brother wear a uniform that stood for national pride and world leadership spurred the now-referred-to "Sammy" to don something similar. He wanted to get into the game of serving his country right there in the hub of influential America, albeit in a different manner.

The fall semester at Monroe welcomed a taste of time management for the young Sommer. While some of his classmates confronted teen stresses like what tune to play on the jukebox at the pool hall or how to dress cool for the dance, Sammy fretted over balancing sports and a new job before the age of sixteen.

He spent his after-school hours and weekends delivering butter, eggs, and meat provisions on a bicycle a few weeks into his sophomore year. Sammy had to quit football to focus on the demands of the new job. He put on a work uniform with pride like Morris wore his and hit the streets working for the father of a close friend who owned a dairy proprietorship.

When asked why he worked so much as a teenager, Sammy said, "I finally found a job that I like."

Max and Anna Sommer tried to guide their youngest son in his juggling of time and priorities. Max's hands burned a tired and rough tale of a worn out working man. He grew to realize that he wanted something better for Sammy now that Morris dutifully found his niche in the world.

Max pushed the importance of homework to his son with a fair degree of success but nothing exceptional. Sammy's gifts carried both an aptitude for business and a line drive off of baseball bats. By spring of '52, Sammy was making money and coaches happy.

The two merging passions kept Sammy focused and out of trouble on the streets. Temptations on sidewalks and in alleyways slowly began to bubble up in New York City in the shape of gangs, cultural clashes, and territorialism. On the flip side, immigrants worked in booming factories, creating a dangling carrot for entrepreneurs and business developers.

Enterprisers on the brink of building a strong economic America embodied a shopping cart full of negotiation skills. Some preferred a handshake; others dealt in written contracts, and a few talked with guns and car rides to no man's land. Past decades gradually dripped steady drops of organized crime behind the scenes. Sammy's deliveries carved out short-cuts over time through alleys and catwalks. That put him in unexpected positions to detect a few deals in the dark, suggesting a changing business landscape.

Sammy recalls knowing what he wanted to do the rest of his life by saying to himself after completing delivery routes, "I was born to serve." He continued to shine around the bases as well. His former introduction to competition by way of a sibling rivalry now morphed into understanding perhaps what he wanted to be when grownup. He struggled, however, to find a twenty-fifth hour of the day.

Max and Anna did their best to slow Sammy down. They vied for him to take a breath and exhale the high school experience. Go to dances, Coney Island, and the like. Perhaps in a demonstration of compartmentalizing his parents' advice, Sammy started a neighborhood stickball league of sorts—rain or shine and even in the dead of winter once in a while. Good fun. Roll up your sleeves, act tough, and nail a ball into oblivion and watch it bounce of off any number of buildings.

The stress reliever and admirable use of youthful bonding succumbed quickly, however, to what was meant to be. Midway through his junior year, Sammy received an offer to play development league baseball in Central Park the next summer. The opportunity bred connections to major league scouts. The prestigious invitation rendered a once-in-a-lifetime shot at professional baseball.

At the same time Sammy's delivery route was increasing due to his ability to build relationships, increasing both repeat and new business for the company. He was just the kind of kid whose big heart and passion for work left such an uplifting mark with everyone he encountered on delivery routes. The busy lifestyle for the sixteen-year-old, however, meant that something had to be taken off of his plate.

Home plate wasn't one of the commitments for removal in Sammy's mind, nor was letting go of his fruitful employment. Therefore, with baseball and work taking priority, quitting high school entered the equation. But why quit with only a year-and-a-half to go? In winter of 1953 he took his dilemma to his mother.

She understood, but urged her son to not let go of his education because of baseball. Anna's heart ached not seeing her second son want to finish high school, especially since he was an upperclassman now, yet she saw a spark in his eye for business. She offered support. A grateful son accepted it, but what would Max think?

Anna broke the ice for her son to his father. In one of those full-circle scenes in a motion picture, Max joined his youngest son on the icicle-filled fire escape for a heart-to-heart, late night talk one pleasant star-filled winter evening. Times were still tough all around despite a local economy getting stronger. Turf wars and racial tensions ushered social competition to go along with a competitive workforce. Mobsters were mixing up the market, causing distrust among merchants and paranoia ran rampant on the street.

Max knew Sammy's jumpstart at a good life wasn't the result of luck. It was meant to be, that's it, period. Sammy was put in the position he was from the good Lord. Don't question it, said his father. The remainder of the spring semester at James Monroe High went on without Sammy Sommer, who made his delivery routes now for an elated boss a fulltime gig at the age of sixteen.

Sammy missed some of his high school buddies. They kept in touch from time-to-time; he would see them at the following fall football games and around the neighborhood a bit. His focus on making money and learning the ropes of food service remained steadfast.

Later that fall Sammy found himself savoring a rare night off from baseball workouts and work. His boss was on a business strip and halted some of his operations for a couple of days. The buzz of young America in a popular billiard hall in the South Bronx lured Sammy to join a few friends from high school for Coca-Cola, rock and roll, and eight ball madness.

The scene at the hall for guys was a James Dean attitude. There were lots of colorful combs showing off in back pockets of blue jeans on a busy night at the hot spot. Within feet of entering the smoky joint, Sammy did a double take at a sight he'd never seen before. For a young man on the go from dusk to dawn mastering the art of delivery, stopping on a dime felt different.

The distraction was a young lady with a shy smile named Elaine.

Elaine Francis Rosen was born in 1938 as the daughter of another hard-working family of second generation Jewish immigrants in New York. A steady wave of resettlement from Europe beginning in the late 1800s and then Eastern Europe after both World Wars built a strong Jewish culture in New York City.

Approximately two million Jews called the Big Apple home by the early 1950s, making up one-quarter of the city's population.[1] Many brought skills with them to the United States, including kosher food preparations, the practice of medicine, making clothes, and various artistic gifts related to the performing arts and music.

The clothing industry swelled, and New York's economy started to ride the coattails of the entrepreneurial spirit of Jewish settlers during a time when Sammy rode success on a bicycle. Elaine's father was one of those successful descendants of the garment business.

Morris Rosen served as a founding partner at a thriving men's clothing factory in mid-town Manhattan, and his wife, Sadie, displayed an eye for design. The location today is infamously known as New York's garment district. Elaine didn't show much interest in the business, and her younger brother, Joel, was in elementary school.

Elaine's big heart navigated her time to soup kitchens and libraries in the Bronx serving the less fortunate. Volunteering trumped socializing; she shied away from common hangouts like pool halls, candy stores, Steeplechase Park, or even Coney Island. On this particular night in 1953, however, her rare jaunt to the land of social butterflies with some friends brought forth a young man named Sammy.

Sammy and Elaine turned their attempt at shooting pool together into a comedy show. Not a lot of noise from balls falling into pockets on this table… probably the first silent pool table ever realized in the joint. Those wanting to play next either split for another table or bought one soda after another. Keen observers knew a love story was unraveling, not a classic game of pool.

Sammy could tell the smoke from the hall started to bother Elaine. The two new acquaintances left the scene after their marathon game and headed outside to sit on a stoop in the well-lit neighborhood. They talked as the night faded into silence. Another motion picture moment.

Sammy's street instinct uttered a familiar feeling in his gut. He knew when nights gave way to no good. A good thing. Elaine's parents would be worried. Sammy walked Elaine home spanning three-four blocks. The two hugged at her doorstep. Sammy's life would change forever from that bottled wink in time.

Elaine was raised in an upper middle-class section of South Bronx in a single-family house—something a bit foreign to Sammy's neck of the concrete woods. His upbringing a bit more to the northeast part of the city was a chorus line of small multilevel tenements that lined streets with fire escape backdrops in rows of perfect symmetry like cornfields in Nebraska. Elaine's neighborhood presented more character in terms of its homes. Her family employed a maid and a servant.

Sammy was drawn to Elaine's grace and gentle-heartedness. She was the first person in his life to make him slow down enough to plan what exit to take off of the proverbial highway of too much, too fast. Two hearts from different sides of the tracks met at the intersection of love at first sight.

New York City in the mid-50s became a centerpiece for both Jewish and Italian settlers. A healthy number of Irish and Puerto Rican immigrants were beginning to call New York City home as well. The business sector straddled a wait-and-see fence. One side was ready to explode from new markets brought on by immigration and a population boom that bore a high spirit of entrepreneurism. Another side included an increasing number of organized crime members who made doing business a tricky undertaking.

Thirty-some years after the major inception of organized crime in the United States triggered by Al Capone, New York City's version of mobsters extended beyond liquor, gambling, and prostitution. With Capone's claws grabbing control in Chicago and parts of New York, a new legion of gangsters popped up in the big city. Their main baits? Clothing and food.

Organization was the name of the game if a company's garments were going to make Fifth Avenue or end up on clearance racks. John Gotti and his extended family were huge players in the garment industry for decades in New York. Apparel jumpstarted a new line of products for Mafia families to advance their agendas at the same time Sammy's dad and father-in-law worked in the industry.

A chilling irony foretold? Sammy and Gotti together? Read on.

Sammy's first-and-only semi-pro baseball season in summer of 1954 didn't amount to any major league scouts calling on him. He reached a crossroads. Thanks to his rock, Elaine, he now knew what something real felt like, something certain.

He believed in her. Where was the certainty behind landing a professional baseball contract? Sammy loved baseball, but he loved Elaine more.

Elaine started her junior year of high school in fall of '54 and Sammy started a new hobby: stashing money. He loved saving money. Big red rubber bands wrapped around wads of green. Sammy also loved Christmas, so he decided to make the season alive and well, 365, with the colors of red and green uniting in the form of bundles of cash. He intentionally saved his cash in this meticulous manner all year long in his bedroom closet.

Making the transition from bicycle to delivery truck meant time to run with the big boys on the commercial streets of New York. No more time for deliveries by way of pedals; Sammy was moving up in the business world. His boss liked his productivity, people skills, and tenacity for sales.

While Elaine offered Sammy her heart, her father offered him a job at his garment factory. Now Sammy had two jobs to juggle. Realizing he should relinquish something from his daily calendar, Sammy chalked up baseball as a destiny he couldn't control. He quit chasing ground balls for a future that looked exceedingly promising for a nineteen year-old in the early summer of 1955.

Morris Rosen's bloodline of family garment proprietors traces back to the turn of the twentieth century. In the 1950s greater technologies emerged onto the production scene, calling for investments of research and implementation of time, capital, and people on the factory floor. The times called for a strategic emphasis on longer-term planning versus just making a go of it day-to-day.

About a third of Rosen's workforce could not read or write, creating havoc on skilled positions relying on fundamental soft skills. What timing for Sammy. He became the go-to-guy at the clothing factory. He did everything from cutting fabric to balancing books to providing frontline customer service. He had to quit his dairy job in early spring of '56 after learning how to drive a variety of delivery trucks for his friend's dad. It was a tough choice. He knew, however, that this career stepping stone would divulge greater meaning later on.

The people Sammy met along his former routes all told a story. What did the person who received eggs and milk on Arthur Avenue do for a living? How did Liebman's deli that everyone was raving about differentiate from Katz's in upscale Manhattan—a joint that's been around since the Ice Age? Those kinds of self-generated valuations fed an inquisitive mind while the company's products fed families and served restaurants.

Elaine Rosen finished high school in 1956, and Sammy didn't wait long to take her forever in marriage. Their life together began on the foundation of youthful imagination, patience, and hard work. Elaine enrolled in a local vocational school to study business. A version of the American Dream was alive and well for these young New Yorkers.

Enamored by the new undertakings with Morris Rosen, Sammy excelled at the garment factory. By the time he hit twenty-one, he was making $15,000 a year in 1957. This is the modern-day equivalent of an annual gross salary of around $133,000.[2]

3.

FULL PLATES

Newlyweds Sam and Elaine Sommer made a go of it in a small South Bronx apartment. For a short stint the couple lived with Elaine's parents, but Sam's growing salary enabled them to get along in this capacity for the time being. "Sammy" transformed into a nickname by family and friends; the name Sam engraved his identity from here on.

Sam left a stash of cash at his parent's house and didn't mind living rough for a bit. He wanted something better for Elaine; yet, it wasn't time to put the money to work yet in that capacity. She was accustomed to finer things and lots of space, but business studies kept her buried in homework and time flew making meals for her around-the-clock working husband. Elaine also worked part-time at her father's garment company.

Blessed from having jobs resulting from the head of the Rosen household, Sam and Elaine sought to write their own ticket. The young couple was on the cusp of change in late fall of 1957 thanks to a business relationship Sam nurtured a couple years earlier as a teenager from his routes. An impression on older folks as a teenager? Herein laid a prelude to the development of one heck of a people person whether anyone saw it coming or not.

Sam ran into a Harlem-based meat and seafood proprietor, Al Lang, from his delivery days. The two stood outside of

Morris Rosen's garment factory and small-talked about the Brooklyn Dodgers' heartbreaking move to Los Angeles.

The conversation shifted to business. Surprised that Sam was no longer delivering to local restaurants, the seasoned Jewish gentleman scheduled a meeting over coffee with the exuberant apprentice a couple days later to talk shop.

Sam's first-ever official business meeting produced an offer to buy one of Lang's meat routes. The established entrepreneur was slowly selling his routes for retirement. He also wanted to help family members in Israel get settled within the young nation's emerging developments, so Lang was set to relocate part of the time in the Middle East.

Here came the unwrapping of red rubber bands around non-interest bearing wads of green. Sam took everything he owned from his bedroom bank and bought a delivery route and rented a used refrigeration truck from Hertz.

The young Sommer couple christened their empty piggy bank and leap of faith by settling into a studio apartment in northwestern Queens. They could almost touch one end of the dwelling to the other with their collective arms extended. Elaine kept working part-time for her dad and finished her studies with a vocational business degree. The apartment downsizing was treated like a mental tradeoff, so to speak, for a couple's quest toward small business ownership.

Sam and Elaine's exuberance of owning a business together snowballed into Elaine expecting. News of her pregnancy prior to the holidays sent Sam into jubilation. Before adding another plate in their tiny apartment, Sam needed to remove a few things from his other plates. They were running over in balancing a full-time job while turning a new investment into an established business.

Sam knew his entrepreneurial gig wouldn't springboard unless he devoted more time to it. Ready to mix faith with small business ownership into a blender named now or never, he pushed the purify button on his life with Elaine. Sam said goodbye to his high-paying garment job to concentrate primarily on one venture for the first time in his underdeveloped yet promising business life. He did remain working at the clothing factory on a limited basis just to have some cash around.

Sam took on the new routes as an entrepreneur at the age of twenty-one—doing paperwork from home and keeping his truck at Morris' company for the time being. Each day was a make-or-break challenge. One day after sixteen hours of pounding the pavement and cutting clothes, Sam came home to heartbreak.

Elaine's mother accompanied her daughter to the doctor that morning. Elaine had miscarried their first child. Devastated, Sam's first introduction to tragedy thwarted his doings in the mecca of influential America. He was beyond sad. The couple grieved in a frozen state and couldn't do much but stare off into the streets.

The home front tragedy marshaled Sam down a one-way street of unprecedented concentration. He absorbed guilt from unsuccessfully juggling work with family and accepted sole responsibility for Elaine's miscarriage. A tough holiday stretch made the husband determined to better manage making money with making a family. He took prayer to a new level.

Remaining grateful for an opportunity to still work for Elaine's father, Sam welcomed 1958 with the opening of Sheppard Meat Company. He rented space from another deli proprietor in the Bronx as a place to cut meat for his wholesale routes and ran the office out of his apartment with Elaine's help.

Within a few months, Sam's routes produced enough money to pay the bills. He quit the garment company but stayed on to do special projects for Morris Rosen, and Elaine switched to full-time there. Mr. Rosen wore a different hat for Sam—he became the young business owner's coach. Sam learned basically every aspect of owning and operating a business thanks to his father-in-law. He also had the backing of both of his parents in nonfinancial areas. They were his cheerleaders and assisted around the apartment with cleaning and so forth.

Consumed with fresh confidence and knowledge, Sam shook relational trees from his old delivery route connections. Those past connections produced a few untapped branches of distribution in the wholesale-to-retail meat business. Born a networker, the young purveyor introduced wholesale kosher sandwich meat service to schools and hospitals in greater New York and parts of New Jersey. Unprecedented.

Sam struck gold. By 1959, he unwrapped innovation by witnessing the unwrapping of deli meats at unheard of establishments. He slowly began monopolizing some business-to-business markets in health care and education. Like when he was sixteen ahead of his time working a privileged delivery route, the now self-acclaimed visionary grabbed a share of exploding new markets at the age of twenty-two.

Raised in a home full of humility, Sam took his cash and started to save it all over again. It wasn't as much as it sounded, though, because the young innovator was astute enough to put money back into the business. He stopped renting equipment in place of purchasing, for starters—almost draining his cash upon earning it.

From a business perspective, what looked good on paper for the young entrepreneur didn't equate to reality. Growing pains and sleep deprivation took over. How would Sam transition from lone delivery man and solo capitalist to owning a fleet of wheels and employing drivers to keep up with new markets? Besides, he was being watched by business buffoons wanting a piece of the action.

Amidst his rise to street stardom, Sam felt nothing toward luxury. He did think about getting a small house for his wife, but for the time being he felt dedicated to saving and roughing life a bit. The stress of owning a company persisted at the same time Elaine became pregnant again.

Both sets of parents aimed their near future plans on retirement, knowing they could assist Sam in his chaotic yet promising ventures. Morris Rosen guided Sam through a challenging immersion of handling "what the hell do I do now." Armed with an education without tuition, books, or lecture halls, Sam's life skill professor showed him at the very least how to keep his head above water. Coupled with a strong work ethic that he learned from his own dad, the young Sommer forged ahead.

He hired two drivers and targeted his resources into fulfilling deliveries for the time being. Sam couldn't devote another second toward acquiring new businesses or setting up long-term goals and estate plans, for instance. He craved reeling in new customers and was damn good at it. Daily survival was the name-of-the-game, however, so frustrated he couldn't grow his company too fast.

The new drivers for Sheppard Meat seized the moment. Sam wanted to hire young immigrants vying for their first buck—those who couldn't afford college or struggled to find a job due to adjusting to life in America. He sought out family men he knew from getting around and helped them get on their feet.

By fall of '59 the grind turned a different direction. Additional vehicles, insurance issues, and time devoted to visiting his larger clients took a toll on Sam. Elaine carried their second child longer than the first, but tragically she experienced another miscarriage.

A doozer... the sadness reminded the couple of their earlier loss. Anger snatched center stage over grief on this one.

Sorrow not withheld, but Elaine soaked up guilt along with Sam, and the two struggled to move forward. Sam lost a few accounts and Elaine quit working. She felt like doing nothing but staring outside their apartment most days and praying.

Then God answered a prayer.

A close colleague of Sam's from Hebrew National, a longstanding manufacturer of kosher deli meats that started in lower Manhattan back in the day, shared with him his family's exuberance of adopting a child. The corporate executive mentioned difficult conditions in Greece during the onset of a political crisis.

The nation was reeling from remnants of a civil war a decade earlier. Heavily reliant on U.S. aid, Greece had appropriated American funds intended for humanitarian and social purposes toward building a strong military. Three tiers of political ideology vied for power. Two initially gave way to a leader who allowed women to vote and attempted to build a pro-American, industrialized nation.

The two opposing parties didn't take long to disrupt Prime Minister Constantine Karamanlis' implementation of industrialism. The resistance thwarted development enough to leave part of Greece desolate. Thousands defected for work abroad, including yes, the United States and New York City. In desperation, some children were left abandoned in Greece.[3]

Elaine viewed Sam's encounter with the Hebrew National executive as divine reception. The hurt couple welcomed a new decade by initiating the process of adoption overseas. They learned of a little orphan boy almost a year old who was abandoned in the streets of Athens and receiving care at a monastery outside of the city. Sam and Elaine departed for Greece in summer of 1960 to adopt the young boy.

Immediately in Greece, the couple's calling intensified. After settling in from a long flight for the night at a hotel in Athens, Sam and Elaine met the adoption agent for breakfast the next morning to discuss the terms prior to seeing the child.

During the meeting, the couple asked a visibly discombobulated agent how she'd been holding up in the chaos. Troubled over what she witnessed that morning before meeting the Sommers, her response unintentionally divulged the fate of twin girls with no home—a few months old and suffering from malnutrition at a nearby hospital. The agent couldn't shake the news of hearing about the little girls that same morning. Sam and Elaine wanted to see the twins.

At the hospital, the couple saw two thin lives waiting for a shot at life. Torn from not wanting to leave the boy, the agent informed the couple that a family from England was scheduled to see him in a couple of days if their original plans took a different turn. Turn it did. The whole visit rode on God's wings, according to Sam and Elaine then and throughout their entire life, so why stop now.

The twin girls barely moved in a tiny crib that resembled a desk drawer. Each breath portrayed a marathon of energy for them. The kids didn't even have names. Time stood still while Sam and Elaine Sommer nodded to the agent in love with the little hearts.

At an Athens' bank, Sam received an advance from Elaine's father to help pay an adoption fee that wasn't anywhere close to what was quoted by the agent earlier. No price tag on life he and Elaine thought. Sam heard a warning back home before leaving to not carry a lot of cash on the trip, so the transaction with Morris basically took shape as a quick loan.

Prior to the electronic wiring of money, the couple had to trek for several blocks in Athens carrying two huge shopping bags full of mostly coins from the bank resulting from a clunky international transaction. Lots of curious spectators … not a lot of inner peace while the couple lugged the mostly metal dough.

Sam and Elaine hurriedly reached their hotel room and secured it with chairs and other furniture against the door. They spent most of the afternoon counting out more than $4,000 on the bed, double-checking the payment in order to satisfy the twin adoption arrangement.

Within a few hours, husband and wife happily accepted the identity of father and mother of two after a pair of failed tries. Before leaving Greece, Sam checked out the city while Elaine reviewed some final terms with the agency. He saw poverty like never before. In New York, the less fortunate were abound but not as visible in his everyday travels. He and Elaine gave generously to their community, but this global eye-opener showed destitution at almost every corner.

The Sommers left New York as a family of two and returned a party of five. Two adults, two children. Did all the hustle and bustle break their calculator? An icing on the cake to the Sommer's jet set around the world came with another surprise: Elaine was carrying again, and the couple didn't know it until returning to New York, although she experienced morning sickness symptoms on the flight back to the States.

At LaGuardia in New York, the couple was met by an entourage of family members. A celebration kicked off right then and there at the airport. Sam skipped a few hugs and stepped outside the airport for a second on his own. Curious family members observed him falling to his knees to kiss the ground.

His sudden act offered a gesture of thankfulness to the Lord for his blessings and in remembrance to the sad sights he witnessed in Athens. Prior to leaving for Greece, he purchased a brand new Buick. The very next day after returning from overseas, he sold the car back to the dealership and donated all the money to a Manhattan church that worked with homeless families both locally and abroad.

Back in the States the conditions of the two adopted girls steadily improved. Linda and Marlene Sommer christened the conversion of a small apartment into their nursery. They owned the joint. Tons of stumbles and piles of household items made the place training grounds for dodgeball. One needed an insurance policy just to visit the apartment. Sam and Elaine didn't care much for how the place presented itself to others. They were on top of the world.

For the first time in their green marriage, Sam could marry his green earnings with a joyful Elaine and blessings of children and another on the way. She raised the twins while Sam returned to the grind. He exhibited a different bounce in his step before the girls took their first steps.

The family of four plus one on the way soon upgraded to a larger apartment within the same building. The Greek girls all but kicked malnutrition into yesterday, and their health improved with each passing day. Elaine remained healthy with her first naturally-born child growing into a later-stage pregnancy.

New York City beat to its own drum, and a steady one at that regarding workforce development at the outset of the '60s. Early morning honks, flashing lights, and lots of doors slamming from illegally parked delivery vehicles captured industry on parade. The city's job outlook started strong, then dipped in the mid-60s, only to pick up again later in the decade, according to Sam's own business peaks, valleys, and observations.

Jobs, yes; social harmony, not so fast. The start of the Vietnam conflict loaded U.S. streets with protestors. The street soldiers in charge of sustaining the daily grind of commerce in the big city, along with those putting on patriotic boots to battle overseas, both met resistance from a new wave of political activism.

Remnants of the real enemy in Vietnam landed domestically on streets, in parks, and so on. Opposition to the nation's involvement in the war was not directed at combat alone; big business perceivably became an enemy of American culture as well. The chaos downtown befell on Sam and his family. The scene curtailed their concentration in growing a family and distracted Sam from doing business. Thoughts of moving out of the inner hub circled in the twenty-four-year-old's mind.

That consideration moved closer to the front burner of reality when the couple welcomed their first naturally-born child into the fold as another sister to Linda and Marlene. Jane Sommer was born in March of 1961.

Needing more space and a little breathing room from growing unrest downtown, the Sommers moved to Commack on Long Island in 1962, joining an existing trend of urbanites who preferred rural residences while maintaining big city jobs. They mortgaged a two-story, four-bedroom home in a recently-developed neighborhood not far from the Jericho Turnpike on Zinnia Court. The easy access to the freeway aided Sam and his deliveries.

Red wagons and ice cream trucks defined sidewalks in this neighborhood. The Sommer house cried for kids and lots of them. The young girls loved going barefoot in the grass without their parents worrying about broken glass and cigarette butts.

The clothing industry budded nationwide, and New York City remained the root of its influence and production. Elaine's parents planned on selling their share of the factory soon to retire in Florida. The pressure to sell partly mounted from the street. Mafia influence appeared to spoil an otherwise vibrant time in the city's commerce; yet, the time neared for the Rosen couple to hit the sunset anyway.

What to eat joined forces with what to wear in New York as food service took off in the early '60s as another big city staple. The previous decade introduced a plethora of fancier restaurants, many of which were Italian, along with candy stores and soda fountain drug stores that kind of portrayed the city in pop culture and the arts. Some delicatessens stood tall like the aforementioned Liebman's and Katz's; now other smaller delis came into play too.

If opportunity knocked; Sam Sommer was a door handle. There were no signs of any kosher delis making it a go on Long Island, much less in the Commack vicinity. It didn't appear that a deli fetish hit Long Island quite as fast as the inner city burbs.

Sam's vision for a deli in Commack intensified. The experiences he chalked up from his wholesale operations where he had been exposed to numerous delis assisted him in this next venture. Plans were underway to put up a deli in central Long Island. That undertaking would also move his main headquarters out of the concrete jungle and into the burbs.

Elaine's business studies came in handy. Sam was wrapped up in daily operations and never found time for administrative duties. Elaine did the best she could to balance her important hand in the family enterprises while looking after three young children in a new home. The couple felt like it needed third-party help with bookkeeping, filing, payroll, and the like but withheld making such a move due to lack of time to train and related issues.

Essentially Sam needed leadership to align with opening a sit-down deli so he could attend to and grow his wholesale ventures in New Jersey. Elaine's uncle, Irving Silver, was in-and-out of jobs due to caring for his ailing wife, Jeanette.

With Sheppard Meat doing pretty good, Sam offered Irving a chance to oversee part of that business with family flexibility to spend time with Jeanette. The fifty-four-year-old relative accepted the offer, enabling Sam's small business to turn another page closer to building a conglomerate.

In spring of 1963, Elaine discovered she was pregnant again. The twins would start preschool the following year, and the timing appeared ripe again for a consecutive successful natural-born child. Like a Norman Rockwell portrait, life was falling in place again for the young Sommer family. Other families were enjoying a ride on Sam's coattails as well—the way he designed the whole thing to be.

Sam set his sights on further legitimizing his operations with trusts, estate planning, and longer-term goals—both personally and professionally. That was a goal that kept eluding him, however, due to the pace of life.

The Sommers' home in Commack included lots of closet space. Clothes and clutter weren't the issue; money was. Closets functioned as branch offices of a bank with convenient deposit hours. Two of them held wads of cash. Sam realized though that he should stop paying his employees and everyone else under the sun with cash and start doing business on paper. That was yet another goal that didn't seem to reach fruition—lots of ideas, little time.

Morris Rosen sold his part of the business and planned to help Sam with some of his entrepreneurial growing pains once he worked out the details of a retirement home in Miami. For the time being, full plates overflowed with sales, deliveries, developing staff, kids, and so forth.

With Irving Silver grabbing the reigns of Sheppard Meat for the time being, Sam focused on starting up the Commack deli. One of his inner-city connections led him to "Sal" Salvatore Spatarella, an aggressive enterpriser who had his hands in New York City's garbage collection business. He served as head of the Suffolk County Carting Association.

As New York City populated, droves of trash filled the streets. Garbage collection prospered. The Mafia, even somewhat to this day and before Sam's introduction to the workforce in the 50s, controlled the trucks, routes, and disposal of waste in the hub. Sometimes the "disposal end" of the operation remained off the radar for discussion.

Just as recent as 2013, more than thirty members of the infamous Luchese, Genovese, and Gambino families were indicted for extortion in the trash-hauling business. A retired New York state trooper, Mario Velez, was also among the individuals charged in the high-profile carting ring and subsequent criminal charges.[4]

All those years organically understudying the heartbeat of New York's streets paid off for a twenty-eight-year-old entrepreneur. Thankfully ahead of his time in concrete jungle wisdom, Sam Sommer kept a guarded distance from the animals preying on small business. Spatarella and his entourage fit the mold of king of the forest.

Spatarella provided conveniently-located rental space for Sam to park his main delivery truck in one of his garages in Brooklyn—one that also stored garbage trucks for the Luchese family. Sam hit it off well with Sal, but again, he massaged the relationship with pinpoint patience and back-of-mind skepticism. He did not, however, completely realize the scope of Spatarella's influence.

The relationship between Sal and Sam naturally exposed Sommer's capital undertakings to a member of the Mafia. Sam called it regretted oversight and to some degree, he felt defenseless anyway. No harm, no foul, he thought. For the time being mutual respect between the gentlemen toward making a buck or two trumped any suspicion of invasion on

Sam's turf. If mobsters were mounting a front against Sam for business reasons, he didn't see it coming.

Back on the home front, the Sommers were prepping for a fourth member of their family. A silver lining canvassed their hearts from the pain of two previous miscarriages during the Christmas season in '63. Elaine gave birth to Karen Sommer on December 23.

At the start of 1964 everything Sam touched continued to turn to gold with the opening of the first delicatessen in Commack—the Deli-Queen. Later the name would change to Rosen's in spirit for the mentorship Sam received from his father-in-law. It didn't take long for the restaurant to become a cash cow. It was conveniently located right off Jericho Turnpike near a courthouse, a shopping mall, and among residential houses for blocks on end.

The deli was a good-sized restaurant, seating about a hundred for lunch Monday thru Friday. Corned beef and pastrami was a smash hit—piled to the ceiling and requiring a mouth like a hippo to eat. Judges, attorneys, legal professionals, and other nearby folks of all walks made up a steady stream of clientele. Even Spatarella frequented there from the big city.

Before long, Sam sculpted an American Dream for more than twenty employees at the Deli-Queen alone, many of whom again emigrated from Europe looking to make a life on U.S. soil. He also opened two hair salons in Queens and grew the Sheppard Meat venture to become a catering business for hospitals and schools. Sam was on the verge of capturing a decent portion of the Eastern Seaboard wholesale meat market.

Irving Silver struggled to sustain the pressure of a booming company while attending to Jeanette. She felt better in '64 compared to the previous year from treatment from cancer. Sam granted Irving some time off and resumed oversight of wholesale sales. His key clients were glad to see him again. Folks around him said he got better with age. He wasn't even thirty.

Inwardly, Sam contemplated his shortcomings. Realizing he could read shifting behavior on the streets when it came to organized crime, his self-admitted downfall encompassed a bit of gullibility. He possessed a sharp eye for the untrustworthy; yet, at times he trusted freely without proper diligence.

Sal Spatarella was one such example and perhaps Irving Silver another. The jury was still out on where the relationship with Spatarella may be heading in Sam's mind. Despite Irving being a blood relative, "family" in the '60s in the big city was as loose of a term as "fake news" is today. Sam kept relying on Irving simply because he was "family."

Child number five for Sam and Elaine was on the way in 1965, and Jeanette Silver seemed to be in remission. Some days Sam and Irving would ride into the inner city together, making deliveries and checking on customers. The carpooling together reintroduced Silver to Sam's work, and it also gave Elaine a chance to hear about Jeanette's condition through Sam on a regular basis. The Silver's lived in Kew Gardens, Queens—not a terrible distance from Commack but a long enough hike to not be able to borrow cups of sugar from one another on a regular basis.

Sam cared about Silver's family. He repeatedly tried to ground Irving in a little stability. He gave him a part-time management position at Rosen's since that endeavor almost coasted on autopilot. Repeat business at the deli pulled customers back in magnetic magic, plus it took Irving only around thirty minutes to get to Deli-Queen compared to traveling bumper-to-bumper into the hub to visit the whole operation.

Silver's old car saw better days, but he didn't have much money left after paying medical bills for Jeanette's treatment to make major repairs or buy new wheels. Sam felt an obligation to soon address Irving's transportation issue since he needed a car for business as well.

Elaine visited Jeanette with the older kids to help around their apartment whenever possible. Her plate also included doing paperwork for her husband while raising four kids. The Silver kids, college-student Ronnie and the younger Barrie, loved seeing their nieces. Irving mentioned to Sam a concern for Ronnie despite going to college at Pace University in Manhattan. He was starting to hang out with much older men who were into gambling.

While Elaine's parents were getting settled into retirement near Miami, Sam's dad had another year before calling it quits. His parents would join the Rosen's in Florida the following year, albeit on the "other side of the track" so to speak in socioeconomic living conditions. The business owner had a bit more of a luxurious retirement than the business laborer. Didn't matter—they were joined together in love. The two couples always enjoyed a close relationship.

The next couple of years brought two more little ones—Robert in '65 and Stephen the following year—the first boys into the fold. By spring of 1967, Elaine and Sam had six kids and owned one deli, two hairs salons, and a thriving wholesale meat proprietorship.

In peculiar irony, the couple's hunch was that their family's future was uncertain. How could that be with bundles of cash stacked in closets like precision-like bricks that shape a decorative wall? Go figure. A growing supply of money would make most people feel good about tomorrow. By all accounts, Sam was on the verge of becoming a millionaire at the age of thirty, and he provided jobs for nearly fifty people.

A credit to his extinct, Sam got his ass rung in 1967 by a newly-hired financial advisor. Come hell or high water it was a must for Sam to begin the process of setting up trusts, estates, and a foundation to protect his business and family's assets. The advisor resembled an angry nun tapping a yardstick in one hand ready to whack sense into her pupil. As smart as Sommer was in business, he was still a pupil when it came to financial management.

Six kids did more than break in the Sommer's Commack home. Sam's intentions of honing in on family and business planning stalled momentarily to make some repairs around the home. The oldest kids would start second grade that fall.

Another roadblock stymied Sam's blueprint for putting in place future financial security arrangements: Jeanette's cancer returned with a vengeance. She passed in July at the age of fifty-five after getting blindsided by the disease's return in a matter of weeks.

The death of Jeanette Silver put Irving's family into a rightful and predictable tailspin. Barrie relocated out of the area for school, and twenty-three-year-old Ronnie finished college, yet he wasn't actively putting his degree to work. Rather, his obsession of the street grabbed the young man and pulled him into playing cards and placing bets—draining his dad's pockets from time to time to get out of hot water.

Sam wanted to do more for Irving and his family. He even offered Ronnie a job, but the young man respectfully declined, adamant about getting into the marketing research field instead. Ronnie did help out occasionally, which came as a relief for many. Fear of him ending up in a tall grassy field with his head down suggested a real possibility based on the characters he ran with.

Unable to appease his financial advisor, the remainder of 1967 came and went with Sam looking at a remodeled home for his family as a priority. The holiday celebration centered around word of the family's seventh child on the way—the original goal of Sam and Elaine. The number seven to them is in tune with God's divinity. The Sommer children were growing up strong in faith while outgrowing their home in Commack.

The start of 1968 saw an opportunity for Sam to help nurture the healing process for the Silver family. He created a special position for Irving to grow Sheppard Meat Company into new markets and secure potential partnerships. In the process of training the sixty-year-old, Irving asked Sam if he would give a friend of his a second shot at rehabilitation after serving time in prison.

Sam acquiesced to Irving's request in the spirit of giving anyone a second chance at life. The two of them brainstormed ideas related to odd jobs the convicted felon released on parole could do for the company. At the same time, Sam mulled going on vacation with his family to Florida.

Both of Sam and Elaine's parents were pressing the couple for more than a year to join them for a visit. The retirees had been back to New York during childbirths and holidays, but Sam's family didn't yet hit the sun to celebrate retirements with both families on tropical turf.

The trip would mean leaving his businesses in the hands of Irving Silver.

4.

DEEP WATERS

Sam and Elaine Sommer decided to hit the brakes on life in the spring of 1968 without even knowing how to do such a thing. The arduous aspiration loomed like a fairy tale for a family of six tykes, another on the way in July, and an around-the-clock husband and father who owned businesses throughout greater New York City.

A fortuitous circumstance to get away for a breather after a long winter grind in the Northeast befell the family. The end of the school year approached for second-graders Linda and Marlene, and Miami in early-May served as the ticket with retired in-laws itching for a chance to see their grandkids.

The respite would also give Elaine downtime from her loving routine of seeing kids off to pre-school and elementary learning from the breakfast table at different times. She was the family rock while Sam climbed the mountain to prosperity. A part-time nanny and housekeeper could take a break as well from the domestic grind.

Prior to leaving on the trip, Sam had to cover more bases than he did during his baseball days. He was leaving an empire behind for an excursion in the sun. The decision to vacate a momentous nest egg to his wife's uncle was more unsettling than dealing with mobsters who eyed his businesses all the time. He had little choice, though, and loved Irving Silver.

Irving Silver's track record of holding jobs, even before the recent death of Jeannette, bordered on head scratching. For whatever reason Silver's employment resume resembled that of a gypsy roadshow. Sam's options were thin in terms of personnel to watch over his operations. He had a few other employees in mind to train for this purpose, but lack of time prevented that objective from unfolding.

For Sam, the vacation also meant focusing on building a fortress around his growing enterprises. He planned to spend time setting up investments, trusts, and the like for his wife and kids without phones ringing, meeting delivery deadlines, and so on. The Florida trip offered an ideal landscape to put into practice a goal that evaded him daily as a budding and busy entrepreneur.

A couple of weeks before heading to Florida, the two men were leaving the Bronx Diner to return to Commack. They walked a half block toward Sam's station wagon parked near the corner when Irving wanted to go across the street to quickly check out a newer deli. Sam told him he noticed the new store too but was in a hurry and that he'd check it out next time they were in the area. He asked Irving to kindly make it quick.

Before he entered his car, Sam noticed a dark four-door Lincoln speeding faster and faster from the other direction heading straight toward Irving.

> **Sitting with a cane in hand at the age of eighty-two, Sam recalled that frightful moment:**
>
> *Irving and I, you know, it was business as usual. I enjoyed taking him around to build connections. He was coming around—had been through so much with his wife's cancer and losing a couple of jobs. Getting him involved in work we prayed would help him make some dough for his family.*

It was a nice early afternoon in a growing southwestern Bronx neighborhood. The two of us headed back to my car after grabbing a bite at the diner. It was a wide street, almost highway-like and a little underdeveloped. Man, we got around in those days—there weren't too many unfamiliar sights or sounds we hadn't experienced.

Until that moment (cocking his head to one side with a neutral smile).

Irving wanted to check out a new deli that I had my eye on as well to pay a visit, but time was getting away from me—a busy afternoon of work was on my plate. I told him I'd be waiting in the car for him, but you know, to kindly hurry it up. Out of the blue this dark car raced down the other side of the street coming straight in his direction. The whole neighborhood went from peace and routine to horror because of this demonic car.

The way it zoomed in Irving's direction made me freeze outside my car. It was like that vehicle was possessed, and the driver didn't care about anything. I looked at Irving, who had not yet made it across the street.

I yelled, 'look out,' but he stood like ice just as I did. The car was almost at the intersection coming toward our block. Suddenly I did not want this car to win, regardless of where it was going and who the target may be. I felt that target was Irving.

I sprinted toward Irving and must have threaded the needle between getting mauled to death and tackling him into a curbside garbage pile. I guess I'm still here so a needle has never been looked at quite the same (smile).

We hit the sidewalk hard, yet our fall was cushioned by some trash. I got up to look and saw that the car had bounced off the curb and sped down the street out of sight. There weren't many other cars around—this was like a newer business district with a few buildings.

A few people came up to us. We were filled with greasy slime. A young man wearing an apron from the deli asked about our condition. It looked like a couple of cars were pulled over as well. We didn't want to drag anyone into whatever mess this was in case the raging machine returned. Irving and I thanked the man and limped out of fear, not injury, back to our car. Never knew you could limp in fear.

We were just dirty from falling and sweating. Shook up, you know. That car veered toward Irving—I'm sure of it. Later on, I learned that a guy who was involved in my case admitted he hired guys to scare or hit people with cars around New York. At the moment I couldn't fathom such a connection, despite Silver and his son running with street thugs. Again, though, the car clearly was aiming at Silver. No one else was around.

It seemed like a crystal ball somewhere out of time foretold that moment, even though I don't believe in crystal balls. That's my point. Evil must have been behind the wheel of that car (shaking his head).

I believe to this day that tackling Irving compromised something in my walk. I can't describe it, but there's a possibility that car, a three-thousand pound metal feather, brushed my side. It's affected my gait by way of a hitch in my walk; however, I can't pinpoint whether or not for sure I was hit.

Scary shit. Broad daylight, too.

NOTE: When this book approached fruition, Sam Sommer began falling in his apartment regularly. In fall of 2018 he underwent hip surgery.

Silver was a target, believed Sam on a hunch. After the attempted rundown, he repeatedly asked Irving if he had any intuition about the near-death experience. Irving didn't say much other than a Hallmark card's worth of "thank yous" to Sam for saving his life. The aftermath of the incident was just as mysterious as the event itself.

Sam didn't tell Elaine about the hit-and-run attempt until much later in life because of her pregnancy. Good move with a trip to Florida on the horizon as well. She did question her husband's hitch. Pulled muscle from lifting a side of beef.

The day before the family would leave for Florida on May 11, Sam directed Irving to what priorities stood tallest in keeping business afloat while away. Irving appeared somewhat distracted to Sam's counsel. When Sam asked Irving what was bothering him thinking it might be the latest shenanigan from Ronnie, Silver expressed some concerns about the man they hired to restore part of the Deli-Queen after a kitchen fire.

***

Irving Silver met Harold Goberman in early 1968, a thirty-year-old general commercial remodeler from Allentown, Pennsylvania, through his son Ronnie. Goberman had been released from prison the previous fall. He was in-and-out of prison several times for crimes related to third-degree assault, armed robbery, kidnapping, hijacking, and grand larceny, to name a few. He even spent time at a state hospital to have his sanity examined.

Goberman would later be involved in two major New York court cases. In 1984, he was part of a ring of selling fake logo wear shirts. That operation enlisted the help of a company in east Pennsylvania to manufacture shirts using the Izod alligator emblem, which was unlawfully reproduced by a design firm with alleged ties to South America. The counterfeit shirts were then sold to retail outlets in the United States, Japan, and Europe.[5]

In 1992, Goberman was part of court testimony involving Long Island auto dealer and developer John McNamara, who was accused of defrauding General Motors for more than $400 million over a decade. Twenty years earlier in 1972 and just four years after Goberman's interactions with Irving Silver, McNamara and a family member hired four men to "intimidate" Goberman, who was working as a contractor in the construction of a new dealership for the auto tycoon.[6]

***

Silver's concerns about Goberman were predicated on the influence he was having on Ronnie, not anything pertaining to his behaver with Sam's staff or work at Rosen's. The restoration project seemed to be working out okay. Sam suggested to Irving to keep an eye on Goberman and to call him in Florida if anything came up. In terms of Ronnie, Sam reiterated to his wife's uncle that he and Elaine warned him of his son hanging around the wrong people for quite some time.

Sam gave Irving the green light to allow Ronnie to help him with deliveries. Sam and Elaine's hearts extended beyond assisting Irving with his time and money; they were devoted to his kids as well. The strategic suggestion was also made, so Irving could keep Ronnie closer to his side while teaching him the value of helping a family member. The Sommers arrived in Miami on Saturday, May 10.

The retired parents of both Sam and Elaine lived within a few miles from one another in a booming coastal retirement community outside of Miami. The close proximity of the families aided Sam and Elaine in the friendly politics of where they'd stay and for how long during vacation. They played their accommodations by ear without an itinerary thanks to a short driving distance between both homes. Finally a chance to do something that didn't require the command of a clock. The almost idle lifestyle felt unusual for the couple, and it took a few days to adjust.

Meanwhile, Irving Silver was not adjusting well to his lifestyle as head of Sam's ventures. He forced a conversation with Sal Spatarella while retrieving Sam's delivery truck for the day that was stored in Sal's Mafia-owned garage in Brooklyn. Spatarella owned the All-American Refuse Removal Corporation, and set his sights on gaining control over the Long Island refuse market as well.

Silver began bugging Spatarella for opportunities to invest in his enterprises, particularly since Sal's family was targeting Long Island in business development. Spatarella didn't appreciate Silver pressuring him on business matters. He told him to take a hike.

Whether it was clothing, delicatessens, or garbage removal, Nassau and Suffolk Counties at the time seemed to lag a bit in development compared to the inner city boroughs. Conversely, Long Island would soon turn out to be the place where everyone moved to as a trend. Work in the big city and live on the Island—that was the ticket.

After a couple days on vacation on Monday night, Sam called Silver to check on how everything was going. Same old song and dance. Silver didn't say much in the way of details. Instead he repeatedly assured Sam that all was well. Sam asked about Goberman, and Silver tiptoed around the subject before informing Sam he hadn't seen him. He then informed Sam that Ronnie was doing well and that he turned out to be a big help.

Sam was pleased to hear things were at least stable for the moment. He sensed, however, something was not right with Irving. The two concluded their conversation without Sam's knowledge of Silver's intrusion at Spatarella's garage. That wasn't the only future surprise waiting in the wings for Sam Sommer concerning Irving Silver.

A few days before Irving and Sam talked long distance, likely around the time the Sommer family left for the sun, Goberman approached Silver at the Deli-Queen about a loan. Silver accepted a check from Goberman made out to Sam's Sheppard Meat Co. for $5,000 in exchange for cash. To this day it remains a mystery regarding what kind of future "favor" Silver was to receive from the bad boy who was supposed to be fixated on rehabilitation. A strong theory is that Goberman wanted to use Silver to get in with Spatarella's undertakings.

Around the time of Irving and Sam's New York-to-Florida conversation or shortly beforehand, Silver discovered that the check he received from Goberman bounced. Upset about being out five grand and taken for a ride from a crook and yet at the same time a colleague or even a "friend," Silver marched into the Suffolk County Second Precinct in Huntington to file a complaint against Goberman.

Silver apparently couldn't find Goberman to confront him— probably a good thing in the buying him of time department and his life. It came out later that Ronnie pled the fifth to his own father about Goberman's whereabouts. Frustrated and perhaps scared shitless because the five grand wasn't his money in the first place, Silver went to the police station just west of Commack. He didn't have that kind of money laying around anyway—not even close.

The police would later validate this event as part of the story of Sam Sommer. Lots of educated guesses to speculate again as to why the money was needed, but one truth remained strong at the time the bogus loan went down: Irving Silver had been swimming with merciless sharks in deep waters.

In tropical waters off the coast of Miami, catching a big fish on vacation dodged Sam's line a few times on Tuesday. That evening, May 14, Sam planned to rise at the crack of dawn. He became moved by the challenge and wanted to hit the Atlantic early. While getting ready to hit the pillow earlier than usual, he got a call from Silver.

Irving said he needed Sam to come back without explaining too much, except that it dealt with the business. Sam believed, and still does to this day, that Silver feared for his life over Goberman. The urgency behind the phone call prompted Sam to catch an evening flight back to New York on Wednesday, May 15. He remarkably caught a swordfish earlier that morning and asked his father to get it mounted.

Sam left his family in Florida to enjoy themselves a while longer. He figured he'd return in a couple of days to resume the family vacation. He even considered staying closer to two weeks at one point. Too much stress now with Silver and his enterprises—a future nugget Sam sought to protect for his family, future offspring, and for his employees and their families.

In New York, Sam and Irving connected on Thursday morning, May 16, at the Hollywood Diner in Commack—one of Sam's competing businesses but better than meeting at Rosen's given the seriousness of their gathering. Sam purposely wanted to keep a low profile while in town anyway. He desired to rectify Irving's dilemma and hit the blue skies for blue waters as soon as possible again to be with his extended family.

Over breakfast, Irving apologetically told Sam about the loan, bounced check, and complaint with Suffolk County police. Irving came across boiled as opposed to battered in shame and embarrassment. His anger protruded at Goberman about the check, while indicating to Sam that he thought by helping Goberman it would improve relationships.

In between dodging questions about what the money was used for and why Irving felt compelled to loan five grand, Sam clutched the breakfast table in Superman-fashion—ready to toss it into tomorrow. Instead, he exhaled a gust and then asked Irving a poignant question. "What relationships?"

Fumbled speech and mumbles followed. Irving's response offered a cross stream between not wanting to ruffle Goberman's feathers and trying to fit in with street kings. The ruffling of feathers dealt with fear, and wanting to be one of the good ole' boys related to preserving Ronnie's connections and a desire to be wanted. Sam got the gist of where Irving's woeful situational state was coming from.

Strangely and impulsively, by going to the police Irving stirred a hornet's nest despite that not being what he wanted. Sam suggested that the two of them resume a normal day of carpooling the next morning to make their rounds—business as usual. In doing so, they would see what might unfold naturally along their routes with respect to Goberman. Sam didn't want to "hunt him down" about the check since Irving went to the police. He thought that changed everything. Something had to give on its own under these circumstances.

Sam spent the rest of the day doing some administrative work alone at his Sheppard Meat office in Commack. He called Elaine and told her he'd likely catch a flight tomorrow afternoon or early evening to rejoin her and family in Miami.

At home that evening, Sam called Irving to remind him of their carpool arrangement.

The carpool typically involved Irving parking his car at Sam's early in the morning (Incidentally, Sam recently purchased a new Buick Skylark for Irving in exchange for his commitment to work.). The two would then often take Sam's car and make a quick stop at Bernie's Diner outside of town for coffee, followed by hitting the big city in Sam's car until they reached a location where one of the company vehicles was parked.

After spending time with the family St. Bernard, Sargent, and thanking a neighbor for watching him and then continuing to do so because of return plans to Florida, Sam went to bed early. Tomorrow had all the makings of two businessmen playing sleuths over $5,000, distrust, and who knew what else. The latter uncertainty, the "what else," would change lives forever.

5.

AVALANCHE ON LONG ISLAND

The alarm sounded around 4:00 a.m. on Friday, May 17, 1968. Anchored by a propensity for hard work, and on this day seeking answers to protect a loved one and his businesses, Sam Sommer awaited Irving Silver's arrival to carpool.

Irving purportedly was running a bit behind that morning. In the driveway, Sam waited in his car with the engine running and the morning news on the radio. He liked to pay particular attention to new business mergers and openings.

About thirty minutes went by and still no Irving Silver. Despite longing to get a move on, Sam calmly replayed in his mind the communications he had with Irving the day before—the morning meeting and reminder phone call. Maybe the Florida trip and Goberman thing threw off their morning's routine together, he pondered.

The 6:00 a.m. hour neared and still no Irving. Sam knew that Irving could drive himself to the office—it's not like he'd be stranded anywhere unless there was car trouble. Then again, with a new Skylark that was unlikely.

A few natural thoughts rolled in Sam's mind in consideration of the circumstance: Irving was ill. He overslept. He was already at the office and overlooked the carpool. Something was up with Ronnie, or something was up with Irving. More thoughts, less comforting in the lonely running car at the crack of dawn. He went inside his house and placed a call to the Silver residence. No answer.

More time passed. Sam needed to hit the road without Irving. He wanted to get back to the southern sun later that day, so he figured maybe his path would cross with Irving's at some point in the morning. Still wanting to maintain anonymity from his staff at the Deli-Queen due to erratic vacation plans and not wanting to confuse anyone, Sam went to the Sheppard Meat office prior to hitting New York City.

He worried about Irving but kept busy, plotting his morning stops in the hub. A couple hours went by and Sam called Irving's place again before heading into the city. Surprisingly on the first ring, a hoarse-voice answered.

"Yeah, Hello."

"Hello, Sam here. Irv?"

"Sam?" a surprised tone inquired.

"Ronnie?"

"Yeah, it's me, Ronnie."

"Where's your father?"

"Sam, I've been meaning to call you but didn't know where you were," Ronnie said in a choppy tone.

Ronnie's disclosure—*I've been meaning to call you but didn't know where you were* came so far out of left field that it resonated from a different stadium, metaphorically speaking. "What the heck was that?" Sam thought.

Once Sam regained composure, he replied. "OK, I'll catch him later." On the verge of hanging up a shout stopped the harrowing conversation from ending.

"Sam, wait! Wait, I... I... gotta tell you something."

Dead air and no time for drum rolls. Sam became frustrated at Ronnie's dramatic stuttering. He wanted directness. "What, Ronnie. What is it?"

Ronnie began whining and then forcefully uttered, "Dad's dead."

The same instinct that led Sam to call Irving a second time that morning before leaving the office morphed into a tussle between a chuckle from a sick joke and his jaw hitting the floor. Middle ground between two tugging emotions produced a cold palpitation at what just came out of Ronnie Silver's mouth. The breaking news lacked authenticity in spite of it coming from a family member.

Zapped from reality, Sam dropped the phone and gazed across his office into nowhere. Mind waves zig zagged from grieving to gripping a current state of devastation. Zoned out.

"Sam, Sam, are you there?" streamed through the end of the receiver like a megaphone. "Sam, please," cried Ronnie in despair.

Hands over his face and lost in a gaze, Sam's thoughts ran the gamut from guilt for leaving on his trip to feeling responsible for Ronnie despite this unbelievable disclosure and odd behavior over the phone—going from drama to directness in seconds. Ronnie continued his attempt to restore Sam's attention on the phone.

"Sam, are you at home?" Ronnie's message changed. He sought Sam's location. His change in cadence and meaning caught Sam's attention. Sam snapped out of his trance and picked up the phone. Clearly the two men needed to talk face-to-face.

"Ronnie, this can't be real."

"I'm so sorry, Sam. It's all so…, so"…

Sam interrupted. "Ronnie, when and how did this happen?"

"I don't know, Sam."

"When did you see him last, Ronnie? Did you call the police?"

"Last night, Sam. I saw him last night at home. They just found his body out west of Melville off of Wheatley Road." Wheatley Road in 1968 was an under-developed artery that ran undefined in infancy south of Highway 25 in a rural setting. Today, the road is more established but still winds all over the board about half way between Commack and Queens on northern Long Island.

When a newspaper delivery driver discovered Irving Silver's body, it was likely by chance due to the tall grass and piles of dirt that staged alongside the road. The location alone added a creepy prelude to a developing story of grief and shock. After Sam verified the tragic spot with Ronnie, the conversation shifted into an accusatory gear.

"Sam, dad was supposed to meet you for work; this is the first you heard?"

Incensed by the young man's tone, Sam fired back. "Been in Florida, Ronnie, came back to help your dad for a bit. What do you know? What's going on?"

His wife's cousin remained silent other than a few clears of his throat. Sam believed he placed Ronnie in the hot seat, so to speak, after challenging his inquisitive tone. Sam changed the subject a little to focus on the police. Ronnie said that is how he found out—Suffolk County detectives visited him at his apartment earlier that morning. He hadn't told his sister yet from still being in shock over the tragedy.

Sam encouraged Ronnie, as difficult as it was, to go to whatever precinct the detectives were from and try to offer whatever help he could toward their investigation. The situation became too emotional for any further phone dialogue. Enough said for now between the two relatives.

Sam invited Ronnie over to his house that evening so they could speak face-to-face.

After hanging up the phone, stunned by the news Sam could do nothing more but think of Elaine and the sadness behind losing her uncle. Proximity recognizably made matters difficult for Sam to tell Elaine. His office didn't serve justice to a place of required solitude to grieve and think, so he left for home. Speaking of justice, who killed Irving Silver and why?

At home, the recent confrontation between Goberman and Silver conflicted with emotions of sorrow. Sam spent most of the afternoon sitting in his living room trying to make sense of the senseless. He couldn't yet find the strength to call Elaine and hadn't factored in getting the family back from Florida as well.

She left a message on the answering machine to see when her husband was going to return to Florida. Sam tentatively informed her before he left for New York that Friday night would be likely. The evening approached, and Sam needed to return to his office because he wanted to grab the subcontractor file on Harold Goberman.

Close to 4:00 p.m. prior to heading out to retrieve the file, Sam received a call from a Detective Thomas Mansel with Suffolk County Homicide, Fourth Precinct in Hauppauge—not far from Commack to the east. The detective asked Sam to meet him concerning the death of his relative. Sam agreed and suggested the Sheppard Meat office since he needed to go back there anyway.

He felt good about the call in the spirit of addressing Irving's death, but it was a tad strange to receive a meeting question before notification of the actual death. Granted, Sam already knew about Irving's demise. How did Mansel know that? It could have been an oversight. If so, maybe Mansel failed Policing 101 during training under how to notify a family member concerning a death. Perhaps Ronnie told Mansel that Sam knew, yet that wasn't brought up in the conversation—one that involved two complete strangers up until the phone call. Either way, it struck Sam between the eyes as a bizarre call.

Within minutes at his office, Sam greeted Mansel and another detective, Jack Brown. Mansel asked Sam to go with him and Brown to the Fourth Precinct to ID the body of Irving Silver. Sam felt queasy. Maybe he was being tested. Is it possible Mansel or Brown didn't say anything about the death to gain his pulse on whether he knew or not? Erring on the side of stating what he knew versus what he didn't know about Irving, Sam mentioned that he heard of the tragedy from the deceased's son just that morning. A glance from both detectives served as a response to the statement.

Sam joined the two detectives in a squad car for the fifteen-minute drive to the homicide unit. Why they didn't have him travel there alone introduced another edge-of-the-seat moment in the already sorrowful and perplexing situation. While Sam sat in the back on the way to the county morgue (adjacent to the homicide precinct), he reviewed in his mind how the officers' eyes danced around his place of business in curiosity.

Was Sam a suspect in the murder of Irving Silver already in the minds of these detectives? Was the "identification of the deceased's body" more of a ploy than a formality?

At the fourth precinct, the detectives brought Sam into a room around twelve feet by twelve feet. They asked him about his business relationship with Silver. At the time, Sam didn't believe he was a suspect; he simply wanted to help law enforcement find out how Silver died. Murder or foul play did not yet surface in any conversation.

Mansel artfully deceived Sam by luring him to the station under the premise that the main purpose of his visit was to ID the body. Sam was all right with Mansel's approach because he wanted to cooperate; yet, he saw it coming with an inner chuckle as a trick-of-the-trade. He stated that Irving was a partner in some aspects of his business and affirmed that he was also Elaine's uncle. He also reminded the detectives about Ronnie Silver and his willingness to help. Sam did so, in part, out of curiosity as to their reaction on whether or not the son has identified the body as well. Tit for tat.

Mansel, with Brown nodding in agreement, informed Sam that Ronnie Silver had been notified about his father's death. Not much more. They did half-heartedly and nonverbally thank Sam for the suggestion in terms of Ronnie identifying the body. Sam thought that was weird—an immediate family member not identifying the body before he did? Unless, of course, they couldn't reach Ronnie, but that would contradict their mention the he was notified of the death. Something wasn't adding up. Rumblings of an avalanche of foul play beset Long Island.

Sam identified Silver's body at the morgue next door, and the two detectives transported him back to Sheppard Meat. Mansel asked Sam if they could continue their conversation with him at the office about his work with Silver and so forth. The bounced check was not part of that solicitation of his time by the officers. Sam had Elaine on his mind above all else. He declined to continue to speak but offered a time around 6:00 or 6:30 at the fourth precinct. He wanted to go home and call his wife about the news first. The detectives agreed to his desire to inform family and meeting later on.

At home Sam called Elaine. Devastated, she handed the phone to her mother and collapsed. She came around thanks to a ton of support around her. Sam made arrangements to have the family flown home the next day right away in the morning. Feeling the pain from hundreds of miles away, he then pounded a few miles into the inner city to get some answers. His emotions traveled from sorrow to fury while he pounded the pavement in one initial direction for some answers: Sal Spatarella.

In his garage, Sal heard the news and then emphatically professed to Sam that Irving had been pestering him about investing in his businesses. He left his garage a few days ago in a rant about Harold Goberman giving him bogus money. Spatarella said Silver told him that Goberman would pay for the shit he did.

After he departed, Spatarella thought about why Silver threw Goberman into the mix of their conversation, albeit a one-sided chat and done so while exiting out the door. It wasn't a surprise to those etched in the inner circle of mobster doings that there was no love lost between Spatarella and Goberman. That was news to Sam. He felt out of the loop, but it was a dangerous noose he didn't want to be part of anyway. What he didn't know wouldn't hurt him he often believed when it came to the dark shadows of the street.

The ah-hah moment for Sam, however, from Sal's proclamation dealt with Silver going behind his back to leverage a relationship for a piece of the Mafia pie. It made Sam realize, if anything, Irving's connection (and perhaps Ronnie's) to Goberman came with more baggage than just his criminal background. Their relationship settled right in the heart of New York's underworld activity. We're not talking small potatoes.

In just days, Sam Sommer wore the hats of a family defender, businessman, detective, grief counselor, and alleged murder suspect with little time to reflect on it all. He headed home after the Spatarella visit like a robot, driving back to Commack on auto pilot, dazed and confused about what the hell happened on Friday, May 17, 1968. At home, he called Elaine back and sat disheartened in his living room for most of the night. He totally forgot about meeting the detectives earlier in the evening.

On Saturday, Sam and Elaine attended the burial of Irving Silver before a floored family and relatives, including both sets of parents who flew back on short notice as well. Per Jewish custom, the deceased is to be buried as soon as possible—typically within twenty-four hours of death.[7] Detectives Mansel and Brown were at the ceremony as well but did not approach Sam about his no show the night before.

The avalanche that hit two families amid a puzzling death on the side of an isolated road and an expeditious turnaround for a burial almost bypassed a significant question. Even Sam focused a lot on who killed Irving, it's the how he was killed that almost fell between the cracks. Ronnie shared with Sam and Elaine that Suffolk County did an autopsy and that the report should be available soon.

Over the next few days, the Sommer and Silver families grieved together. Sam's parents flew back to Florida within a couple of days; Elaine's remained at the house. Ronnie started driving his father's Buick, which raised Sam's eyebrows. The car was found next to his father's dead body a few days earlier and now the son was driving it, plus it belonged to Sam even though he planned to give the car to Ronnie (which he did that summer).

A lot of little things started to infiltrate an already weird investigation in Sam's head. It was Tuesday, and Sam decided to volunteer his time to help the police. There was no follow up to his absenteeism from last Friday evening on behalf of the two Suffolk County detectives, which Sam naturally brushed off as they had adequate information for the time being.

In the meantime, Sam devised a plan to assist in the investigation out of frustration for the Silver family. No progress and not much communication took place for a number of days. He intended to pay to a visit to the Fourth

Precinct on Thursday, May 23, almost a week after the death of Irving to discuss the following:

- The status of the Autopsy Report. No one appeared to be pushing its completion and findings.

- His own contributions toward the investigation, particularly Harold Goberman's potential involvement.

- What was the theory from the detectives' perspective on Irving's death?

Sam also planned to ask Ronnie about Goberman, but decided to wait due to the family's grieving. In between these plans, Sam returned to running his business ventures—tragically without Irving Silver. On Wednesday, May 22, he spent most of the day catching up on orders, scheduling, making deliveries—putting in a complete day for the first time in weeks. Clearing the decks for maybe another week entailed Sam's thinking here, wanting to devote energy toward Silver's investigation.

During dinner on Wednesday evening Harold Goberman called the Sommer household. He asked Sam to meet him at a nearby Dunkin' Donuts a few blocks from the Sommer's house. Goberman had been on Sam's mind. Surprised by the call, Sam nervously agreed to meet Goberman in the sinking twilight on a warm Wednesday evening.

Elaine trembled. She adamantly resisted Sam meeting with the son-of-a-bitch. In addition, the couple was expecting a visit from their dear friends, Phil and Susan Cirrone, for a chance to catch up on the recent incident. Their visit to the Sommer home originally was intended to hear about the family's adventures in Florida, but the mood and dynamic changed for obvious reasons. Sam and Elaine had a ton of respect for the couple and adored their company; they welcomed the visit in a therapeutic kind of spirit.

Guarded due to a late-stage pregnancy and confused small children over the latest turmoil, Sam believed the scheduled visit could comfort Elaine in his absence. He assured Elaine that he'd be back right away. If not, he urged her to come and check on him at Dunkin' Donuts with the Cirrones.

What happened next at Dunkin' Donuts in Commack, New York was the kidnapping of Sam Sommer on the evening of May 17, 1968. From that point forward, the young couple's hopes for the American Dream and giving others a shot at it would be smothered under Long Island's first targeted avalanche of hate and corruption.

6.

GHOSTLY GAVEL

Finally, the four-hour physical torture ended. Sam Sommer was transferred to a hospital in Riverhead, New York, and treated for multiple injuries. He then slept a few winks in a cell at the Suffolk County Riverhead Police Station.

***

At daybreak, Sam tried to shake off cobwebs inside his taxed mind while his lifeless eyes fixated on cobwebs around the dusty cot that he rested on. The web's meticulous design inches away fostered a strange form of peace. While he laid in agony with a left eye too smashed to open, bruises covered his pummeled head. It hurt to move. It hurt worse to remember.

"They might come back," he thought. "Those assholes could still be around. Pure evil."

Sam's six-by-nine accommodations came with rusty vertical bars and smelly bedding, along with a lot of uncertainty. His throbbing head just wanted to go dormant on a beach in Miami—a recent memory that jerked a tear from his sore eye thinking of Elaine and the kids. He figured a bad dream was overtaking him and that a snap of the fingers would make everything better.

The wishful thinking eroded at the sight of his orange institutional attire. Bandages on Sam's arms and hands, discoloration around his stomach, and a gooey tenderness from stitches stole the day. He grappled with the reality of where he was and how he got there. It took him several minutes to realize that it was Thursday morning, May 23.

Real fear introduced itself to the thirty-one-year-old family man in 1968. He now lived inside the century-old adage that truth is stranger than fiction. Such a realization bred a brand of terror beyond any movie, book, or backroom mobster death ritual. He shivered, shaking his cot.

The sound of something metal or tin hit the floor in a nearby cell, and Sam's temporary trance stopped. He tried looking around a bit and was drawn to a beautiful ray of light shooting through a small window from above. Too painful to look up and enjoy the light, the opening sparked his memory for some reason. He knew he hadn't been in that cell long.

Sam's wounds couldn't hide the story behind them. His healthy physique from wrestling with sides of beef over the years likely contributed toward surviving the night. A slightly larger room without the bedding and toilet further tripped his memory of a horrific state of affairs that occurred the night before.

Kidnapped and then brought to a police station where he had been beaten into another galaxy was the last thing Sam remembered, causing another teardrop. His gazes at peaceful cobwebs blurred in sadness. He wondered where that horror chamber from last night was located. Lots of cigarette smoke. Telephone books turned into weaponry. Cops. One was named Gill, another Mansel.

Sam started to piece a puzzle together. Then a strong voice emerged from outside his jail cell, commanding him to get up. He struggled at every turn to sit up on the hard cot. Two jailers came in and placed his feet on the floor, followed by a scream from sunburned bruises and cuts. He noticed their shirts displayed the name Riverhead Police on them. They informed Sam that a visitor stopped by to see him.

"Shit," thought Sam, "not those damn detectives." To his surprise, a tall, pleasant-looking man introduced himself as Joe Scibilia, a Long Island defense attorney who specialized in insurance matters dealing with personal injuries. Not knowing of Sam's condition ahead of time, the attorney simply expected to explore with Sam the reason why he was jailed—preliminary stuff most likely to assist another lawyer well-versed in criminality.

Shocked by a dominating sight of bruises, Scibilia told Sam that Phil Cirrone referred him to help. Sam cracked a hurtful, yet comforting smile in hearing Phil's name. Scibilia inquired about the bruises. Sam countered with a question concerning his own whereabouts the night before.

"Suffolk County Fourth Precinct, Homicide," Scibilia noted. Sam's throat flinched. His heavy head fell on Scibilia's shoulder.

"Get me outta here."

"Who beat you, Mr. Sommer?"

"Almost killed me, those bastards. Where's my wife?"

Scibilia held Sam and told him that Mrs. Sommer was with the Cirrones and that he'd see her in a couple of hours in court.

"Court?"

"You're being arraigned this morning for confessing to the murder of Irving Silver."

"What?" A burst of energy awoke Sam's spirit. He stood as if the physical pain delayed reaching his brain for nearly a day. The pain shifted from Sam's body to his heart. The hell with getting beaten. This was a set up turned cover up, and the victim was Sam Sommer.

Sam could have taken another punch or two even after an overnight assault in exchange for serving as a target of a set up. There were no words to describe being abducted, much less accused of murder or lied to about a confession. The whole situation wreaked of a personal agenda. Some sort of fate met Sam from a predetermined plan involving bad police.

In a timely twist of irony around the same time, police officers in mostly Brooklyn, along with parts of Harlem and the Bronx, were under growing scrutiny on behalf of a free-wheeling hippie cop named Frank Serpico. As portrayed in the 1973 blockbuster motion picture, *Serpico,* the courage of one New York City plainclothes cop exposed police corruption into a legendary unraveling of disgrace and dishonor to the badge.

Bribery, racketeering, gambling, and a surge of drugs were among the favorite palm greasers for Big Apple cops in the 1960s when the problem swelled to notoriety. At the time of Sommer's demise, however, not a lot of attention toward Long Island law enforcement occurred yet regarding such probes, despite the fact criminal cops were abound in this part of influential America as well.

If he wasn't spending time nurturing a young family, Sam's days and nights found him building lives. That's why the human heist at Dunkin' Donuts, which came without warning except for Harold Goberman at the eleventh hour, baffled Scibilia and another newcomer who arrived at the scene in Sam's defense, Eugene Lamb.

Lamb, a respected lawman and war veteran in his late thirties of Sayville, Long Island, got right down to business. The three men explored a plethora of theories and facts. What was Goberman's role in the kidnapping? Was it a set up? Sam grew leery of Goberman, but was not afraid of him. Goberman must have run with the mob, Sam figured, because why else would a former felon be perceivably held in high esteem by cops? He started to connect some dots with Scibilia and Lamb.

Sadly, Sam's mental sleuthing with the two gentlemen brought on more concern. He felt trapped and suffocated. A runaway train derailed the law at his expense. He felt like there was no way out from standing as a poster child to the ill-effects of abuse and power.

Encouraged by his two attorneys to remain upbeat, Sam switched his outlook to fighting. Enough doom and defeat. Sam moved from one emotion to the other like a viewfinder flips scenes with the clutch of a finger. "We were in Florida, you guys, one minute, and then this."

Sam shed light on Silver's run in with Goberman over a bad check and Ronnie's strange behavior after his father's death. Scibilia and Lamb took note of these claims and learned that Sam never confessed to the murder. Sam couldn't have delivered the gumption to say anything substantial anyway in between getting annihilated during the Suffolk County ambush. Lamb left the cell to make some phone calls. He would join Scibilia in court and lead Sam's defense. Sam was due in court later that morning.

Phil Cirrone arrived with a bag of clothes and told Sam that Susan was watching over Elaine. The Cirrones arranged for babysitting not only for obvious reasons but to protect the kids from seeing a mother in distress. The situation could incite another miscarriage resulting from an emotional collapse.

Phil helped Sam get cleaned up and dressed for court. Scibilia reviewed a few more details with Sam, rejoined Lamb for a conversation outside the cell, and departed westward to Commack for arraignment at the Suffolk County District Courthouse. The building was located just blocks away from the same Dunkin' Donuts in which Sam was kidnapped and another block or two from his home, deli, and main office.

The forthcoming hearing provided a stark contradiction to Sam's daily grind of countless cups of coffee and making cash registers ring for fifteen hours. He instead found himself in a boxing ring, outnumbered and outwitted for the time being.

A lot of miles were racked up the night before with Sam traveling as a black-and-blue passenger. On the way to Commack for arraignment against Suffolk County, he learned from Lamb how much law enforcement had moved him around overnight.

From his kidnapping in Commack to Smithtown for a beating, Sam was then transported in the wee hours almost an hour east to the hub of Long Island's bay in Riverhead. There he received medical attention at Riverhead Hospital and then lodged in the Riverhead Police Station until he awoke to cobwebs and two defense lawyers.

Lamb insisted on wanting to know why his client needed medical attention from an alleged arrest and confession. The only thing he learned from one of the desk detectives at the Fourth Precinct was that Sam suffered minor self-inflicted injuries from resisting arrest—that's all that was offered as an explanation.

As expected, this information didn't sit well with the defense team in comparison to what Sam revealed about the beating. Moreover, it is unclear to this day why Sam needed to travel so far to receive treatment for injuries that a *MASH*-unit physician could have performed. There were other health care providers in the Smithtown/Commack vicinity who could have treated him.

So many head shakes on the way to the courthouse rusted the men's necks in disbelief. An oil can remedy could only be found in another dimension of reality. Could Long Island police, or any other jurisdiction of cops, really behave like this? Everything Sam believed about police contradicted what happened. He had held them in the highest of esteem until now.

Sam arrived at the Suffolk County District Courthouse near noon to the sight of his pregnant wife. Elaine was waiting outside the entrance shouting her husband's name. Susan Cirrone's lovingly contained Elaine while Sam's escort pulled up to the bottom of the stairs that led into the main entrance. Her shadowing of Elaine's every move with tireless love and courage assumed an unheralded responsibility that perhaps saved two lives.

After a quick, yet panda-strong hug with her husband, Elaine felt Susan's clutch. She robotically ushered Elaine into the courthouse behind Sam, his defense entourage, and police foot escort. There didn't appear to be media present for what would have the makings of a news frenzy by today's standards. The quick turnaround of events in less than fifteen hours, however, may have played a factor in the absence of reporters back in the day before digital communications and social media.

Or was there a different reason cameras weren't flashing on this particular day? After all, it's been common practice for members of the media to check daily logs for court proceedings, according to one of the author's twenty-seven years of experience in working with reporters. Given this case dealt with murder, the May 23, 1968, arraignment of Sam Sommer was headed for the history books as one of the quieter publicity proceedings, at least at the outset. The coverage that did run in the local paper, *Newsday*, was one-sided—basically hanging the accused out to dry before due process. Where have we seen this before in America?

Another speculative angle was that maybe the kidnapping and subsequent fast arraignment were prearranged in an orchestration of collective power. Sam pondered the creepy nature of all that went down in a war against him that stunk like a cover up. 'But why me?' he ached in thought while big wooden courtroom doors swung open.

Lamb, Scibilia, and Sam settled behind an enormous, heavily-nicked table inside the courtroom. Their table counterparts were three gentlemen representing Suffolk County District Attorney (DA) George Aspland's office, including Aspland himself. Detectives Thomas Gill and Thomas Mansel were present in the gallery. In the back of the courtroom Elaine remained distraught from the sight of Sam's abrasions, which drew the attention of other onlookers as well thanks to obvious leans and whispers under hands that covered mouths. It was difficult for her to take a seat.

The arraignment was called to order by Suffolk County Judge Frank DeLuca. Sam needed help to stand from the pain, and DeLuca obviously took notice of his condition. Then an extended and bizarre look took place between Sam and the judge. It's like they'd seen one another before.

The hiccup in the proceeding was enough to throw off any momentum of starting an arraignment under normal protocol. Everyone sat down in disorderly fashion, taken aback by the curious stare down. DeLuca had to restart his own arraignment by asking everyone to take their seats, even after the bailiff made the same gesture seconds ago.

Then something came over Sam. He pictured the judge in his mind, sitting at a corner table in front of a mouthwatering pastrami on rye piled to the top floor of Empire State Building. The justice was a regular at the Deli-Queen. For a brief moment, Sam considered that maybe DeLuca's patronage boded well for his case if he drew the same connection. That glimmer of hope in a neighborhood sense swelled a sense of home field advantage for Sam. The deli stood just a block away from the courthouse.

The arraignment opened with yet another stray from protocol. Intentionally or accidentally, it curtain-called the quirky glances between the two men a moment ago. DeLuca commented on Sam's physical condition with a degree of empathy. He asked Lamb if his defendant was in the right frame of health to proceed. Lamb took Sam's cue to continue. Sam thanked the judge for his concern.

Just like that a couple of golden chances slipped through the cracks. Sam wanted to acknowledge the judge's patronage at Deli-Queen but felt it was not the place or time. He figured there would be an opportunity at some point during or after the proceeding to make that connection with the judge.

In addition, Lamb thought that the early recognition of Sam's bruises from the judge aided in their defense, and that it set the table for a promising outcome. He assumed that DeLuca's observation would lead to a discussion of brutality, thus introducing an X-factor of sorts in Sam's favor. That didn't happen due to a sudden sidetrack that came from behind the bench. DeLuca fumbled through some papers and then looked at the DA.

The justice inquired to the prosecution about why he hadn't received a copy of the grand jury indictment relating to the defendant's arrest. Aspland apologized and said that it was supposed to be delivered to the courtroom at any time by the assistant DA. A perplexed-looking DeLuca asked about the reason for its delay.

Aspland played the oversight card, using the excuse of a quick turnaround time from arrest-to-arraignment as rationale for the missing paperwork. Lamb stood and adamantly objected, claiming a procedure of this nature dealing with a murder charge should be thrown out without a grand jury indictment.

In a gasp of stillness the courtroom air thickened in a potential turning point moment. DeLuca asked the two respective counsels to approach the bench. Elaine Sommer, the Cirrones, and some family supporters stood in the gallery, anticipating this was a momentous break in the arraignment. Basically the toss of a coin could determine Sam Sommer's fate right then and there. Where in the name of justice was this indictment?

On paper in virtually every law book ever written (with exception to certain state laws), no indictment, no arrest. Without an arrest, no charges, No charges, no jail time and arraignment. That snowbell effect in thinking mirrored what most, if not all, judicial experts would deem a standard recipe for mistrial.

The two men left the judge's bench and returned toward their tables. Lamb looked pissed. Sam lowered his head in foretold defeat from the nonverbal cue of his attorney. One defeat, Sam thought, could still not win the war against him. His mind raced again while Lamb sat next to him with a despaired look. He didn't need to say anything to Sam.

The sound of a ghostly gavel hit the wooden block. DeLuca said that the arraignment would assume a twenty-four-hour recess, so the prosecution could present its grand jury indictment. The coin toss landed on the wrong end of justice for the Sommer family.

Ready to rip the courtroom into yesterday, Elaine submitted to an escort by Phil and Susan out of the room at the pleasure of the bailiffs. DeLuca continued his discernment that in the preservation of justice both sides ought to conduct their proceedings based on the indictment. He fell for Aspland's argument and apology that the indictment was temporarily misplaced.

So much for justice by the book. Subjective call in favor of an apology and against the rule of the land. DeLuca concluded the hearing with another gavel bang and a reminder of the arraignment's one-day extension. Lamb repeated his displeasure to the justice from his table. Deaf ears. The judge vacated the bench to his chambers, and the prosecution headed for the exit.

Lamb, Scibilia, and Sommer remained at their table stunned and in shock. Dejected, they now knew that perhaps their defense was up against an army in Suffolk County. Too early to tell for sure, but this unexpected twist certainly suggested a playing field that leaned toward power and authority over truth and impartiality.

One more day for Sam behind bars while the other side got another day to right a wrong. The whole court proceeding felt like starting the Indy 500 without a track. What no one put together at the time was what if there actually wasn't an indictment? Everyone was caught up in the subjectivity of the judge that this question didn't sink in as part of the oddly-run court proceeding.

Sam remained seated while two police officers approached him for his transport to the Smithtown jail—the original horror chamber from the night before. Elaine returned to the back of the courtroom in tears. Susan led her outside again, assuring Elaine that she could visit Sam in the afternoon. The arraignment would continue the next day on Friday under the assumption that an official Grand Jury Indictment would be rendered into court.

The extended arraignment, however, would now be held in a state supreme court in Riverhead under the presiding direction of New York State Judge Thomas Stark. The fact that a plea and trial couldn't be set in a lower court precipitated the move to a higher court in which no one argued. Technically, the lower court in Commack ended on appeal due to the absence of a grand jury indictment.

Only one other United States murder case resembled Sam's demise at the expense of an absent grand jury indictment, and that was in the 1950s in New York State also. The May

23, 1968, arraignment of Samuel L. Sommer vs. Suffolk County coughed up unprecedented legal practices that were morphing into case study stardom in college law courses.

Meanwhile, Sam's defense team still remained astonished at its table while their client walked out in cuffs, escorted to the Smithtown jail for the night. They would soon go back to the drawing board before heading over to see him later in the day to discuss round two at the circus on Friday.

7.
OFF THE RAILS

Back in jail in Hauppauge, Sam wore orange again for the remainder of the day on Thursday, May 23. He forcefully tried to placate all those around him. Consumed with forecasting his own release based on one big misunderstanding, Sam just wanted to stay cool for another day and ride out a storm of injustice.

Through heavy eyes, Sam saw a lineup of people waiting to see him. Feeling like an attraction at the state fair, he spotted Elaine and rose in a rush of adrenaline. She followed him to the Fourth Precinct Homicide in the company of the Cirrones after the bizarre arraignment in Commack.

Elaine was allowed to see her husband from outside the bars. Sam remained strong while her sandpaper voice cried for his release. Eugene Lamb and Joe Scibilia arrived on the scene as well, conversing with the Cirrones off to the side out of respect for Sam and Elaine's time together.

Elaine's anger over observing a loving husband, dignified community leader, and father minimized to a jumpsuit in a small cell sent her over the edge. Sam canvassed Elaine with love and reminded her of child number seven on the way.

"What about that guy my husband was supposed to meet last night at Dunkin' Donuts?" she shouted to whomever may have been within a hundred miles. Her echoes deflected off the tight corridor walls. Elaine's rage caught the attention of the guards and the heart of her husband.

Sam signaled to Phil and Susan Cirrone to remove Elaine from the police station. Before doing so, he assured his wife everything was going to be all right and that she needed to take care of their unborn child. He said he'd be home before she knew it, and from the deepest part of his heart, he believed that truly was going to happen.

The couple exchanged tears and Elaine left. On her way out she left Sam a set of clean clothes and lowered a ringing bellow intended at two guards by the cell door and at his defense attorneys. "It's a damn disgrace he didn't have any underwear last night," she said with a look of disgust. Between the lines, Elaine's comment meant: *You better make sure Sam's inhumane treatment is addressed or else.*

Sam and his attorneys were moved to a nearby larger room with a table to discuss their strategy for the next day. During their short walk down the hall, Sam struggled to deal with mind traps of *Is this really happening?* to *What now?* One part of him grappled with anger for being nabbed and punched around while naked the night before. His other opposing thoughts required attention toward developing a defense plan.

Lamb and Scibilia felt Sam's swirl of emotions. They were faced with an unprecedented conundrum. So many questions veered from a myriad of angles based on their defendant's disclosures. Motive? Sam and Irving Silver were business partners of sorts—so how could that play out? Alibi? Sam mentioned that he and Irving were to visit Bernie's Diner the morning of May 17 for coffee before heading into Commack and New York City for a day of work. Maybe Irving was seen that morning at Bernie's without Sam?

Then there was the belief of prejudice. Sam is Jewish-American and was a successful businessman at a young age. Jews held their own as a culture throughout New York; however, their rivaled history with Italians dates back to even biblical days. Greed? Was his cash cow conglomerate a target of growing mafia-affiliated takeovers in New York City? The fabric of organized crime wove a foul entanglement of resentment and jealousy toward Jews. They stood in the way of the Sicilian mob's quest to monopolize commerce in the Big Apple.

One aspect of Mafia influence leading up to Sam's dilemma, especially in cities like New York and Chicago, was control of the media. For the most part society didn't fathom gangsters having newspaper reporters on the payroll because news is not a "tangible" product like drugs, booze, clothing, guns, prostitutes, etc. People, even today, only see the finished product of articles on pages; they don't understand "how" stories make it in.

In the opinion of a seasoned public relations professional, the art of journalism in its pure roots is an objective understudy of reporting information predicated on trends, hard news, lifestyles, economic developments, business initiatives, global and national events, and so forth. Corrupt journalism accepts money and favors to determine what gets covered. Today we see one political party control the majority of the mainstream press; back in the day it was the Mafia. Same form of dishonesty with different entities pulling the cash strings.

Any takeover of a Jewish business would be hard pressed to make the news at the time Sam was building American Dreams. The grappling questions he tossed around with his defense team were better suited prepping for an actual trial, not an arraignment or even a second crack at going through one. The three men were trying to nip the preliminary prelude to a murder trial in the bud so it could never be realized. That's how unbelievable the whole situation played out. A newspaper reporter who knew the Sommer family years later would comment on this case being so eerily real that no one would believe it.

Lamb and Scibilia tried to comprehend Sam's erratic arguments to earn his confidence. Sam ranted all over the board. The speedy beeline from "arrest" to arraignment caught everyone out of sync. A perceived urgency to arraign Sam loomed a mystery.

The two defense counsels complied with Sam's utterances of absurdity toward the whole situation. Police brutality and a meeting with a felon at a donut shop supported strong alibis like Irving Silver's dispute with a convicted felon over money and the Bernie's Diner wild card.

Scibilia back checked with wait staff at the restaurant and learned they didn't remember seeing Sam there the morning Silver was killed. The same employees did recall seeing Silver with another man the same morning. Lamb took that discovery and capped it in a bottle like a piece of gold for future reference, if needed.

Ronnie Silver's quirks about his father's death added more substance to the big picture. All of these arguments created a favorable yet challenging predicament for Lamb and Scibilia. How would they handle another arraignment when their client shouldn't be in a courtroom in the first place?

Should their defense focus on the unlawful practice of arrest and interrogation or the aforementioned alibis? The unpredictability resulting from the first failed crack at a Suffolk County arraignment made the three men scratch their heads on an approach to Friday's judicial sequel—this time in a different venue and in a higher court.

Thursday afternoon progressed in a manner of shooting darts. What was the best target for Friday morning's arraignment in which Sam would enter a not-guilty plea? The preliminary hearing wouldn't allow for a trial-like exchange of arguments. The prosecution already had an alleged confession to play off of.

Sam needed rest. All three gentlemen basically agreed to bring up Sam's physical appearance to stonewall the case from going to trial since it was fortuitously brought up already by Judge DeLuca. In blind faith they assumed DeLuca would have translated such a message to Judge Thomas Stark in time for the Riverhead proceeding. That should do it, they thought. There was no platform or time to introduce other arguments anyway, regrettably.

Friday morning, May 24, 1968, arrived as a dark milestone for Sam Sommer and his young family. The date marked one week from the tragic death of Irving Silver, which unexpectedly also triggered a battle in Sam's life. He would either stand trial for the murder of his business partner and relative or find the madness dropped for good.

Whether the latter would result from simple skepticism because a defendant's rights were neglected, it didn't matter. Sam, along with his family, friends, and even a number of employees who made the hour-plus drive eastward to gather at the courthouse for support, believed by day's end that he'd be freed.

Judge Stark called the Friday morning arraignment to order at the state courthouse in Riverhead. Stark was a well-respected, middle-aged justice who served in the Navy during World War II and was a gifted musician, known for volunteering his talents at various community functions. Many legal professionals would often send young defense attorneys to his proceedings to learn how lawyers should conduct themselves in a courtroom.

Later in his career, Stark would preside over the infamous "Amityville Horror" murders and a $1 billion property tax case involving the Long Island Lighting Company.[8] Scibilia mentioned to Sam and Eugene Lamb on the way to the courthouse about Stark's stellar reputation—the first testimonial of sorts that landed positively thus far on the ears of the defense. Maybe the circus act shenanigans from round one of the arraignment would take a back seat now under the direction of Stark.

Stark began the Friday proceeding without any comment on Sam's battered appearance as a continuation from the day before, nor did any reference to a grand jury indictment come up. He basically went right into the plea phase in a business-as-usual persona. For a few seconds everyone in the courtroom followed his suit, naturally.

Lamb thought the indictment issue must have been satisfied by the judge. He figured if there was something out of sorts, Stark would have brought it up. With the indictment momentarily out of Lamb's mind, he waited for a break in the action to address the beating of his client—a gamble he felt he had to take to drown the arraignment's anticipated outcome.

Stark previewed the proceeding by reminding everyone that his intention was to arraign the defendant in the name of justice under a plea. He summed up yesterday's lower court hearing as a failed attempt to finish the proceeding. He continued by offering brief arguments from either bench pertaining to anything that caused a do-over in the lower court's proceedings. In other words, this was the break in the sky that opened light on any judicial wounds or complaints both sides could state for the record.

Stark impressively set the tone in his courtroom by asking why the heck there was a need for another arraignment. He tactfully insinuated accountability for the do-over on the hands of the legal teams, not in the name of any injustice from the day before. Sam believed Stark knew about the beating and mysterious indictment but waited for someone to fess up in the name of integrity.

Lamb leaped at the opportunity, almost spraying the floor with spit from an eager mouth. He thanked Stark for a chance to quickly address his defendant's appearance first. The judge answered by acknowledging the appearance of the defendant and then asked Lamb how many other arguments he planned to bring up.

A thunderous roar then stole the show before Lamb could utter a response. Suffolk County District Attorney George Aspland loudly objected to the purpose behind the arraignment. He indicated the proceeding had nothing to do with the defendant's appearance and everything to do with his plea prior to going to trial.

Stark didn't take the objection too kindly. He slammed his gavel. Overruled. He warned Aspland to tread lightly on assuming judgeship in his courtroom. Aspland apologized, yet he made sure to interject that the argument wasn't deemed serious enough to discuss in the lower court so why would it warrant such attention now.

Lamb shot back at Aspland. Stark suspended his gavel in midair to signal to Lamb to redirect the argument to him in the heated moment, not at the DA. Lamb turned away from the DA and calmed his voice toward the bench. He submitted to Stark that his defendant required medical attention the night he was allegedly arrested. He then stated that Mr. Sommer took on wounds from being beaten by police and they extended to his stomach area.

Objection. Aspland argued that there was no proof that Mr. Sommer's appearance resulted from police brutality. Overruled. Stark rebuked Aspland's argument by saying that his admission of Mr. Sommer's altered appearance was enough to get to the bottom of that issue pertinent to the overall case. Aspland knew his objection was ill-advised in the way Stark disseminated the argument—more or less admitting that Sommer's body was compromised, period. Dejected, Aspland sat down.

Stark noted the condition of Mr. Lamb's defendant held credence to extending the pretrial phase of his case. Gasps of support for Sam Sommer sounded from the back of the courtroom. The state's table looked transparently pissed. On the verge of expounding on his extension to a pretrial hearing of Mr. Sommer's case, Judge Stark interrupted himself with a hiccup in thought.

He suddenly sifted through some papers at his bench. He asked both sides to be patient for a moment. Then detective Thomas Mansel abruptly left the courtroom from the front of gallery. Bizarre to say the least, Sam recalled. A nonverbal masquerade stole the courtroom, flipping the verbal fireworks from a moment ago completely upside down.

Mansel's urgent exit distracted everyone for a smidgeon of time. Lamb used the glitch in procedural flow and huddled with Sam and Scibilia at their table. Feeling momentous, they quickly strategized about the missing grand jury indictment that had not yet been brought up. Maybe, they collectively thought, that's what Stark was looking for at his bench.

The judge restored order with a look of frustration toward the prosecution.

Stark asked the DA as to the whereabouts of a grand jury indictment, citing a notation that carried over from yesterday's Commack hearing. Aspland stood with his hands spread in a gesture of amiable confusion. "Your honor, we apologize."

The "a" word that means the same as "sorry" reared its ugly head again and made the other side squirm in disbelief. Sam's faith in justice prevailing over right from wrong slipped into reverse. Apologize, again? Law school-like simulations had no place in determining a man's life. The state's amateur hour needed to stop.

Lamb objected and then realized he couldn't object to an apology—that's how bad it became in dealing with the schemes of the prosecution. Something phony was almost expected every time the DA's side would speak, making an objection virtually automatic in knee-jerk fashion. Lamb quickly apologized for his premature objection.

On the verge of Stark addressing Ashland's apology, the DA spun around in unison with a wave of onlookers toward the back of the courtroom. The main doors had been thrown open and smashed loudly against the wall. A grandiose display turned all eyes on two well-dressed men who entered the courtroom in dramatic form. Mansel stood at the opening and watched them march toward the well. One man shouted, "Your honor, please!" He waved a piece of paper. "Please, excuse us, but this urgent!"

There was no time for any reaction to the Shakespearean-like interlude. Aspland told the judge that the other person was part of his team to curb any potential fear of someone going postal. Lamb couldn't produce a word. Before anyone knew it, the two men reached Aspland's table and the DA held a hot commodity in his hands.

"Here's the indictment, your honor," said Aspland. He handed it to the bailiff to give to Stark. "Sorry for the delay." Another apology. Sam felt like jumping in the game and apologizing for going to Dunkin' Donuts two nights ago out of a sarcastic show of frustration. He refrained from playing a game of apology.

Mansel returned to his spot in the gallery, and the other men left the courtroom. Stunned spectators peered hypnotized in resemblance to the 1980 Russian Olympic hockey team—that famous scene when they astoundingly gazed with chins resting atop their sticks at a celebrating Team USA in that snapshot in time known as "Miracle on Ice." Sam didn't know then if he should laugh, cry, or ask for Bellevue. Lamb stood with hands on hips. He shook his head repeatedly with mouth agape.

For years, Sam recalled a piece of Lamb's vent from that moment. "That's it, your honor?" inquired a bedazzled Lamb. "We're going to let life-changing documents just enter the court out of nowhere?"

Gavel met wood. "Order. Fifteen-minute recess," announced Stark. The judge departed to his chambers and in a guard-the-empire manner, bailiffs stood in front of his door.

Scibilia comforted Sam. Chatter overtook the room. Sam tried to block out hearing Elaine cry. The whole hearing absorbed peaks and valleys of momentum. It was heading off the rails in emotion and doubt. One hell of a fight commenced. One side threw out all the stops to get Sam to trial for murder; the defense wanted justice to reign over corrupt police and paper airplanes flying onto a hall of justice as official affidavits.

"What gives?" Lamb asked Aspland and the two detectives who were already half way out the room to take a break together. Aspland just professionally wrinkled his closed lips at Lamb in acknowledgement of his frustration and then departed.

Family and friends wanted to see Sam, but he had to leave the room with his defense team for another nearby meeting space until it was time to resume the arraignment. "What the hell is going on?" Sam asked Lamb.

"I honestly don't know, Sam." He took his client out of the courtroom down a short hallway and into another room. There they sat bewildered and devastated. "It will work out somehow," Scibilia chimed. He added that the recess was a good sign.

In retrospect, the zoom in time travel from Point A in which Sam was "arrested" to Point B of his arraignment presented a peculiar timetable. The defense, prosecution, or presiding judges could never really get their seatbelts fastened for the uncontrollable runaway coaster that rushed toward convicting a man so fast. What pushed this speedy pathway to justice, or perhaps injustice?

Judge Stark recalled the arraignment to order and issued copies of the late-arriving indictment to each side. He seemed somewhat unhinged but retained a professional persona. Both counsels were called to his bench. Stark shared his displeasure about the arrival of an eleventh-hour grand jury indictment which also exposed a crossed off date on it and a few other blemishes of penmanship.

Stark asked the DA about the authenticity of the indictment and the nature in which it was hurriedly admitted into his courtroom. Aspland said the indictment was genuine and that it was rushed into play because of the fast turnaround from arrest to arraignment. Stark countered with basically putting that timetable back in the DA office's lap. Aspland indicated that they wanted to speed the process a bit due to the severity of the crime.

Stark's displeasure from the DA's oversight grew evident. He asked both counsels to return to their tables. The judge then previewed a ruling that was forthcoming based on the recess and gathering of both counsels at the bench. He announced first that the arraignment had to officially record a plea from the defendant. Stark kindly asked the defendant to stand.

"Mr. Lamb, does your defendant wish to enter a plea?"

"Yes, your honor. Not guilty."

The defense team was seated, and Stark openly ruled that the arraignment was suspended in order to first determine police protocol and a defendant's rights while being arrested. In other words, the duly "notation" of Sam's condition (as expressed in day one of the arraignment by Judge DeLuca) came to life in a turn of events once again—this time fortuitously for the defense.

In other words, for the time being Sam Sommer was found Not Guilty. Such a ruling concerning his freedom is recorded to this very day, stained from a plethora of photocopies but visible to the human eye. It is in print on two documents (see Illustrations): **Police Department, County of Suffolk, Court Disposition Report,** dated May 22, 1968 (prior to this hearing, interestingly) and **Police Department, County of Suffolk, Supplementary Report,** dated April 22, 1971. More on the latter is referenced again in Chapter 16.

Stark ordered a Huntley Hearing. Gasps of life found their way back into the air on behalf Sam's family and supporters. A Huntley Hearing is a pretrial proceeding unique to New York State. It's designed for the purpose of reviewing the manner in which police obtain statements from a defendant and his or her rights associated with such mannerisms.[9] The hearing would serve as another pretrial condition prior to Sam's murder trial. It could bode well for his overall defense and perhaps end the case altogether.

The Huntley Hearing would begin on January 20, 1969. Sam Sommer was released on bond with conditions of no travel outside Suffolk County for the next seven months. Like that the state-run second round at one of the strangest arraignments ever run ended with no arraignment at all.

In considering the big picture, things looked up for Sam Sommer and his family. He had avoided going to trial for murder for the time being, and if his defense could prove misconduct by Suffolk County police, he could be freed from a crime he did not commit in the first place.

Or would his plight continue in disturbing notoriety as the start of remarkable cover ups in modern judicial history that have spanned decades?

8.

A HAUNTED PRELUDE

Home at 8 Zinnia Court in Commack and released on bail posted in cash, Sam Sommer reeled from three days of mental whiplash and excruciating pain. He needed rest and isolation. Throbs of discomfort worsened from his sunburned skin getting acquainted with an inventory of bruises.

It was Saturday, May 25, and Sam wanted to get his feet wet again on the home front after a tour of injustice. Between comforting his family and keeping his business afloat, one immediate thing Sam's lawyers had him do was to get re-examined by a doctor with an assessment on what could have caused his injuries.

The two oldest Sommer kids would soon be out of school for the summer and a new baby was weeks away. Thanks to all the support from friends like the Cirrones and many of Sam's employees, Elaine's pregnancy was miraculously uncompromised despite an abundance of stress. Sam hired an extra nanny to help around the house.

As if the last three days weren't enough to shake off and digest, half of Elaine's family doubted Sam's innocence. Regaining trust from extended family members would take time, while time itself would be hard pressed to heal the loss of Irving Silver over a lifetime. The situation appeared that grim—a family tree now bared loose branches. It was ugly.

A lot of doubt made it hard to concentrate on what loomed: a life behind bars or one behind shadows.

Either way, family ties were already ruined. Sam would either be found guilty of a crime he did not commit or guilty of Irving's absence from the earth. Or he would be found not guilty of the crime and still guilty of making Irving disappear in some form or fashion within the guts of relatives.

An immediate emphasis on making up for lost time with family and work came with a related priority. Elaine's parents were visiting since the burial ceremony; however, Sam's mom and dad were unaware of their son's recent turbulence. Sam was in the midst of contacting them to make arrangement for a visit to not only delicately break the news in person but to also make them part of relocating his family to a different community. New scenery would help the family get a fresh outlook on life.

Ever since Sam's one-way trip to Dunkin' Donuts and subsequent shellacking that resulted in two court appearances, he and Elaine did not want to upset his parents. They kept their woes off to the side, so to speak. It was like they had to weather the storm first before contacting them.

Problem.

This certain storm wasn't in the mood for weathering. It moved in a beeline to Miami in the shape of bad news. Max Sommer read about his son's potential pending murder trial in a Florida newspaper and died on the spot of a heart attack right on the couch at the age of seventy.

Coincidently, it happened while Sam was on the verge of calling his parents about the flight and desire to have them come back. Same day, same time. Instead of calling to make arrangements to fly his folks back as planned and discuss what happened to Irving Silver, Sam received a call that made neither he nor Elaine ever want to answer the phone again. Anna Sommer shrieked the news to her son over the phone just minutes after paramedics arrived attempting to revitalize her husband.

In less than two weeks in May of 1968, two family deaths, a kidnapping, a defenseless beating, and at times a third-grade run courtroom instigated uncontrollable darkness for the family. A clean slate and restart button appeared all that was left in the tank for the Sommers. Easier said than done. Starting over had to be manufactured by the grace of the Lord. They needed something to grip, control, direct. It was time to find new tracks for a train in derailment mode.

Even a spurt of optimism that resulted from Judge Stark's ruling for another hearing in place of an immediate murder trial couldn't curb the inky blackness that hung over the family. The Sommers felt haunted from the death of Sam's dad. They were afraid to face the world. Who would fall next?

The young kids' strife and Elaine's late-stage pregnancy aided the couple in not throwing in the towel from all the grief and suffering. Sam revisited earlier thoughts about retiring early and traveling the world with his wife at the time their last child left home. The two often discussed returning to family roots in Israel later in life and giving back as much as they could in honor of their ancestors' humble beginnings.

Those pipes in Sam's dreams were now rusty from being too far out of reach at the moment, but the thoughts functioned as sunny fodder for souls that needed repair. The couple diverted its attention on getting Max Sommer back to New York for a proper funeral and to celebrate his life. Once his loving father was laid to rest, Sam threw himself into his wife and kids, along with a now widowed wife and mother.

To further reduce anguish, the couple made Sam's mom part of a process to help the family look for a new house in Stony Brook near Smithtown Bay—about twelve miles northeast of Commack (still residing in Suffolk County due to bail conditions). The Sommers landed a comfortable two-story home a few blocks away from the bay. The excitement of a fresh start alleviated some anxiety. It's like everyone came together to take this project on, and the task created fun.

Sam just turned thirty-two in June as well; Elaine was due in a matter of a few weeks, and the new home would officially be theirs in July. It provided more space and welcomed another swimming pool like the house in Commack. Still suffering from the loss of his father, Sam tuned out his forthcoming hearing and focused on family. He didn't even want to see Eugene Lamb or Joe Scibilia for an indefinite amount of time, making the two lawyers a bit anxious.

Cash was going fast, however, for a family man who was on the brink of becoming a true business tycoon prior to being kidnapped. Legal bills, a new home, posting bail, an additional nanny, and another child combined with lost revenue from the recent disarray of his ventures shrunk a lot of green. Reserve bundles from those closets converted into bank vaults offered a smidgeon of relief, but a once promising financial future looked unsure.

Despite uncertainties across the board, Sam made sure the summer of 1968 was filled with backyard barbecues and happy gatherings. It was an escape into heartfelt moments with loved ones and close friends—a natural diversion from all the distractions. In July, Elaine gave birth to Eugene Sommer, named after the valiant work of their attorney. It would be the couple's last child in an already traditionally-large Jewish family.

Another new name came into the mix during the summer of 1968. Sam renamed the Deli-Queen to Rosen's in honor of Morris' mentorship over the years. Morris increasingly became more like a dad to Sam since the passing of Max. He always remembered where his work ethic came from, through--his late father. And that drive to succeed reenergized Sam to restore his businesses to their cash happy days.

Anna Sommer spent the summer at her son's home. Her delicate state was offset with love, a new grandchild, and seven young kids everywhere running rampant. Sam and Elaine intentionally kept her busy with little tasks around the house. In mid-August she returned to her retirement home in Florida.

In Florida, Elaine's parents helped Anna get acclimated to life as a widow and as a mother of a son who could lose his freedom. Thinking of Elaine raising kids without a father pummeled her heart with agony. It wasn't long before Anna sold her retirement home and returned to live with her son's family on Long Island until later getting her own place near the house. The Rosen's made numerous trips back to New York that year to support the family in whatever way they could.

It took a while, but Sam finally threw himself back into his businesses later that fall. What he didn't account for at the time is how much his absence from the grind threw off the vitality of his enterprises. Sheppard Meat Company lost accounts and his deli suffered in management, resulting in lower patronage. The rumor mill around Commack on allegations against him didn't help business either.

Fueled by his late father's love and work ethic, Sam returned to the fifteen-hour grind to make amends for lost sales. He resumed full responsibility of his endeavors. Hustle and bustle also served as a chance to maybe unearth a clue or two to find out what really happened to Irving Silver.

Incidentally, Sam did not encounter much in the way of confrontations from his staff given his pending hearing and perception of being a killer. In fact, his staff supported him, at least openly. In between a weird look here and there, his travels around New York City grew a curiosity about Silver's death. The windshield time gave him a chance to look back on a night when he was supposed to meet Harold Goberman at Dunkin' Donuts.

The leaves started to turn Stony Brook into a fall haven. Sam fell into a smooth routine of working all day and then relaxing at home in the serenity of the picturesque community. The routine became a new norm. He wrestled, however, in knowing a time would soon come to prepare for the hearing—an event that would determine the rest of his life.

Sam started to make money again from basically restoring a bunch of business relationships that went south since he left for Florida. A few of his customers, however, reached the South Pole in ditching him for good because of the alleged murder. They turned their back on him in such coldness—basically not even saying a word to him. His financial health still had a ways to go to where it was before he left for Florida and turned the reins over to a now-deceased Silver.

The sight of seeing good business deals and budding relationships suffer caused Sam to want to find Goberman even more and get to the bottom of the mess. Goberman was nowhere to be found. Sam was careful in how he sought his whereabouts because of the future Huntley Hearing. Strangely, there was no trace of him. Even Sal Spatarella alleged he didn't know where Goberman was hiding at the time—a believable assertion since the convicted felon wasn't on top of Sal's black book of friends anyway.

During his travels while playing detective Sam met a rising kosher purveyor named Robert Greenbaum. He ran into Greenbaum at a Harlem coffee shop and the two began talking business. The older Greenbaum settled in the Bronx with a deli and meat company as part of the Ellis Island experiment from Germany. The two aficionados of kosher cuts hit it off from the get-go.

Greenbaum invited Sam to see his business. While following Greenbaum to his store in the Bronx, Sam's radar went up. He approached a neighborhood of recent memory where the Bronx Diner was located—one of his favorite inner city stops until a wicked event went down months earlier. Greenbaum's business sat right at the very spot Sam and Irving Silver were almost mauled by a speeding vehicle last spring.

Sam kept the worrisome memory under wraps for the time being to focus on creating turkey, ham, and roast beef wraps as newer menu items with his new partner. The two proprietors set up new morning routes as part of a partnership into developing parts of Manhattan and Staten Island, which included the increasingly popular sandwich wraps as the main attraction.

Their business model turned into a money machine. The two men agreed to put the money back into the business under an investment arrangement. Greenbaum and Sommer's ventures seemed to break exciting ground on the dynamic link between wholesale and retail deli meats. It was like a scene out of the Roaring 20s—two men working in rhythm making a go of it to an upbeat tempo of buying, selling, and delivering goods. Good timing for Sam, too, because some of the extra money would soon get absorbed into the hands of Lamb and Scibilia.

In late October, Sam finally told Robert Greenbaum about his situation as a christening of their close friendship. He also brought up the attempted hit-and-run that occurred by Greenbaum's store about a half a year ago. Not connecting the dots until this moment, Greenbaum recalled the incident from one of his employees. By the time he came outside Sam and Irving were gone. The two gentlemen sipped coffee outside Greenbaum's store, and Sam relived the horror with his partner in hope of maybe finding a clue. Greenbaum insisted to Sam that he was available to do whatever he could to help. No clue other than the mention of his employee running to the back of the store at the time to tell him.

The discussion was interrupted when Robert noticed a car across the street and pointed it out to Sam. He told Sam that he'd seen that same vehicle before parked near places they'd visited over the past couple of weeks. Sam shrugged off the suspicious car, but not completely in his mind. He found himself trapped between being concerned and appearing to be untroubled. On one hand, there wasn't much Sam hadn't seen in 1968 that would either surprise or scare him as the end of this troubling year inched closer to the holidays.

On the other hand, Sam couldn't really trust anyone or anything thanks to an involuntary car ride from Dunkin' Donuts and subsequent thrashing. Furthermore, flashbacks lingered from when he and Irving Silver were nearly run down before the Florida trip close to the very spot he now occupied with Greenbaum.

Sam couldn't totally dismiss, however, this suspicious car—especially since the identity of the driver was concealed behind tinted glass. Greenbaum commented that the driver always donned a low-hanging hat and dark sunglasses. A "normal" Sam Sommer would have approached the car and called a spade a spade. Not now.

On another occasion over the next week Sam noticed the car again while in the company of Greenbaum. Sam was tempted to approach it, but he restrained in the best interest of his upcoming court appearance.

The men's growing customer base introduced them to a young man that Sam recalls was named Sly. The Manhattan entrepreneur discovered an untapped niche that was waiting to explode on the retail scene dealing with a new brand of pork loin. The three men masterfully merged their synergies and set up an operation where they pre-sliced the pork on the wholesale end and then sold the meat to retail delis ready to land on bread and sell. This reduced labor on the fast-paced retail side while redefining, and perhaps introducing, succulence in deli-style pork.

Sam and Robert fell into a groove serving the greater metro New York region with the fresh concept. Although part of their coattails of success, Sly didn't feel any love in the venture. He wanted more. Rather than focusing on what the three men were doing and expanding their trade nationally by giving more people a shot at success, Sly was not content. He was overcome by greed.

In addition to the kosher deli market bursting at the seams in New York, as mentioned earlier the garbage collection industry was a hidden gem in both profit and control of yet another piece of the streets. Sly wanted Sam and Robert to invest in a garbage collection operation that he had close ties to through the Mafia.

Greenbaum immediately declined citing personal reasons, and Sam refused to acquiesce to Sly's proposal as well for obvious reasons heading into a new year (in which he didn't disclose the upcoming hearing to Sly—his trust wasn't there as it was with Robert).

Sly became openly hurt by the dual declines. He turned an invitation to invest into an ultimatum, more or less through a verbal threat. Sam believed that the solicitation to invest could have precipitated a clash between organized business families at the time in New York... the Jewish and Italian Mafias.

Within a couple of days of both Robert Greenbaum and Sam Sommer turning down Sly, two employees of Sly's were gunned down in an alley behind his Manhattan office. Sly was never heard from again; his store changed hands in a heartbeat and the whole operation the three men were involved in vanished. The pre-sliced pork sales continued with new owners but without Sommer and Greenbaum. Walk away. That was a good move for the two men.

In another development, Lamb informed Sam that a Judge George McInerney ordered the Suffolk County Medical Examiner's office to furnish a copy of the Autopsy Report performed on Irving Silver in case they would need it down the road. The judge made the order on October 21. The prosecution would have five days to provide the documentation to Sam's defense lawyers. McInerney would soon take on a vital presence in Sam's life.

Incidentally, while this paragraph was being written, Sam Sommer is still waiting for a copy of the aforementioned Suffolk County Autopsy Report after 17,965 days.

Contempt of Court? Something to hide? Where is it?

Shortly after the too-close-to-home murder of Sly's employees, Sam parted ways professionally with Greenbaum during the holiday season in 1968. The two men profited from their joint ventures, aiding Sam in working again with his defense team. Greenbaum knew what he faced in terms of his family and his life, and Sam didn't want to pull a friend and business associate into a complex mix.

After months of turmoil and change, Sam slammed the brakes on life. He made the most of the holidays with his family in their new home and worked tirelessly with Lamb on a defense strategy. All Sam had been through since that fateful night in May with his family functioned as a haunted prelude to a do-or-die life event waiting in the wings in a matter of days.

The New Year rang in and Sam would greet it shortly on hardwood floors and big tables with robes, swearing to tell the whole truth and nothing but the truth. No time for New Year's resolutions at the outset of 1969—it was all about justice. The Huntley Hearing would begin in mid-January in Riverhead.

9.

TRUE COLORS

Black. Blue. Red. Purple.

A spectrum of colors characterized the identity of Sam Sommer more than half a year ago, and their importance wrought judicial contrast. His bodily hues came with pain yet they bore evidence—battle marks from a one-sided battlefield.

A late night car ride through Long Island's eastern peninsula (technically, Long Island is not an island) involuntarily and inevitably brought Sam to a medical facility in Riverhead. There he was treated for scars, bruises, cuts, and more resulting from the hands of Suffolk County detectives. The detectives could not cover up Sam's marks of brutality like they were able to cover up everything else about his "arrest" up to this point.

Black and blue primarily around one eye, red stains from stitches and scars, and a rather distinctive purple on the stomach defined Sam's already sunburn body in May of '68. Although more storytellers of the skin were concealed with clothes in public during his two arraignments, photos from a private physician afterward illuminated them for future purposes. That impending event finally came in the long-awaited Huntley Hearing at the county courthouse in Riverhead.

Bitter Long Island winds whipped off of Smithtown Bay onto the Stony Brook community the morning of January 21, 1969, as an equally-bitter Sam and Elaine prepared for a moment of truth. The biggest forthcoming event of their lives painted a contradiction to the warm summer backyard gatherings months earlier. The couple held hands in their bedroom before getting dressed for Sam's hearing. Would justice finally show its true colors and spring a blueprint of redemption for the young couple?

The 1965 case of *People vs. Huntley* sparked the need for a criminal pretrial hearing that scrutinizes the voluntariness of a confession. It's unique to the State of New York and seeks to determine if a statement made to a public official or one working in cooperation with a public official was voluntarily made, and therefore admissible. The prosecution has the burden of showing beyond a reasonable doubt that such a statement was made of the defendant's own volition.

In Sam's unique case, his defense team convinced Judge Stark in May at the county pretrial "do-over" to take another look at how detectives brought their suspect into custody. It took, however, a well-rounded judge to take the nourishment from spoon-fed arguments that primarily took shape from Sam's physical appearance alone. It remains to be seen whether or not the amateur submission of a grand jury indictment aided in the decision to not bring his case straight to trial for murder.

After making it through a kidnapping, beating, strip job, and circus-run arraignment the first time around, justice didn't appear too promising for Sam. Now the Huntley Hearing believed to be the stop gate against an unjust string of circumstances that hit his family so quickly.

The Honorable Gordon Lipetz, a native of Riverhead, presided over the Huntley Hearing. The fifty-nine-year-old welcomed the hearing as one of his first from behind the bench after serving four decades as a trial and appellate attorney. His January 1969 judgeship of Sam's hearing was held at the Suffolk County Riverhead courthouse—the same building as Stark's proceeding. Lipetz would end up serving as a Suffolk County judge until 1973, when he was elected to the State Supreme Court—a position he held until his retirement from the bench at the age of seventy in 1979.

The proceeding began with Suffolk County Assistant District Attorney Edward Connors leading the prosecution with a couple of aides. George Aspland, DA, who was involved in the pretrial proceedings, would partake behind the County's table as more of an advisor. The long-anticipated do or die criminal appellate hearing for Sam Sommer enlisted his two legal defense champions from last May: Eugene Lamb and Joe Scibilia.

No jurors made up the Huntley Hearing, but a splattering of key witnesses embodied its atmosphere, including Elaine Sommer. Little did anyone know at the time, particularly Lipetz given this was one of his early major trials as a judge, is that *People vs. Sommer, 34 App. Div. 2nd 817* would end up as a law study of notoriety.

The transcript is published in a St. John's Law Library book, *Criminal Procedure in New York, Part II, Revised, Criminal Evidence* (Paperno and Goldstein, Acme, 1980). It became almost an instant learning tool as a first edition in the early '70s related to assessing the voluntariness of a confession.

Suffolk County homicide detective Thomas Mansel took the stand for the People first. Mansel was assigned to the case of Irving Silver's death. Sam drew a nerve at the sight of seeing this hard ass again from last spring on numerous occasions.

Mansel was the one who took Sam to the station to discuss Irving Silver's plight and then to ID his body on the day Silver was purportedly killed on May 17, 1968. Ironically, that accusatory joyride to the precinct precluded another car adventure of harsher variety the night Sam was kidnapped five days later. At the Huntley Hearing Mansel would be front and center at its outset.

Summary of Primary Huntley Hearing Testimonies (translated)

Italicized narrative does not reflect testimony.

Some narrative paraphrased to preserve space and sustain story progression.

The first four witnesses who took the stand were the detectives primarily responsible for the apprehension and assumed arrest of Sam Sommer: Mansel, Brown, Gill, and Dunn. Mansel's testimony established key points from direct examination for the benefit of those who followed to avoid summative repetitiveness.

—— (start of testimony summary)

Connors initiated Mansel's testimony with an account of his encounter with the defendant on the day of Irving Silver's reported death. Mansel indicated that he and a detective Brown found Mr. Sommer at his Sheppard Meat Company office in Commack later that afternoon on May 17, 1968. He continued to say that Mr. Sommer agreed to travel back with him and Brown to the Homicide Squad in Smithtown.

After a couple of questions about when Mr. Sommer saw Silver last, Mansel voluntarily accompanied him across the street to a morgue to ID the deceased's body, which the defendant did (paraphrase). Mansel then claimed he asked Mr. Sommer to join him at his office to shed light on his business arrangements with the deceased. Mr. Sommer declined because he wanted to go home to inform his wife about what happened to her uncle. Before doing so, he did make a later arrangement that same day to meet Mansel at the squad's office that night but never showed up.

Mansel then said the next time he saw Mr. Sommer was at the cemetery in which Mr. Silver was laid to rest (apparently that was over the weekend, according to sources today). There was no interaction between Mansel and Sommer at the cemetery.

Still under the direction of Connors, Mansel's next testimony remained glued to when he saw Mr. Sommer again. The detective noted the evening of May 22 at Dunkin' Donuts near Jericho Turnpike (the one a few blocks from the Sommer home as affirmed by the court). He stated that detective Gill approached Sam, who was sitting in a parked car, about coming down to the precinct to answer some questions. Furthermore, he inferred that Gill was peaceful in his approach and read Sam his Miranda Rights (paraphrase).

Mansel spent the next few minutes re-establishing logistics and that the third detective involved in the Dunkin' Donuts "meeting" was Suffolk County Detective Sargent Dunn. Lamb casted his first objection after Mansel started placing Mr. Sommer in an interrogation room at the Fourth Precinct Homicide unit in Smithtown. Lamb claimed Connors was getting ahead of himself in leading the witness into statements of assumption (paraphrase). It would be the first of a menagerie of objections by both sides that would characterize a heated Huntley Hearing.

The next set of disclosures pertained to references of a card that all detectives carried regarding Miranda Rights, Mansel said these rights were read again to Mr. Sommer, followed by asking him if he preferred to have a lawyer present. Mr. Sommer responded by saying he didn't do anything wrong, so a lawyer wasn't necessary.

Mansel added that he and his team of detectives showed Mr. Sommer photographs of a deceased Silver, followed by the start of a confession made by the accused of the crime. Gill handwrote the beginning of a confession and read it back to Mr. Sommer based on insinuations that put him at the scene of the crime. The accused agreed to its message but refused to sign the paper. The entire party then went across a parking lot to fingerprint Mr. Sommer and process some paperwork under the assumption he had been officially arrested (paraphrase).

The remainder of Mansel's direct testimony included snippets of approximate times when Mr. Sommer was transferred back to a cell for lodging and the arrival of an attorney for the accused. Lamb started his redirect with a fury after Connors was finished with Mansel.

He introduced the use of force into the hearing. Mansel denied the use of force on Mr. Sommer. Lamb's cross-examination of Mansel continued with a recap of his various dialogues with Mr. Sommer on the fateful day of May 17, 1968.

In cross-examination, Mansel couldn't recall the official language that was used when he told Mr. Sommer about the death of Irving Silver during his visit to Sheppard Meat Company. Lamb then inquired about Mansel's disclosure to Mr. Sommer about where and how Mr. Silver was killed. Here the court learned that Silver was killed near Melville on Long Island as the result of being struck by a vehicle around five in the morning (paraphrase).

Lamb resumed by bringing the deceased's son, Ronnie, into the picture by asking Mansel if he spoke with him on May 17. That question was met with harsh objection by Connors due to his opinion on the materiality of Mr. Silver's son (paraphrase). Lipetz sustained the objection. Lamb promised the court Mr. Silver's son will be part of the hearing's arguments later on (kind of done so with a "like or not" attitude per Sam's recollection).

Questions about Ronnie Silver triggered a poke from Lamb at Mansel about how he knew Mr. Silver was involved with Sam in business. That, too, was met with objections from Connors. Finally, Mansel said he "believed Irv Silver" was a partner of Sam's based on registration papers or papers found in the vehicle indicating a partnership at Sheppard Meat Company.

More fireworks over Ronnie Silver ensued after Lamb reviewed a few details about the morgue, and according to Mansel, Mr. Sommer last spoke to Irving Silver the night of May 16. Apparently Sam suggested to Mansel that he contact Irving's son for potential answers and to ID the body as well. Mansel said they couldn't reach him until later in the day on the seventeenth after Sommer identified Silver. *That dialogue didn't bode well with Connors.* More objections.

Lamb and Connors exchanged aggressive comments (based on the flow of the transcript—a fair share of interruptions and dialogue went down before Lipetz intervened). Connors spoke on the materiality of Ronnie Silver—Lamb on potential coercion during Sam's perceived confession and facts on the timeline in which the defendant identified the deceased.

Connors openly tried to put to bed anything about Ronnie Silver and reminded the court that the hearing should remain focused on the nature in which the defendant was taken into custody. Most of Connors' objections were sustained with direction given to Lamb to get somewhere with his flow of questioning.

Moving on, Lamb asked Mansel about when he saw Mr. Sommer next after the cemetery. Dunkin' Donuts again enters into play on May 22—all seemingly consistent from the original questioning by Connors. The detective asserted that he and his fellow officers "saw" Mr. Sommer pulling into the Dunkin' Donuts parking lot on the way to visit

RAILROADED | 131

him at his house (paraphrase). An implication was made by Lamb that Mansel's party knew Mr. Sommer wasn't home, and then this direct citation from the testimony occurred (names inserted by authors):

> Q (Lamb): Isn't it a fact, Detective Mansel, that you knew that he (Sommer) was going to be at the Dunkin' Donut at eight o'clock because it was pre-arranged?
>
> A (Mansel): No, sir.
>
> Q: You say that that's not so?
>
> A: I did not know that.
>
> Q: Oh, you didn't know that?
>
> A; No, sir. (529)

The cross-examination switches gears to how and where Mr. Sommer was parked at the restaurant. The meticulous questioning soon caused Connors to object on the ground of irrelevant detail. Lamb defended his line of questioning saying that his intent was to establish that Mr. Sommer's vehicle was left running with a dog barking wildly in the back seat, corroborated by witnesses (paraphrase). The two counsels go back and forth on the materiality of the dog. Judge Lipetz allowed Lamb to continue with notice of swiftly getting to the point.

Mansel held his ground about the parking lot encounter in that Mr. Sommer went to the police station voluntarily and peacefully (paraphrase). Lamb jabbed between those details with a reminder that a dog was left barking in a running car after the three detectives and Mr. Sommer left the scene.

The next phase of cross-examination consisted of the interrogation at the Homicide Unit. Part of that event introduced details of an investigation that contradicted Mr.

Sommer's personal story after he returned from Florida. *He was set to resume work again with Mr. Silver under their normal carpool arrangement.*

Mansel contended that his team's investigation revealed that Mr. Sommer talked to Mr. Silver last around 3:30 a.m. by phone on May 17 (versus Mr. Sommer's indication of around 6:00 p.m. the night before per later testimony and his personal recollection). Mansel couldn't answer where Mr. Sommer made the alleged call from. That statement was met by another objection. Sustained on immateriality.

It is believed Lamb used this tactic throughout the Huntley Hearing knowing that based on admissions from four different detectives pertaining to the same events, a hiccup in inconsistencies would surface. The harsh objections from the prosecution didn't bother him for this strategic purpose.

While in the interrogation room, Mansel said Mr. Sommer was informed that they knew of someone who drove him to Kew Gardens (Silver's residence) on the evening of May 16. There Mr. Sommer was dropped off under a plan to kill Mr. Silver by striking him with a lead pipe and then throwing him in front of a moving vehicle.

The interrogation, according to Mansel, led to Mr. Sommer's admittance to meeting a Harold Goberman an hour before carpooling with Mr. Silver the early morning of May 17. The assumed confession at some point included Mr. Silver joining Misters Goberman and Sommer in a car. Then supposedly an argument arose over money matters. Silver got out of the car upset, and Mr. Sommer took advantage of the situation and ran him over.

This all happened, Mansel explained, from Mr. Sommer's mouth late in the evening on May 22 in a room at the Fourth Precinct Homicide. It was captured on paper by Detective Gill in the form of a handwritten (paraphrase) confession.

The court then learned from Lamb's cross-examination with Mansel that there was no warrant issued to arrest Mr. Sommer on the evening of May 22. The arrest concept snowballed into further contention between Connors and Lamb for some time. Lamb made it known about the discrepancies in time when his defendant was actually "placed under arrest."

Connors claimed his witness was not responsible nor in a position to "record" the exact time in which Mr. Sommer was under arrest. Both parties fired placations to let Lipetz know that the desk officer responsible for documenting the time of the defendant's arrest should take the stand (paraphrase), if it pleases the court (paraphrase).

Lamb pushed the timeline of the presumed arrest of his client up to a point where he then prodded at Mansel about force. Mansel said that no physical force was ever used against Mr. Sommer. Lamb countered by asking Mansel if he noticed marks on Mr. Sommer's body on that evening of May 22 during the questioning of the defendant. Mansel answered yes, behind Mr. Sommer's knee—a discoloration of black and blue.

The end of Lamb's cross-examination of Mansel explored the manner in which the detective became aware of a black and blue mark on Mr. Sommer behind his knee. He admitted asking Mr. Sommer to lower his pants during questioning because he was notified by an informant that the defendant was in a recent accident.

Lamb asked Mansel to expound on Mr. Sommer's marks and anything else noticeable around that area of black and blue. The detective mentioned he didn't recall if Mr. Sommer was wearing underpants during the interrogation. He also stated that Mr. Sommer did not have any marks on his face.

Lamb left his time with Mansel under oath recounting why Mr. Sommer had to be read his rights twice. Mansel answered with a remark about using the (Miranda Rights) card while at the station. Cross-examination of Mansel over.

Detective Jack Brown then took the stand. *It's noteworthy to mention that Brown was not part of the trio that met Mr. Sommer in the parking lot of Dunkin' Donuts.* He joined Mansel, Gill, and Dunn in the interrogation room at the Homicide Unit near Smithtown (also referred to as Hauppauge). The first notable aspect of Brown's cross-examination dealt with the aforementioned black and blue mark behind Mr. Sommer's knee, but his observation shed a different light. Brown said that he didn't observe the defendant wearing any underwear while the detectives looked at the black and blue mark.

Brown corroborated Mansel's testimony that Mr. Sommer refused to sign the drawn up confession by Detective Gill. Brown, too, mentioned that Mr. Sommer said that he accidently ran over the deceased. The questioning then navigated toward the informant piece of the puzzle like previously introduced by Mansel.

Here Brown said that Mr. Sommer offered $5,000 to the informant to have Mr. Silver killed. The informant refused the offer. Brown stated that Mr. Sommer denied the allegation and further contended that the informant was "crazy."

The unmasking of the informant didn't take long once Thomas Gill took the stand after Brown. The court discovered that a Harry Masterson, aka Harold Goberman, was the informant in reference throughout the Huntley Hearing thus far. *In addition to the fresh name drop at this point in proceeding, part of Gill's sworn to tell the whole truth and nothing but the truth dropped a few innuendos of head-scratching proportions.*

Gill was the second detective during the hearing who ended up referring to the deceased as *"Irv."* He didn't recall whether or not Mr. Sommer wore underwear either like

Mansel, and there was a contentious go-around between Gill and Lamb about discrepancies in time concerning the defendant's arrest and detainment procedures.

Finally, Detective Robert Dunn, Jr. was sworn in. His testimony jumped ship a few times in contradiction to his three colleagues during their cross-examinations. Initially, Dunn claimed he didn't recall whether or not Mr. Sommer had any clothing removed from his body during questioning at the police station. Then, later in Lamb's redirect he recanted by thinking he recalled Mr. Sommer dropping his pants.

Lamb emphasized that a police officer of eight years on the force should be able to remember anything noticeable about a person with his or her clothes off. *In Sam's reflection of this moment, Lamb basically inferred that one would have to be removed from common sense not to recall seeing a man's private parts.*

The end of Dunn's testimony raised a harrowing showdown between both sides that summoned them to the bench. Lamb brought up a subpoena 'duces tecum' (a court order requiring the person named in it to produce certain books, papers, or other tangible things for the court). It dealt with the desk clerk at the Fourth Precinct.

After convening with both counsels at his bench, Judge Lipetz ordered a recess until the next morning at 9:30.

—— (end of testimony summary)

Sam Sommer would take the stand first on day two of the soon-to-be infamous Huntley Hearing.

10.

KNEE JERKS

The aftermath of the first battle in Riverhead was treated like the end of a Presidential debate when pundits from two sides hit the spin machine to recap who got the upper hand. Sam Sommer felt good about his chances after the initial tussle. Small coverage in print media painted him as a villain. He didn't like how his instinct was polarized from what was being reported. In his mind, lots of separation from the truth coalesced with an orchestrated cover up; yet, he knew everything was going to be straightened out.

Sam and his wife, along with some friends and defense team, gathered outside his cell after the hearing. They shared echoes of encouragement together. After listening to four detectives try to polish their spew in consistent harmony, Sam believed Lamb orchestrated a good enough fight to illustrate the following ambiguities or rehashes of injustice to introduce reasonable doubt:

- No warrant for an arrest was issued; therefore, arguments about Sam's car left running at Dunkin' Donuts made his ultimate "arrest" look pre-planned. Doubts raised over the manner in which the car was found, soon to be reaffirmed by witnesses, boded well for the reason behind the Huntley Hearing in the first place: the use of force. Moreover, why was the car left running with a dog in the back seat if Sam left voluntarily with three detectives? Sam's departure from the parking lot under his own will represented a consistent claim by the prosecution.

- The no arrest warrant compounded another problem for the prosecution. It played conspicuously into the previous proceedings through the troublesome means in which a grand jury indictment for Sam's arrest found its way into court.

- Three detectives just "happened" to ride by a local donut shop on a Wednesday night on their way to a suspect's home, and "happened" to see Mr. Sommer in a parking lot in his vehicle at a precise time. The cherry on top of this Vegas-type longshot of a coincidence also puts the very person who called Sam to meet him at Dunkin' Donuts (Goberman, aka Masterson) in connection with the detectives since they admitted he was an informant. The timing of the call to the Sommer home and arrival of the detectives thread the needle of precision.

- Papers found in a car about a business partnership certainly made vehicle registration documentation seem unimportant in a glove compartment. This admission seemed weak. Who carries papers of a business partnership with them in a car? There was no evidence that these papers were presented to the court. Did Mr. Silver have pre-existing relationships prior to his death with any of the detectives? Two detectives referred to him by the name "Irv" during testimony.

- The informant was referred to as "informant" but also by two different names (it is noteworthy to point out that "Harold Goberman" was this person's primary known name based on research). How deep were these relationships? Whose side was the informant really on? Who did he work for? The more questions... the more reasonable doubt.

- The issue of whether Sam was wearing underwear or not while being interrogated appeared laughable. Obviously the four men of the badge supposedly trained to know what to look for during this kind of procedure didn't rehearse their aligned responses very well.

- The black and blue mark behind Sam's knee from a prior accident was not expounded on by either side until later on in the Huntley Hearing. Off the record Sam said he didn't make a big deal out of these marks compared to others around his body of more noticeable nature. The backside knee colors likely came from when he was jerked out of the car in the parking lot. In a dual instant of multiple pain, he hit the ground and then was kicked to his side behind the knee. He kind of took this minor pain for granted as it was overpowered later with other force at the police station. That episode of violence caused multiple cuts and bruises. Most of those marks, according to Sam, came into play after he was observed out of curiosity behind the knee.

- Inconsistencies as to the time of Sam's "arrest" were abound, as well as how and when he confessed to the crime from the collective statements of four detectives.

- The deceased's son, Ronnie Silver, was introduced into the testimony with furious objection by the People. Clearly no discussion on this man's role was going to take place come hell or high water in Connors' mind.

- The testimony behind two rounds of rights being read to Sam could be viewed as either nothing or overkill. If the latter was true, why didn't the reading of Miranda Rights suffice when they should have upon the heist, or alleged "first" arrest, of Sam at Dunkin' Donuts?

- The use of force on the defendant was rejected by each detective, setting the stage for a showdown of oil or water at the Huntley Hearing. A defendant months earlier sat at his arraignment transparently beaten and battered. Something had to give.

Day two of the Huntley Hearing was called to order on January 22, 1969. Sam Sommer took the stand on surprisingly a good night's rest. He would have raised his right hand on the Bible next to any judge in the world a second after his do-over arraignment seven months ago. Sam has been that ready to clear his name graciously and without holding grudges in the spirit of some sort of huge blunder, albeit one tainted with increased signs of evil and power. That said, his sights were confidently set on resuming life with a young loving family and thriving businesses, while doing whatever he could to aid the Silver family.

Summary of Primary Huntley Hearing Testimonies (translated)

Italicized narrative does not reflect testimony.

Some narrative paraphrased to preserve space and sustain story progression.

The trial transcriptions resume from the book noted in the previous chapter, *Criminal Procedure in New York, Part II, Revised, Criminal Evidence* (Paperno and Goldstein, Acme, 1980)—acquired from the St. John's Law Library.

—— (start of testimony summary)

In direct examination from Eugene Lamb, Sam Sommer immediately brought up Ronnie Silver. He mentioned that he asked him to help the police without hesitation concerning his father's identification and more, if needed. Lamb seemed careful enough to not delve too deeply on Ronnie Silver for sake of Suffolk County Assistant District Attorney Edward Connors' earlier objectionable tirade. He let Sommer briefly recount his interaction with the deceased's son and then moved on to another subject in what appeared to be seconds, not minutes.

Sommer said he knew Harry Masterson (Goberman) for around five months through business. The principle statements on Masterson were two-fold: First, Masterson's call to the Sommer home on the evening of May 22, 1968, came with insistance on Dunkin' Donuts as a meeting place. Masterson pushed Sommer to meet with him. Second, a bounced check briefly entered the court record with ties to Masterson and Silver.

The deposition then switched to the Dunkin' Donuts property. Sommer alleged he never went inside the store. He contended that right after pulling into the store's lot, he slowly proceeded to drive away from the store while remaining on its property (paraphrase) (*presumably away from other foot traffic and vehicle congestion to make it easier for Masterson (Goberman) to find him*).

Sommer's car was still in motion when the (soon-to-be revealed) detectives approached him in their car. Three detectives, led by Mansel, quickly exited their vehicle and approached his car on foot. Before even reaching Sommer's station wagon, Mansel said to him, "You're coming with me." Sommer continued to say that he was taken from his automobile physically, cuffed (from the front), shoved all the way to the men's car, and thrown into their vehicle.

Declarations from the defendant resumed with his attorney about being sandwiched (paraphrase) between detectives Mansel and Gill in the back seat. Detective Gill called him a "son-of-a-bitch." Sommer repeatedly pleaded that his wife would be worried, and his dog needed attention (paraphrase). Detective Gill then punched him in the mouth. Sommer told the court he was too scared to say anything else after getting hit.

Verbal onslaughts (paraphrase) from Gill lingered, according to Sommer. "We know you know something" was one example. The noted location and description of the interrogation room at the Fourth Precinct Homicide Unit on Long Island was consistent with the detectives' portrayals of the same place. Sommer told the court his handcuffs were removed after he was shoved from the shoulders downward onto a stool in the aforementioned room.

After begging to call his wife again, Sommer's request was met with responses from the detectives that had nothing to do with Mrs. Sommer. Instead, his appeal was met with the following decrees…

> "You fucking son-of-a-bitch, bastard, we're going to get you. We're going to make you cooperate. We know. We know that you know something to help us. We've been working on this damn lousy case for four days without no sleep, and we're going to find out what it is—whether you like it or not." (622)

The testimony continued without any objections. Sommer went on to say he was hit over the head with a telephone directory. Punches to the stomach followed by another detective, culminated by more lashes from the directory to the ribs and lower back. The defendant kept asking what they wanted from him; deaf ears followed in the form of more "son of a bitch" and "we know you know something" language.

Sommer alleged that this interrogation tactic (paraphrase) lasted an hour. The detectives then lifted Sommer up from his stool and kicked him from behind, causing the then-suspect to hit the ground. At that point they stripped him. He described a lot of pain in his head, stomach, and sides while being disrobed. Once stripped to his underpants and a t-shirt, more kicking and punching ensued. The detectives placed Sommer back on his stool.

"You mother fucking son-of-a-bitch" highlighted (paraphrase) another round of threats from the detectives. They remained congruent with claims that Sommer was going to help them because he knew something. The interrogated followed with repetitive answers that he didn't know anything about the death. He wanted to call his wife and confer (paraphrase) with a lawyer.

After getting his t-shirt ripped off of him and receiving another punch, Sommer heard one of the detectives (supposedly Dunn) holler, "Don't hit him in the face" twice over (paraphrase). The detectives left the room except for Dunn, who told Sommer the questioning would go easier if he would cooperate. Sommer countered with a rehash of wanting to speak to his wife and a lawyer.

The other detectives returned with photographs of the deceased's body. After he viewed the pictures, Sommer confronted the group of officers and submitted that he couldn't help them. He sustained his dialogue by telling them this whole thing (paraphrase) was ridiculous and that they were insane animals.

> "You're hitting me; you're punching me; you're giving me something, you're making up a story. I don't understand." (626)

The men then ripped off Sommer's shorts. Standing in the nude, Sommer conveyed to the court that he was humiliated and embarrassed. He continued by saying how could this happen in America; it wasn't Germany or some other place where these things happened. He couldn't fathom what was going on and hollered. That triggered another throw down to the floor and a kick in the testicles.

Sommer started vomiting and throwing up blood. He had to move his bowels from the lashing (paraphrase). He asked to move his bowels and used the word please. The reply from one of the men of the badge:

> "You'll shit all over yourself until we get whatever cooperation we want." (626)

Scared to death is how the defendant described his feelings. Presumably still laying down, Sommer was shown photos again of Silver's compromised (paraphrase) body. Gill held a pipe in his hand and addressed the detained, "Sommer, you see that picture? You see this pipe? Would you like to look like that? Cooperate with us." Sommer remained adamant that if he knew something he would help; after all it was his wife's uncle (paraphrase).

Sommer, alone with Dunn again, asked him if he could talk to his wife and obtain a lawyer while citing that his mother-in-law must be worried, too (paraphrase). Then the other detectives returned to the room after a short exodus. Sommer was offered a final chance to either sign a confession or he'd be booked. *It's deduced that the commands to Sommer "to cooperate" by the detectives up to this point meant sign a confession.*

Sommer refused to sign anything because he didn't do anything. He prolonged that stance by saying you (the homicide detectives) beat me like animals. One detective met that comment with a directive to get dressed because you're going to be booked. Sommer said he couldn't get dressed because he couldn't move.

According to the defendant, Gill and Mansel dressed him but without any underwear. Then, as Sommer declared, Mansel and another cop exchanged a conversation while leading him out of the interrogation room. Its gist was to not cuff Sommer while taking him across the street (for fingerprinting and photos). Sommer heard one of the detectives say, "It would go easier on him and us if he ran."

After 10:30 in the evening on May 22, 1968, Sommer was allowed to call his wife. He then answered a question from Lamb that appeared to arduously drive a stake in the ground that he did not admit to killing Silver (paraphrase). After being processed across the street, his entourage brought him back to the Homicide Unit and placed him in a cell (not an interrogation room).

Herein presents a problem to the prosecution. Recall **Sommer was offered a final chance to either sign a confession or he'd be booked** *from just a few paragraphs ago. If there was record of photos, fingerprints, and documents pertaining to his booking, then is it plausible to assume that he didn't confess to the murder? This is perhaps a classic case of having one's cake and eating it, too.*

In a cell, Sommer examined his own body (we assume at this point he was alone for the first time since being taken to the police station). In particular, he noticed a purple color around his abdomen and sides. The defendant said he was in shock and couldn't move.

Sommer's closing statements from Lamb's direct examination included his wife visiting him sometime after 11:00 p.m. She cried while he showed her his marks, recalling also not being able to move his hands much from them being stepped on. He asked her to get him some underwear. At the approval of a patrolman, Elaine Sommer was able to give her husband a pill to ease some pain.

The men in charge still wouldn't allow Sommer to place a phone call to a lawyer; they wanted him to sign a confession. That exchange with the detectives was assumed to be brief without force and after Elaine departed due to the transcription.

It was time for cross-examination from Suffolk County Assistant DA Edward Connors. The initial questions centered on Sommer's businesses and their ownership infrastructure. The accused listed Rosen's Deli, the Deli-Queen Restaurant, and S. Sommer Provision Company (meat distribution).

The meat distributorship came with a partnership with the deceased, Mr. Silver, according to the defendant. Relative to that business, it was established that Sommer had a $50,000 insurance policy with Silver tied to the company. Lamb objected a few times to see where Connors was going with this line of questioning. Judge Gordon Lipetz gave Connors a little leeway.

After seeking said background on Sommer's business ventures, Connors' jabs at the defendant encompassed an insinuation about his St. Bernard not attacking the detectives at Dunkin' Donuts if he was taken involuntarily (paraphrase). Nothing was said about the dog's location in the car with respect to this notion, although it was brought up in previous testimony (backseat).

Some smaller details about the makeup of the interrogation room and the amount of time it took for the detectives to supposedly use force on Sommer precluded a deeper dive into the use of phone books as weapons (paraphrase). Connors pried to get the names of the detectives who perceivably hit Sommer with phone books. The defendant couldn't recall exactly who hit him (by name) at the given moment.

Then Connors raised "inferred" (paraphrase) concerns over Sommer's inability to remember who hit him with phone books during a thirty-minute duration. For the next several minutes Connors asked Sommer short questions in what *gave the impression of choking his credibility. His pokes perceivably sought times, names, and places regarding Sommer's body where he purportedly and specifically was beaten* (paraphrase).

The gist of Connors' cross-examination changed into a contentious fight for a while compared to the length of other exchanges up to this point. The issue recounted the scrapes on Sam's knees and whether they resulted from an accident prior to May 22, 1968.

Note: During the detectives' testimony, the knee section of Sam's body was referenced in numerous capacities. Now, Connors navigated his inquiries about the same body location by repeatedly using the word "scrapes."

To better understand these important roadblocks in the consistent use of terminology since the prosecution decided to draw attention to this part of Sommer's body, here is a recap from the detectives' earlier testimony related to his knee area:

> Black and blue behind the knee, after first saying "around the knee area" (Mansel testimony, 551)
>
> Bruises on his right leg (Brown testimony, 564)
>
> To observe his body… then… Behind his right knee on the calf of his leg (Gill testimony, 586)

I saw that he had marks on his body. As I recall, the back of his right leg (Dunn testimony, 605)

The type of injury Sommer professedly sustained from "a prior accident" moved to actual details on the whereabouts and manner in which it went down. Countless objections by Lamb were overruled while Connors methodically peeled back an incident introduced in Chapter 3.

Ironically, nothing really strayed from Sam's original account of a fiery mid-day hit-and-run-like event during Connors' long cross-examination. It was fairly obvious Connors was vying for a belief that Sam's knee area marks resulted from an earlier brush with death against him and Mr. Silver by way of an automobile.

That cross-examination from Connors went as far as making it look like the defendant stretched the truth a bit about the incident actually being a hit-and-run. By doing so, a natural contradiction in his questioning surfaced. If Connors' intent was to establish a mark behind Sam's knee resulting from an emergency situation, why then did he question the urgency behind the event? He downplayed it to look like Sam didn't need to get out of the way of a speeding car so desperately.

On one hand, Connors kind of poo-pooed the hit-and-run situation to deflect any possibility that it had a bearing on Silver's death. On the other hand, the assistant district attorney seemed to want the court to know that the discoloration behind Sommer's knee was not caused by police force.

Judge Lipetz eventually asked Connors to get to the point about the experience with Sommer and the deathly car and if any injuries were sustained. Sommer denied any injuries. Connors then made an issue about the distance at which the car was in conjunction with when Sommer pushed Silver into the ditch (gutter) for safety. Connors questioned

Sommer's credibility in terms of whether or not the episode ever happened.

The defendant admitted to another accident after Connors asked if there were others of recent memory. Sommer said that he and Sal Spatarella were in a car together near East Northport approximately a month before Silver's death. Sommer said Spatarella struck a car that was in front of them. Here Connors tried to connect scrapes on Sommer's knees to this occasion like the other. Connors and Sommer traded verbal punches at one another in sarcasm; those were interrupted by the court and a call for a new witness.

Lipetz issued a temporary interruption to Sommer's time on the stand to call on a Dr. Fred Frankel of Riverhead—a licensed medical professional in which Connors conceded to his qualifications. He was there to testify for the defense, but the two sides agreed the timing fit the moment due to escalating contention over bodily marks on Sommer.

Frankel told the court that he examined Mr. Sommer on May 24, 1968, in a Suffolk County cell and in the presence of a deputy warden. His findings first noted a tenderness on the back of Sommer's head without signs of laceration or swelling. Sommer said it hurt when he had palpitated that area during examination. Frankel admitted that this part of the Sommer's body could have been caused from being struck by something.

Further observations from the doctor did not reveal any serious wounds or lacerations to the face of Sommer except for possibly the cheek bone area, although it wasn't documented at that time of examination. Basically, the cumulative testimony from this physician gave Sommer a clean bill of health other than the tenderness and cheek bone assumptions, with one exception.

A meatier disclosure surfaced on behalf of Frankel in terms of Sommer's abdomen region below the rib cage. Frankel said that area was consistent with being struck by something; he found it to be contused and ecchymotic (a discolored condition on the skin or membrane caused by blood seeping into the tissue as the result of a contusion).

Lamb started to end his direct examination by revisiting the condition of Sommer's face. Frankel "wasn't sure he saw anything of that nature" (paraphrase). Connors objected. That led to a verbal tiff between both sides. Lamb offered evidence that gave him perceived momentum.

Lipetz allowed a full transcript from Lamb from the May 23, 1968, arraignment of his defendant before Judge Frank De Luca. In reference to page seven of said document, Lamb noted that De Luca acknowledged a "'slight swelling on the left cheek bone (of Mr. Sommer)."

Using that acknowledgment from an earlier justice, Lamb proceeded to ask Frankel a parting query. If Sommer was struck on the face a couple of times on the left side (paraphrased in combined testimonial sentences), can you say with any degree of medical certainty that the absence of the swelling on the twenty-fourth ruled out the fact that he was struck on the twenty-second? Frankel replied, "No, it doesn't rule it out" (669).

Connors approached the witness in cross-examination. His only testimonial solicitation from Frankel dealt with the tenderness behind Sommer's head. Frankel told Connors that his assessment was based on pressure, not on visible evidence of the area. He concluded his response by saying he took the defendant's word for it that he felt pain in the referenced area.

All said and done with Frankel, his testimony appeared to be a coin toss on whether or not it aided Sommer. Lamb gambled with Frankel. Sam believed he was part of the Suffolk County establishment and cowardly couldn't utter the truth for the duration of his testimony.

After a recess, Sam Sommer resumed his testimony in cross-examination from Edward Connors. Primary digs involved Sommer's absence of underwear while presumptively (paraphrase) being interrogated and the whereabouts with Silver the day before he was reported dead. *The underwear prods were believed to be an attempt to contradict elements of time.*

Conversely, circumstances revolving around May 16 and 17 of 1968 got ugly in what is arguably the most combative part of this notorious Huntley Hearing. Connors ambushed Sommer about his activities the day before and early morning of Silver's death. Lamb countered with disputes that such questioning strayed from the voluntariness of a confession.

In other words, Connors wanted this to turn into a murder trial; Lamb worked to keep it under the framework of a customized hearing for sake of voluntary admittance. Sam had a front row view of a fierce rivalry that came to life when his own life depended on its outcome.

He sat on the stand and watched a prosecution obsess over taking him down right then and there for murder.

—— (end of testimony summary)

11.

A RIVALRY AND A ROCK STAR

Move over Yankees, Red Sox... North Carolina and Duke. A new rivalry in influential America was coming into the world at the time of these heated rivalries in the 1960s. Nestled under the radar in a rickety old courtroom in Riverhead, New York, Suffolk County Assistant District Attorney Edward Connors and attorney Eugene Lamb went for broke against one another over the life of a young husband, father, and employer.

The hardwood in which these two distinguished gentlemen fought didn't draw national attention or bragging rights for thousands of sports enthusiasts like Tobacco Road's hardwood courts yielded. This court didn't see spiked sales like Tar Heel or Blue Devil apparel did resulting from hype. The Riverhead court simply sought justice. Little did anyone know at the time that this little public place would be the launch of Long Island's continued dilemma today—corruption. And it all stemmed from the case of Samuel Leonard Sommer.

The end point of Suffolk County's judicial and law enforcement malpractices still remains at large today. Sommer's 1969 Huntley Hearing heeded a warning for Suffolk County to clean up its act. That objective to this day is still a fuzzy mirage.

Let's delve deeper into an unheralded rivalry in day two of the historic Huntley Hearing. Long Island's pangs of persuasion and an American Dream maker wrangled over credibility and confession.

Summary of Primary Huntley Hearing Testimonies (translated)

Italicized narrative does not reflect testimony.

Some narrative paraphrased to preserve space and sustain story progression.

The trial transcriptions resume from the book noted in the previous chapter, *Criminal Procedure in New York, Part II, Revised, Criminal Evidence* (Paperno and Goldstein, Acme, 1980)—acquired from the St. John's Law Library.

—— (start of testimony summary)

The initial impetus behind the Connors-Lamb dispute stemmed from the assistant DA's hammering of Sommer about when he and Irving Silver were together last before the deceased met his fate (paraphrase). Lamb rebuked the attacks on his defendant by saying that the evidentiary aspect of the Huntley Hearing is irrelevant to the authenticity of an oral admission (paraphrase).

Furthermore, Lamb said the testimony of Sommer pertaining to May 16 and 17 was already brought up by the detectives. He reminded the court that any testimony either supporting or circumventing guilt or non-guilt as to the murder of Silver for purposes of this hearing was immaterial (paraphrase). Overruled.

Connors dove into rough waters with Sommer, bombarding him about those two days in-and-out of overruled objections from Lamb. He kept reminding Judge Lipetz that he wanted to gauge the credibility of the witness. Eventually Lipetz drew warry of the tactic, but Connors evidentially had Sommer on the defensive based on his sense of impatience and anger toward the prosecutor (assertion).

Sommer didn't waver much from his earlier accounts of what happened on the sixteenth of May and the early morning of the seventeenth; however, his responses grew shorter in this section of the transcript perhaps out of frustration (assertion). A sample ploy (assertion) to trip up Sommer occurred when Connors asked the defendant about who called whom around 3:30 a.m. on the seventeenth and from what phone.

An overkill of detail occurred here. Connors had been preemptively repeating answers by Sommer (typically shorter answers) for speculative reasoning of trying to catch him off guard (paraphrase and assertion). In fact, the court needed to intervene and correct a testimony that confirmed Sommer made a call to reach Silver (not the other way around). It got that confusing with all the repeating of testimony—almost game like (assertion).

After that admittance was settled, Connors and Lamb took over the courtroom. Among the contested, uninterrupted dialogue between the two men for quite some time was Lamb's steady hand on keeping the trial fixed on voluntary confession. Connors, on the other hand, relentlessly threw inquiries at Sommer to openly determine witness credibility.

Connors played the credibility card with Lipetz on a few occasions to convince the robe to keep his line of questioning alive. It worked for a while until the judge insisted on Connors asking more direct questions to Sommer. Shortly after the pause in questioning, Connors grilled Sommer over who answered the phone at the Silver residence early on the seventeenth. Sommer admitted speaking to Silver, yet at one point he believed his son, Ronnie, answered the actual placed call.

At last, one of Lamb's objections got more than a slap on the wrist from Lipetz on Connors in light of his stream of guilty/not-guilty pokes at Sommer. He cited Supreme Court cases that apparently set precedence in defense of alibis. Lipetz allowed their admishis court after a short recess.

Lamb was directed to resume the post-recess Thursday proceeding by presenting legal findings comparative to Connors' line of questioning. He cited a Supreme Court decision, *Jackson vs. Denno*, 378, U.S. 368. A Court of Appeals returned a second Huntley case in which a Justice Geller reviewed the history of *Jackson vs. Denno* in this summation (provided by Lamb):

> "... cross-examination on the guilt of the defendant or the truthfulness of the alleged confession is not proper in such a hearing because it deprives the defendant of a right to a fair trial and for him to have a fair chance under due process to attack the confession as being involuntary (681)." (More)... "cross-examination as to the guilt of the defendant or the truthfulness of the confession plays no part and should not be permitted (681)."

Lamb submitted that the precedence included a statement from the defendant concerning his innocence of the crime. He then observed that this Huntley Hearing, *People vs. Sommer* (paraphrase), had yet to do that. He offered, "The only statement that has been elicited is that he (Sommer) did not give a statement as the acts of going into the voluntariness or admissibility to the beatings (681)."

Furthermore, Lamb remarked that nothing about Sommer's innocence or guilt had been addressed, yet was inferred in questioning (paraphrase). He stated that the *Jackson vs. Denno* Huntley Hearing allowed for a direct examination from the defendant's lawyer as to his innocence of the crime charged. A Judge Geller, on exception, permitted this type of examination to continue in *Jackson vs. Denno.*

Connors asked to be heard. He said Lamb was the one who raised the issue of voluntariness of confession when he wanted to know of the substance of the admission. Connors told the court he did not intend on getting at the defendant's guilt or innocence of the charged crime (paraphrase).

Lamb assured the court that he never asked about the truthfulness of the context of confession but rather whether or not the defendant admitted to it. Again, he brought up the Supreme Court precedence. Connors disagreed and said Lamb insisted on the context. He said that Lamb believed it had bearing on the voluntariness (paraphrase).

Artfully (perceived), Connors told Lipetz that he felt entitled to continue his questioning about what the defendant did the evening of May 16 and early morning of May 17. He did so arguing that Sommer (as a witness) already repudiated the whole statement (confession) anyway. Connors underscored not going down the path again with Sommer in regard to the statement itself.

Reminding the court that the defense already interposed a defense of alibi between the hours of 3:00 and 6:00 a.m. on May 17, Lamb indicated it had a direct bearing on the case. Connors didn't disagree, yet he said, "And it also has a direct bearing on the credibility of the witnesses that are going to be offered to this court (684)."

Lamb fought back by stating that Sommer's wife was a witness and called Connors out for aligning with viciousness (paraphrase). The assistant DA hammered credibility again. He summated that if one of the eight witnesses lie on one subject for the defense, they will all lie. Lipetz seemingly tossed a light-hearted response into the mix interjecting that the court won't go down that path (paraphrase).

After all the hubbub comparable in intensity to two champion ping pong players exchanging returns every second, Lipetz granted Connors a continuance of cross-examination. It was now solely (paraphrase), however, to pinpoint what Sommer did on May 17 related to his credibility. Sommer said he and Silver were to meet for coffee at the Pioneer Diner at 3:30 but his business partner was a no show.

Following the quizzing of Sommer about his call to Silver and where it was made from, how long the call took, and so on, Connors and the witness finally met at an intersection of substance. Sommer indicated Silver never picked him up at his house around 4:30 a.m. Tempted to ask the witness if he ever saw the deceased again, Connors withdrew his question (per the transcript he started to go there).

Then Connors threw Goberman (aka Harry Masterson) into the next round of questions at Sommer. That was met with fury by Lamb and a revisit of *Jackson vs. Denno*. Connors kept the compass of his cross-examination pointed at credibility of the witness. Lipetz allowed him to continue on noted exception from Lamb.

Connors inquired about Sommer seeing Goberman after about the tenth of May, 1968, (that was the estimated time in which the defendant said he saw him last in earlier testimony and interrogation). *Connors was ostensibly repeating the same questions to try and catch Sommer in a lie. If Sommer said the tenth of May was approximately the last time he saw Goberman, the same question was popped here—just framed differently.*

Sommer remained consistent with not seeing Goberman after May 10 and that he spoke to him on the phone the evening of May 22. That conversation, according to Sommer, was again in regard to a meeting at Dunkin' Donuts. *Since Connors appeared pleased (or displeased depending on* how this prodding can be viewed) with Sommer's responses, he changed his tactic.

He now went into the relationship between Sommer and Goberman. Such a premise found its way into the hearing earlier when Goberman worked as a subcontractor (paraphrase) to make repairs at Deli-Queen and before that was part of constructing the store (later testimony, 708). This time Connors wanted to know how often Sommer saw him.

Lipetz informed Connors that this testimony was brought up earlier, so the assistant DA rephrased his nudge at Sommers to discover specifics about where he met with Goberman within two months of May 17, 1968 (paraphrase). Sommer said once at his office and another time at the Pioneer Diner within that time parameter.

After going into detail about the thickness of New York regional telephone directories and how they were used against the witness, Connors abruptly ended his cross-examination. Lamb's redirect landed only one question to Sommer. He asked about a partner in Rosen's deli by the name of Frank Biancci being bought out in 1966 by Sommer's wife, Elaine. Elaine Sommer was then asked to take the stand for the defense.

Sam left the stand while his wife approached his spot next to the bench with a look of determination. He remembered that look on her face; it meant business—at the same time he left a scene that seemed like a whole bunch of monkey business. His confidence never wavered leading up to the hearing, but now he realized after being grilled in a microcosm of desperation (as he put it) by the prosecution that Suffolk County had an agenda.

In matter-of-fact style sprinkled with confidence (as Sam put it), Mrs. Sommer recapped the evening of May 22, 1968, at the opening of Lamb's direct examination. She alluded to a call received by her husband at home close to 8:00 p.m. from a Harry Masterson (aka Harold Goberman). She described her husband's hesitancy to go to Dunkin' Donuts to meet him. Elaine said that Sam even offered to have Masterson come to the house.

Mrs. Sommer continued to say that she didn't want her husband to go, but he insisted (paraphrase). Under her advice, he took the family dog. After he left, Phil and Susan Cirrone visited the house to see Elaine Sommer's mother-in-law under a previously-made arrangement. *Note: The Cirrones were close friends of the Sommer family. Sam's mother was visiting from Florida at the time. The family recently traveled down to see both sets of parents in Florida for a few days in mid-May* (see Chapter 4).

Elaine submitted to the court Phil Cirrone's background as a corrections officer with the New York City Department of Corrections against Connors' objection, which was overruled. Sommer's wife made it clear to Lamb that the visiting couple didn't even get settled in their home because she asked Mr. Cirrone to keep his coat on (paraphrase). She told him about her husband's meeting at Dunkin' Donuts.

Mr. Cirrone suggested calling the store, in which Elaine Sommer said she did. Lamb established for the court that Mrs. Sommer knew the owner, and she stated she spoke to this same person on the phone. She remained on the phone while the donut shop owner looked for Mr. Sommer.

He returned to the phone and said, according to Mrs. Sommer, "The (his) car was (seen) outside with the dog in it, but Mr. Sommer (paraphrase) wasn't there." The three then proceeded to Dunkin' Donuts in Mr. Cirrone's vehicle. Mrs. Sommer shared with the court that they arrived to a dog that was barking, foaming, and howling behind foggy windows. She stated she next sat in the car, turned off the engine, and took the keys.

Mrs. Sommer then asked Mr. Cirrone to go inside the store and find the owner and Mrs. Cirrone to call the Sommer (paraphrase) attorney. Those actions were followed by the arrival of a Suffolk County patrolman, Officer Ryan. He told Mrs. Sommer that he was there to secure the car. She responded by saying, "What for?"

Her testimony carried on, pressing the patrolman for answers as to where her husband was. Ryan kept replying that he didn't know. The witness then revealed that the patrolman asked her if she would like to go across the street (paraphrase) to the (paraphrase) Mayfair Shopping Center to make a call to the Fourth Precinct. Maybe they would get some answers from the police station.

Mrs. Sommer said she agreed to walk with the officer to the center to make a call from a pay phone (paraphrase). At the pay phone she heard Officer Ryan say, "Yes, there are three witnesses," followed by an apology and an echoed disclosure to release the car.

A family pulled up to make an unrelated, separate complaint about something at the center, but Mrs. Sommer told the officer that she needed to go back to her car (the station wagon with dog). Mrs. Sommer walked back to the Dunkin' Donuts lot and checked in with Mr. and Mrs. Cirrone (it was determined later in cross-examination that the distance from Dunkin' Donuts to said payphone at Mayfair was around a half a block).

Mr. Cirrone handed the phone to Mrs. Sommer with an attorney on the line named Joe Scibilia. He instructed her to go to the Fourth Precinct and file a kidnapping report. She drove her car home with the dog and rode in Cirrone's car to the precinct. There she was told to wait for a sergeant before she could file a kidnapping report.

During her twenty-minute wait, the officer in charge got very nasty, according to Mrs. Sommer. She elaborated (paraphrase) that his tone was nasty, and he started talking about her uncle. He allegedly knew him. The officer then threw questions at Mrs. Sommer related to the delicatessen and why she thought her husband was missing. She said she expected him in ten minutes while rehashing what looked like an abbreviated summation of the Dunkin' Donuts incident, according to the transcript.

In uninterrupted momentum, Mrs. Sommer submitted to the court that a Sergeant Lyons arrived at the station to meet with her. He gave her the report to complete and tried calling Homicide but no one answered. Mrs. Sommer gave Lyons a few more details about her husband while Mr. and Mrs. Cirrone were by her side the whole time.

Lyons informed Mrs. Sommer there wasn't anything that anyone could do at the moment. She was told to go home and wait for a call. Once home, Mrs. Sommer indicated that she immediately called the Fourth Precinct back to find out if anything had been discovered (paraphrase) about her husband.

She learned from a Detective Garrity that her husband was being booked for "murder one." The witness then went on to say to the detective that he was "crazy" and asked to see her husband. He declined, telling her that she could see him tomorrow morning at the First District Court in Commack for his arraignment.

Following that call, Sam Sommer called his wife at home. She told him a Detective Garrity said she couldn't see him until morning at arraignment. Sam checked with someone at the jail and informed his wife that she could visit and to come down with some belongings. It was guesstimated by Mrs. Sommer to be around 11:00 p.m. (on May 22, 1968).

Mrs. Sommer called and updated attorney Scibilia on her husband and then headed to the Fourth Precinct. Upon arrival, she was placed in a room where her husband was brought to her. She saw her husband in the following condition:

> He (Sam Sommer) was white as a ghost. He was trembling. He could barely talk; the words were slurring out of his mouth. I couldn't make heads or tails out of what he was saying. His hands were stark white. His cheek was swollen. He opened his shirt and said that they ripped his underwear off him, and that he had no underwear. Would I please bring him some (an OK to do so, not a question). And he showed me that his whole abdominal area was all red and purplish. He said that he had the beating of his life like never in his whole life (705).

For a few minutes (paraphrase) Mrs. Sommer and Lamb spoke on details that were already presented to the court in amiable flow. She told Lamb that the precinct officers only gave her five minutes with her husband in the aforementioned room at the precinct later in the night. On her way out of the station, she was given a large envelope containing his belongings. There was no underwear in the envelope.

Mrs. Sommer refused to sign for her husband's belongings because of the absence of underwear. Detective Lyons told her he (Sam Sommer) was wearing it. She disagreed and made note on the receipt of the envelope that his underwear was missing. The envelope was presented as evidence to the court.

Lamb's closing on direct examination with Mrs. Sommer touched on underwear provided for her husband the morning of his arraignment and that the article of clothing (paraphrase) was noted on record with Judge De Luca. She then asserted that her husband had no physical marks on his face when he left home to meet Harry Masterson (aka Harold Goberman) at Dunkin' Donuts.

Connors now approached Mrs. Sommer in cross-examination. He cemented for the court that she knew Harold Goberman (aka Harry Masterson) and for how long. *The admission was congruent to that of her husband's based on the overall transcript.* His questioning proceeded to bob-and-weave through details about what Mr. and Mrs. Cirrone did to aid her, the Mayfair Shopping Center call with Officer Ryan, and the primary goings on (paraphrase) when she and the couple arrived at the Fourth Precinct to file a kidnapping report.

The witness gave her answers with the clarity of a right angle, giving Connors nothing to go by that was controversial. Connors chipped into the night of May 16, 1968, a little ways but couldn't carve the witness into testifying about May 17 due to Lipetz supporting Lamb's objections. Mrs. Sommer told the court she didn't sleep well from time-to-time nor that night from being on medication (paraphrase).

She closed Connors' cross-examination by saying her husband was home the evening of the sixteenth, succeeded in reply to a direct question from Connors about whether or not she retired that night. Mrs. Sommer said, "No, I didn't."

——— (end of testimony summary)

If ink could speak, this latest transcript of the Huntley Hearing oozed with tension. Arguments between two lawyers cranked up the heat on Long Island in January. Sam and Elaine Sommer taking the stand, along with a Supreme Court case serving as hopeful precedence for the defense, added to the character of a newborn rivalry that would run for decades.

Four Suffolk County detectives, a physician, and even the defendant at times reverberated the witness stand in shaky testimony until a rock, an anchor, took it over by the name of

Elaine Sommer. Her resolute testimony stole the courtroom like a rock star moves a crowd of thousands to music.

Looking back, Sam admitted his experience on the witness stand threw him. He thought his confidence coupled with the absurdity behind the whole case would carry the weight of his testimony. He sincerely slam-dunked his presumed innocence with a go-through-the-motions attitude until he realized what he was up against in Suffolk County's obsession to bring him down. It was Elaine Sommer who was the showstopper.

Judge Lipetz ordered a recess at 2:40.

***

12.

BACK PEDDLING

"I received a call from the Sommers' dear friend, Phil Cirrone, at a Dunkin' Donuts in Commack," said former Long Island lawyer Joe Scibilia. "I heard that Sam was in some kind of trouble. Where do you need me and when? That was my response."

The now-retired Scibilia reflected with dog in one arm on the phone while the finishing touches of this book were in the works. The kind of generosity and humility that he portrayed fifty years ago when a friend was in trouble rang true today in talking with him from his south Florida home. The honor was ours; he survived long enough to escape the atrocities of Suffolk County. One of the few courageous individuals to take on evil back in the day during Sam Sommer's ordeal was still around in 2018 when he was in his early 80s.

For decades, Joe Scibilia fixated his time on New Yorkers obsessed with commas and zeros. Money. More money. Never enough money. A seasoned attorney who specialized in insurance legalities was the first sounding board of judicial hope for the Sommer family when Sam was snatched from a donut chain parking lot on May 22, 1968.

Elated to learn that Sam was also still living and forging his story into the open, Scibilia chimed sentiments of compassion toward the project. "I can tell you that the whole thing from the get-go didn't seem right. There was gambling and bad money involved with his uncle and the Mafia, and a convicted felon had one final chance to stay out of prison by working for the police. From start-to-finish it seemed like there was an effort to protect a criminal more than a working class family man."

***

The homestretch of Sam Sommer's case was nearing fruition. The remainder of day two of the combative three-day Huntley Hearing proceeding in 1969 in Suffolk County, New York, resumed below.

The Honorable Gordon Lipetz reopened the hearing around 3:20 on January 22 after a needed recess. Elaine Sommer, on paper by way of both the aged transcript and her husband's recollection today, was a hard act to follow. She definitely gave the defense a shot in the arm from her resoluteness. Eugene Lamb needed to maintain that spark and ride Mrs. Sommer's coattails. Momentously and fortuitously in arrangement of a line of witnesses, he looked to "one of them" as the next witness for the defendant.

Phil Cirrone was called to the stand. His profession probably marshaled instant respect by way of being part of the region's governmental establishment. The New York City Department of Corrections officer placed his left hand on the Bible and prepared to deliver his accounts of Mr. Sommer's plight.

Summary of Primary Huntley Hearing
Testimonies (translated)

Italicized narrative does not reflect testimony.

Some narrative paraphrased to preserve
space and sustain story progression.

The trial transcriptions resume from the book noted in the previous chapter, *Criminal Procedure in New York, Part II, Revised, Criminal Evidence* (Paperno and Goldstein, Acme, 1980)—acquired from the St. John's Law Library.

—— (start of testimony summary)

The onset of Mr. Cirrone's testimony pretty much placed all of the defense's previous testimony on the same shelf in terms of accuracy. He replayed arriving at the Sommer household the evening of May 22, 1968, encountering Elaine's distress (paraphrase), her calling Dunkin' Donuts, and so on leading up to arriving at the restaurant.

Mr. Cirrone recapped the immediate donut shop scene with a bit more specificity compared to other testimonies. He noted that a group of teenagers inside the store witnessed four men getting out of a car and then grabbing another man from his vehicle (paraphrase). One of the teens said a man among the group of four carried a gun at his side (paraphrase). Mr. Cirrone indicated that the owner of the donut shop basically affirmed what the teens said (paraphrase).

Recounts of calling attorney Joe Scibilia from inside the store and observing Mrs. Sommer go with an officer who arrived on the scene at a shopping center to make a call from a phone box (paraphrase) highlighted the continuation of Mr. Cirrone's testimony. The congruent statements that mirrored Mrs. Sommer's up to this point transitioned to the three (Phil and Susan Cirrone and Mrs. Sommer) arriving at the Fourth Precinct in Hauppauge.

There, according to Mr. Cirrone, the desk clerk said he did not see a "Mr. Sommer" in the building (Note: It has been understood and accepted by basically all parties that the Homicide unit was located in a separate building but not far from the main entrance to the police station. Consequently, the term 'building' is inferred loosely throughout the hearing. That could have let the prosecution off the hook when it came to details surrounding Mr. Sommer's whereabouts). The clerk proceeded in a manner like what Mrs. Sommer described in her testimony—all consistent. Mr. Cirrone said the clerk placed an unsuccessful call (paraphrase) to Homicide.

Mr. Cirrone closed his testimony by stating that he and his wife welcomed a babysitter that night. They both brought Mrs. Sommer home and left for their house (paraphrase). Suffolk County Assistant Edward Connors had no questions for Mr. Cirrone.

Susan Cirrone followed her husband in testimony for the defense while the weary proceeding inched deeper into the afternoon. Again, basically the same testimonial roadmap from arrival to the Sommer home to what transpired at Dunkin' Donuts and Fourth Precinct followed suit from her predecessors on the stand. It should be noted also that both Mr. and Mrs. Cirrone corroborated Mrs. Sommer's actions after they visited her house and leading up to when she returned home later that evening.

Mrs. Cirrone brought up, however, a brief yet striking sliver of dialogue between Mrs. Sommer and the desk sergeant at the Fourth Precinct. Mrs. Sommer informed the sergeant that she wanted to report her husband (paraphrase) "kidnapped." Mrs. Cirrone heard the officer reply, "Why?" (731).

Unlike her husband, Mrs. Cirrone's direct examination from Lamb didn't end the questioning. She met a cross-examination. Connors sought her recollection on where Mr. Sommer's vehicle was precisely parked at Dunkin' Donuts and what the lot was made of, i.e., blacktop, cement, etc. (paraphrase). He continued to ask her about how many cars were there and whether or not Mr. Sommer's vehicle was obstructing any vehicles from coming into or leaving the establishment's parking area (paraphrase).

Other Huntley Hearing testimony to this point danced with this same topic of where Mr. Sommer's vehicle was parked; however, nothing surfaced relative to his car being parked that close to the Dunkin' Donuts entrance/exit. *In retrospect, we're certain where Connors was going here. Objectively, he came across during this hearing more than respectable based on the cited law book, yet here his line of questioning maybe backfired on the People's case.*

Connors' meticulous navigation of Mrs. Cirrone's memory of a parking lot and how many weeds grew alongside it perhaps didn't produce the outcome he wanted. Facetiousness aside, that level of detail figured to bring a hiccup against her husband or Mrs. Sommer's testimony, subsequently turning out favorably for the prosecution. Instead, the DA's prodding hit a detour along the way in realizing such a result.

In twisted irony, Connors did get her to cough up new testimony as to the nearly-exact positon of Mr. Sommer's station wagon. Did her portrayal aid in Connors' strategy? In other words, why didn't the previous defense witnesses dip to this level of descriptive depth (even though the prosecution witnesses didn't either)? Oversight by all? Maybe.

She said that his (Mr. Sommer's) vehicle was barely (paraphrase) inside the lot from the street, and it was blocking the flow of traffic from one side of the lot near the store (paraphrase). If anything, Mr. Sommer's erratic parking in the lot spread more reasonable doubt about voluntariness of confession than it did inconsistency of witness testimony.

You could argue both sides hit a detour in detail here and there during the hearing, but the majority of the reasonable doubt plunged into the hands of the prosecution. Not done yet, though.

A layperson's overview of a parking lot's characteristics (paraphrase) in testimony from Mrs. Cirrone ended her time on the witness stand. It also ended day two of the Huntley Hearing around 3:50 p.m. until 9:30 the following morning, January 23.

Through a supposed subpoena in November of 1968, a Suffolk County officer attached to the Fourth Precinct named Michael Ryan kicked off day three of the Huntley Hearing as a witness for the defense on Thursday, January 23. Ryan denied the subpoena (It remains to this day if he was summoned to appear in court or if he did so voluntarily. Connors claimed he came to court on his own.

Lamb referred to a Judge George McInerney of the State Supreme Court in the representation of subpoenas of additional officers for this hearing).

McInerney is the same judge who ordered Sam Sommer's Huntley Hearing on May 24, 1968, after a second arraignment was held. In that proceeding, a Judge Thomas Stark in essence found Mr. Sommer not guilty according to documentation that has served over the years as a bone of contention for the defense (refer to Photo Gallery in the middle of the book).

Ryan was the one sent by the Fourth Precinct to secure a car with a dog in it at Dunkin' Donuts. His contributions to the proceeding amounted to primarily forgetfulness and uncertainty. One of his moments of blankness applied to not remembering a complaint made about some youth (paraphrase) at the Mayfair phone box (whether that incident was true or not, it is noted here about him forgetting as it was brought up in earlier testimony). Lamb nudged Ryan with insinuations that a happening like that would not be hard to recall (paraphrase). *In other words, the event either happened or it didn't.*

That exchange led to Lamb quizzing Ryan on why incidents like those and even information provided by Mrs. Sommer on the evening of May 22, 1968, weren't recorded in a notepad (paraphrase). Lamb asked Ryan if he brought the notepad that would have documented events around that time to court (paraphrase). He did not.

Ryan's brief witness-stand performance included informing the court that a Sergeant Lyons said no one was brought in under arrest based on his call to the Fourth Precinct from the Mayfair phone (paraphrase, 742). Originally, Ryan said he ascertained this information down at headquarters, but then said it was done from the phone box (paraphrase, 742).

Again, both sides tripped on smaller details during the hearing, but this particular testimony related directly to the interrogation and processing of the defendant. If any aspect(s) of analyzing the voluntariness of confession ought to be considered in a hearing that examines such testimony, it's the processing, booking, interrogation, reading of rights, etc., of a defendant.

This part of the hearing connected some more dots. Aside from another glitch in accuracy among men of the badge, why would an officer be called to secure a vehicle unless the command was tied to something that happened to a driver? Officer Ryan showed up without any notification from the Sommer rescue party comprised of Sam's wife and the Cirrone couple.

If Mr. Sommer was taken against his will by testimonies of a running motor, a wild dog, and the arrival of an officer on the scene from an internal command, then reasonable doubt must have filled the courtroom air. These head-scratchers fit the framework of a Huntley Hearing and its purpose of unearthing the voluntariness of confession and arrest procedures.

The subpoena mess at the conclusion of Ryan's direct examination between Lamb and Connors resembled classic he said/she said. Lamb said his investigator noticed Ryan and other officers talking at the end of the hall in the justice building with Mr. Connors before the hearing commenced on January 23. Connors said they were discussing dogs (744).

Connors contested that Ryan never received a subpoena. Rather, he received a phone call at 6:00 that morning (paraphrase) to come down on his day off to testify. Lipetz sustained a Connors' objection a few moments earlier that basically dealt with Lamb poking Ryan about coming in on his day off when he was earlier subpoenaed (paraphrase).

Either way, subpoenas were issued or they weren't. Only Judge Lipetz knew the answer to this mystery, and perhaps the subpoena subject factored into his ultimate decision. Lipetz is deceased. He died at the age of 86 in 1994.

Sergeant Francis Lyons was sworn in next under direct examination by Lamb. Lyons disclosed assuming the role of desk sergeant at the Fourth Precinct on the evening of May 22, 1968, and receiving confirmation from Officer Ryan that there was a vehicle at Dunkin' Donuts (paraphrase). The dialogue turned to what types of calls are logged by a desk sergeant when received from patrolmen (like every hour, for example).

Lyons then disclosed that he learned about a vacant vehicle with a dog in it (paraphrase) by a detective. He thought it was Detective Dunn who informed him but wasn't certain as to the name. Lyons proceeded by saying he found out from a duty officer that a Mr. Sommer (paraphrase) was not on record of being arrested.

In support of the previous assertion on how police would have known to secure a car with a dog in it at a specific location, the court learned here that Detective Dunn (likely) made the revelation.

At the Fourth Precinct, Lyons acknowledged Mrs. Sommer telling him about the death of Irving Silver, followed by a denial that he knew the deceased (paraphrase). Next, Lyons indicated he finally got through to Homicide and discovered that he (Mr. Sommer) was arrested (paraphrase). Then he said he told Mrs. Sommer this, *but what came next flipped the witness stand upside down.* Lyons told Lamb that he called Mrs. Sommer later at her home to inform her that Mr. Sommer was arrested (paraphrase, 749, 750).

Lamb then attempted to solidify time estimates with Lyons on when these interactions went down. To no avail. Connors objected, saying the witness already said he didn't know (paraphrase). Overruled. Lamb unloaded on Lyons with a green light from Lipetz, seeking to understand when these disclosures of arrest occurred. At one point he asked Lyons if he was a trained police officer.

The Lamb/Lyons interaction showed the defense attorney's skill. What may have been frustrating to Lyons (he, for instance, said "I assume so" in response to Lamb's question about being a trained officer) looked momentous to Lamb. It's like he had him where he wanted him. Lamb jumped from the professional training reference to whether or not Lyons knew about police routines. The transitory push kind of fed off the other to discredit the witness.

After an objection from Connors as to the form of Lamb asking Lyons if he could assume that Homicide had the driver of the car at Dunkin' Donuts (paraphrase), Lamb modified his question:

> Q: Well, could you assume that Homicide was involved in some way with that car, couldn't you?
>
> A: You could assume that, yes (751).

Lamb artfully advanced the direct examination with Lyons by wondering what procedures the Fourth Precinct has in place concerning telephone communications between officers and desk personnel (paraphrase*). Sam attested later that this was likely Lamb's finest hour of the Huntley Hearing for his defense. By poking holes in procedural protocol or discrediting witness testimony tied to such organizational operations—didn't matter. An impression of Suffolk County law enforcement running a circus instead of a public safety agency ushered more reasonable doubt.*

Part of Lyons' proclamations to Lamb brought forth subjectivity in events related to when Mrs. Sommer was at the desk with him at the Fourth Precinct. The sergeant said when a person comes in with a complaint that records of those complains are always kept if they're "valid" (paraphrase, 753).

Then this cherry landed on the top of Lamb's artful examination of Sergeant Lyons right at the end of their time together:

> Q: You weren't sure on May 28th - May 22nd (corrected) when the woman (Mrs. Sommer) came in that there was a valid complaint, is that correct?
>
> A: I was not sure that there was a valid complaint as given. She stated it was a kidnap by the mafia. And I was unsure at the time whether it was a kidnap by the mafia or an—an arrest. Or something else (753).

Lamb said, "All right. Or an arrest."

Above all the banter about when Mr. Sommer was arrested, now the court knows that a sergeant with Suffolk County law enforcement couldn't decide if he (Mr. Sommer) was arrested or kidnapped. Too much contradiction. Too much reasonable doubt, in addition to wondering to this day what constitutes a "valid" complaint at the ole' Fourth Precinct in Hauppauge. Jay walking, yes. Kidnapping, no.

The prosecution was back peddling. Unlike Ryan's testimony, Connors felt a need to cross-exam Lyons. The People's case fled into retreat from so much reasonable doubt.

Lyons told Connors that when Mr. Sommer was about to be lodged (Connors scratched "booked" from his question) that he didn't notice any marks on his body. The rest of the short cross exam described a procedural plan that's in place (paraphrase) at the Fourth Precinct in response to the assistant DA's question about what officers do when a suspect (paraphrase) complains of a pain or injury. Lyons provided substance that suggested a plan is on the books (paraphrase).

Lamb's redirect of Lyons regenerated the subpoena puzzle. Lyons said he was not subpoenaed from the defendant's investigator, but he did receive a subpoena last November from a Judge McInerney (paraphrase). He also declined receiving a subpoena to be present (on the day this testimony was going on) from the DA's office. Lyons finished this line of questioning saying, "I said—he (Connors) said there was a possibility that I might be called up, yes (755)."

The McInerney subpoenas opened the ring for another round of verbal punches between the two lawmen. Connors raised a point about the McInerney subpoenas were supposedly directed at the proprietor of Dunkin' Donuts (paraphrase). In so many words, Connors insinuated that this witness (Lyons) would not have been properly instructed to appear in court since McInerney's remarks were as far he knew directed to the proprietor (paraphrase).

In rebuke of Connors' insight, Lamb said those police officers who were subpoenaed did not return to McInerney for next steps in December (paraphrase). He continued to utter that someone from the DA's office assured the judge that the officers would be notified. The latest heated chapter of brawling near the bench was culminated in an unpredictable, yet welcomed interjection from Lipetz. "It's really immaterial, gentlemen (757)."

Only a legal pro could imply if this level of clashing between two attorneys during any hearing is unusual. In this case it's assumptive that Lipetz's interjection warranted a bit of refocus by way of humor. The fact the witnesses were present was of most importance. The preceding rant between lawyers, however, further planted a legacy for this hearing as one for the ages (at least on paper).

The People called Officer Arthur Fries to testify from the Suffolk County Police Department Identification "Section." Fries testified that as part of his role he often takes photographs of suspects (paraphrase). He denied seeing any marks on Mr. Sommer while taking his photograph.

That was all for Connors as Lamb approached the witness. Fries told the court he typically takes two photos of a suspect (paraphrase) on one negative. The negative was not brought to court. Lamb showed him a black-and-white mug shot (paraphrase) photo of Mr. Sommer to Fries and asked him if it refreshed his memory with respect to Mr. Sommer having any marks on his face. Fries said "no" (it did not).

In Connors' redirect, the topic of squinting versus swelling arose. Showtime again for Lamb and Connors about the officer's expertise in photography, and this time Lipetz joined the fray by declaring to the assistant DA that he has to qualify the witness. Connors did.

All said and done here, the prosecution was trying to show that Mr. Sommer could have been blinking when the shutter of the camera went off. In doing so, such an argument would suggest that his left eye (the eye in question over the use of force and swelling) closed from the picture (paraphrase).

Conversely, in Lamb's second cross-examination of Fries, he offered to the court that a person can have both eyes closed when squinting from a camera's flash (paraphrase). Fries didn't disagree, but he added that sometimes those photographed anticipate a shot then squint on impulse (paraphrase). Fries added that the equipment the department uses is set up to help partially reduce squinting in the end shot (paraphrase).

That ended the lineup of witnesses in Sam Sommer's Huntley Hearing. According to the transcript for which this narrative still resides inside a testimonial summary, the three-day proceeding culminated as follows after both the prosecution and defense rested:

- Eugene Lamb responded to Judge Lipetz's inquiry if he wanted to submit anything to the court. Lamb indicated that the defense would need a little time to submit a memorandum of law to the court in context of voluntariness and admissibility. Lamb then raised these closing remarks:

> ...the district attorney has failed to prove beyond a reasonable doubt that this confession and this statement was voluntarily given by the defendant. One of the things the district attorney must prove to the satisfaction of the Court beyond a reasonable doubt when unexplained physical injuries are found and for which there has been testimony, both under the United States Law and the New York State Law, the district attorney must establish satisfactorily how the injuries came into being and to explain how they came to be (768).

- Lamb proceeded by referring to United States vs. Follett (May 8, 1968), 393 Fed. 2d, 879, Decision of the Second Circuit, citing as foundations for the New York cases People vs. Moccio and People vs. Cerullo, etc., (768). Lipetz granted Lamb until February 3 to produce his memorandum with copies for the DA's office. Connors agreed to the time parameter and then asked if he could address the court orally for he had nothing to submit in writing. Both Lamb and Lipetz gave him the floor (paraphrase).

• Connors' conclusory address chewed up nearly all of the final six pages of *Criminal Procedure in New York, Part II, Revised, Criminal Evidence* (Paperno and Goldstein, Acme, 1980)—acquired from the St. John's Law Library.

> *His swan song before the court declared an immediate implosion. In a hearing centered on the confession of a defendant, an eloquent member of the DA's office dropped the mother lode when it came to a confession.* An earlier testimony by Detective Mansel in chapter eight revealed that the four detectives did not know that Mr. Sommer was going to be at Dunkin' Donuts at a given time.

While the curtain was about to drop on the hearing and Lipetz would soon begin deliberation, Connors said this: **First of all, I think it's a fair conclusion on the part of the Court or anyone listening to this case that these police officers set up this appointment through an informant in order to get this defendant into their custody (769).**

He continued to say that it's assumed the defendant was avoiding them (meaning law enforcement, paraphrase); therefore, they (detectives) resorted to the scheme (paraphrase). *It is important to point out that earlier testimony by detectives and Mr. Sommer indicated that the police were able to track him (Mr. Sommer) down on more than one occasion days before May 22, 1968 (his office and the cemetery, for example). Plus, they were, again based on their own statements, going to his house anyway on May 22 for alleged purposes of "finding him."*

Yes, Connors' first breath signified a gasping prelude to an exhaustive conclusion. Whatever he said next, unless it was dropping the murder charges against Sam Sommer, would not hold any water to that jaw-dropper of a confession.

In replaying this account with Sam all these years later, it's theorized that Connors was either putting out this eye-opener deliberately or as an act of charity. If deliberate, it's believed he wanted to get the orchestrated apprehension of Sam out the way so to speak in place of a greater argument. The other assumption is that he was trying to play a heartstring with the judge by suddenly demonstrating a sense of humanity toward the defendant.

Either way, it didn't take Connors long to move into lecture mode in a rather persuasive curtain call on behalf of the prosecution.

- Connors argued to the court that Mr. Sommer self-inflicted his injuries. Based on various testimonies there wasn't a single mark on his body, except for the stomach area, and that the photo (in question) was debatable (paraphrase). The photographer told the court he noticed nothing unusual about the defendant's face. In so many words, Connors made it look like Mr. Sommer exaggerated on the amount of times he was hit and where he received the beating on his body by the detectives, otherwise, there would have been noticeable marks (paraphrase).

- Lipetz inquired about building configurations again pertaining to where Mr. Sommer was moved around during his interrogation, booking, and lodging (paraphrase).

Connors described the makeup of the Fourth Precinct and its adjacent facilities. Connors then downplayed the stomach injury since the defendant "conveniently" forgot about the knee-area injuries from a previous accident. He said the detectives wanted to check that part of his body from a recent accident (paraphrase).

> *Questions remain: What bearing would that knee "exam" have on this case? Did the detectives feel they would have to account for that injury for some reason? If the detectives were bent on checking behind Mr. Sommer's knees in the first place, then they must have been privy to a previous accident. From whom? Was their checking of his knee area a gesture of goodwill? They were detectives, not doctors, like said earlier in testimony by Sergeant Lyons himself.*

- Connors entered another member of his DA's office, a Mr. Berler, into the late mix. He said Berler didn't observe any injury or swelling to Mr. Sommer's face. This observation occurred at the District Court arraignment of Mr. Sommer in Commack on May 23, 1968.

- *The assistant DA perceivably jacked up his argument about the defendant self-inflicting his injuries.* His now nearly-finished closing remarks brought that point up again, believing that the detectives told the truth (paraphrase).

- Finally, Connors hammered home that if the defendant was beaten as badly as he wanted everyone to think, why would the detectives take him over to be photographed and fingerprinted, etc. (paraphrase)? He said Mr. Sommer was never beaten, and that any marks on his body happened by harming himself when left alone in the interrogation room for a few minutes to think about giving a confession (paraphrase). He said no one from the Fourth Squad (a different unit from Homicide) said anything about his condition either (paraphrase).

- *Testimony from the detectives did not reference Mr. Sommer ever being left alone during interrogation. There was always one detective in the room with him.*

Lipetz made sure Connors would receive the forthcoming memorandum from Lamb and that he should acknowledge its receipt (paraphrase). The Huntley Hearing then ended at 11:19 a.m. to chambers.

——— (end of testimony summary)

All parties received the February 3 memorandum as promised from the defense. Judge Lipetz dug in.

13.

HATRED

A 2016 FBI report cited hate crimes on the rise for a second consecutive year with nearly six in ten targeting the victim's race or ethnicity. Of the incidents spurred by hatred of a particular religion, anti-Semitism again led the cause, motivating about 55% of those episodes, followed by anti-Muslim sentiment of about 25%.

Hatred against Jews is not only a growing and to some a trendy realization in the United States; it's a worldwide epidemic. No statistical data is needed to corroborate the previous statement—just do a Google search on United Nations/Israel (discrimination abound), former President Obama's support of Iran (Israel's biggest enemy according to a 2018 interview with Benjamin Netanyahu), daily weaponry onslaughts against Israel from radical Muslims at Gaza and the northern border, and a growing threat to U.S. Jewish centers and to Jews on U.S. college campuses.

The Center for the Study of Hate and Extremism at California State University—San Bernardino released a 2018 study that shows Jews being the most consistently targeted religious group, making up 19% of all hate crimes reported in major U.S. cities. Nothing unusual here, but you won't see it on *CNN*, for instance, so to many this is new information.

Increased alliances in Syria against a culture and nation no bigger than the state of New Jersey is prophesized anyway, most importantly. Historically and ironically, a state right next to New Jersey has heralded a tragedy and cover up against a Jewish-American like never seen before in this nation. Everything Sam Sommer has stood for—creating jobs for immigrants, building a strong family and local economy, and leading by way of a robust work ethic and commitment to innovation has been destroyed in one word: hatred.

Instead of openly targeting Jews on college campuses and in streets like today, in the 1960s powerful people in Suffolk County, New York, attacked them with a few winks and schemes behind closed doors. Judges, cops, and DAs concocted deals with mobsters to gain control over enterprises at a time when Mafia undertakings were defining the Big Apple business climate. Some of this dark history has already been touched on, but more is found later in the book, as well as a dark, present-day Long Island.

The 1969 Huntley Hearing of Sam Sommer draws a scary link to the hatred of Jews in America today. One family who built American Dreams for people of all walks represents the victimization of hatred longer than any single crime on record in the U.S.

Once the hearing adjourned, Sam and his family took a deep breath that would have blown the snow off their Commack, Long Island driveway. The couple felt good about what took place in the Riverhead courtroom. Still out on bail, Sam tossed himself back into a lot of domestic duties, wanting to remove himself as much as he could from his current case.

The hardest part was waiting for Judge Lipetz's decision. If victorious, the whole madness of murder accusations could end along with such a ruling. A win for the prosecution on the other hand would certainly transform the landscape of the Sommer family's future. At the same time and cautiously optimistic, Eugene Lamb and Joe Scibilia kept in close contact with Sam—waiting in the wings like a dove covered in a cloud. They were also cueing up a rising young private investigator named John Darnell to potentially dive into the deceit, if needed.

Sam's businesses started to slide, especially his wholesale meat operation. He didn't have the time to personally grease the well-oiled machine as steady as before. Rosen's and Deli-Queen were doing fair, but the accusations against him the past several months dampened his foot traffic. Sam went into his stores when he could, but basically for the time being he turned over the day-to-day management to other folks.

Sam started losing money. He dipped into his closets of cash quite heftily to pay two attorneys for nearly a year, a new mortgage, extra help around the house, and to post his bond. It wasn't in his heart to lay off staff. The belt had to tighten.

The month of February went by and nothing from the court in Riverhead. Sam and Elaine thought by now Lipetz would have sunk his teeth into Lamb's memorandum and the trial transcripts enough to know he did not confess to the murder of Irving Silver. They kept the faith that too many gray areas encroached any black and white clarity the assistant DA tried to show during the hearing.

Another 'trial' lingered while waiting for the court's judgment, one without pounding gavels and witnesses on the stand. The Sommers longed to comfort the Silver family during this emotional period. That intention walked a fine line, however, since the extended family members of the Silver tree were split on their beliefs toward Sam. Half thought he killed Irving while the other side believed in his innocence. Nonetheless, that didn't stop Sam and Elaine from reaching out to offer condolences, prayers, and a helping hand.

Naturally, trying to bond Elaine's bloodline cross-functioned as a means to keep an eye on Ronnie Silver as well. The troubled young man grew distant from his own family except for his sister, Barrie. Ronnie's past potential involvement in this case was not scrutinized. Out of respect for losing both a father and mother within two years, everyone around Ronnie treaded on a slippery slope when it came to watching over him. He returned to school as maybe somewhat of a façade to still play the streets in gambling and who knew whatever else. Lamb suggested to Sam to do his best in keeping tabs on him in case they needed to bring him back into the judicial fray at some point.

March crawled. Time was not on anyone's side. Two months since the hearing ended and no word from chambers. Sam tried to return to work after a few weeks of maintaining a low profile at home. It wasn't the same, sadly, for a man ahead of his time and one on the brink of shaping New York's culinary heritage. Some put Sam right up there with the legendary Willie Katz of infamous Katz's Deli—a thriving, world class eatery in New York with lines of people waiting to get inside each day. It has been a finger-pointer in the big city for more than one-hundred thirty years.

In the early afternoon on March 28, 1969, Sam was going over some papers on the kitchen table in contemplation of what to do with his businesses when the doorbell rang. It was Lamb. He donned a happy persona despite the frigid air outside. Sam invited him inside; the two hadn't seen each other in a while yet conversed by phone a few times since the hearing.

"We did it," followed by a hug right in the doorway as Elaine shouted from upstairs about who the visitor was. Sam was speechless. Elaine heard cries and laughter in place of verbalization. She sprinted down the steps and was greeted by four arms in a huddle of joy. Judge Gordon Lipetz ruled to suppress the voluntariness of confession after deliberating for fifty-three days. Sam Sommer won the Huntley Hearing.

Lamb handed Sam the official court decree. Those unsettling mind-grinders from a moment ago at the kitchen table concerning his future evaporated. The weight of injustice slid off his mind. He could breathe again. Sam said the weight of injustice cripples the air. The family celebrated in the simplest of means: hugs, food, and an uptick in heartbeats. Time to get back to life.

A technicality still needed to make the ruling official. Judge George McInerney acknowledged the motion to suppress on April 21. Sam got his employees together and restored relationships with them and many customers. The delis were set to undergo a rejuvenation of appearance and menu, and Sam's spirit by the Grace of God put him on the streets of commerce once again. He had lots of visits to make. As of late April, 1969, it appeared he was cleared of murder. There was no indication that he would have to stand trial for the death of Irving Silver.

Prepared to dedicate his time to work and family again, Sam's newfound outlook included the Silver family in his plans. He also wanted to keep working with Scibilia and Lamb to see who was responsible for killing his wife's uncle. The loving and upbeat course of action halted in early May to a screeching stop that shook everyone between the ears.

The Suffolk County DA decided to appeal the Huntley Hearing ruling.

Windless sails took over the hearts of the Sommer family, befalling to a huge level of confusion. Why didn't the prosecution just walk away from the court's decision? Why the appeal? This appeal became horrifyingly personal. Lamb and Scibilia did all they could to assure the Sommers that the motion was a formality.

It didn't feel that way. The news about the appeal felt like hatred. The family, in particular Sam, was now a target. Suffolk County was out for blood. There were plenty of other pressing issues going on around the island (like Silver's real killer). To focus on one man and a crime that he did not commit set the table for nothing like this nation's judicial system had ever seen before.

By late fall, a federal court overturned Lipetz and McInerney's rulings from the Huntley Hearing. Five judges who were former members of the Suffolk County DA's office upheld the appeal on the merit that Sam Sommer created his own injuries. He would now stand trial next year for the murder of Irving Silver.

Welcome to evil. Welcome to Suffolk County.

***

14.

BOXES IN TIME

A long road trip to hell came at least with a view of the best autumn could give. The picturesque Hudson River from mid-state New York southeast toward Long Island filled part of a nearly four-hour drive to Yaphank with October colors. Sam Sommer and his son-in-law, Robert DiNezza, were all business making the trek from New Windsor back to the land of horrors: Suffolk County.

The two gentlemen started their long drive at the crack of dawn on October 19, 2015, in hope of finding a crack in a nearly fifty-year case that has haunted Sam for a lifetime. Sitting with a cane on his lap, he peered out the window with squints of pain. Sam's eyes didn't hurt; his heart ached. As Robert entered Long Island from I-495, Sam relived the sights with a few memories of where his life was stripped eons ago while Robert chewed up gray en route to a Suffolk County archives bank.

Once parked at a police station in Yaphank, Sam's first few steps on the sidewalk toward the entrance hurt his frail legs. He and Robert arrived at what has always been perceived as another battlefield in the shape of a Suffolk County building of justice, so to speak. Sam didn't know what to expect inside even though the Freedom Of Information Act (FOIA) blessed him with this long-anticipated opportunity.

For decades, he was denied to see transcripts of his court proceedings by Suffolk County in a manner of mostly no replies. Even a federal magistrate judge going to bat for him was deprived of finding an important document on his behalf in 2006. More on that later.

At age seventy-nine, could Sam really be treated like a hate doll again inside a Suffolk County government building? He stopped right before the entrance door, smiled at Robert, and entered with dignity. Upon approaching the main desk, Sam felt like he owned a place that once owned him, albeit in a different city. It's like he was ready for the worst all over again, but this time his son-in-law was by his side. Sam considered himself a marked survivor who paid dues unfathomable to anyone around these parts.

A dark tug swallowed his confidence for a second prior to a desk clerk asking if he and his son-in-law could be helped. After all, Suffolk County is still Suffolk County in tainted veracity. In 2014, Suffolk County District Attorney Thomas Spota diminished the importance of an FBI investigation into one of his lieutenants for allegedly taking more than $50,000 in overtime pay that he didn't work for. A couple months later that year Suffolk County Police Chief James Burke was involved in a misconduct case.[10]

These recent episodes of soap opera proportions have pathetically run a long, tragic course. They've regularly surfaced since Sam involuntarily landed in an interrogation room after driving to a donut shop in Commack, Long Island, in 1968. Now, to his surprise, two warm hearts greeted him and Robert inside a Suffolk police station after the desk clerk called for them. They were expecting the gentlemen under an appointment made through the FOIA process.

An FOIA officer and a principal clerk went above and beyond to accompany the men to the archives in the basement. The welcoming atmosphere came as a shock to

Sam. Their kindness manufactured tears in his eyes. Even in recent years calling the Suffolk County DA's office in matters related to his appeals resulted in mean behavior and hang ups from the other end of the line.

Dusty boxes anchored in time stood on two carts ready for Sam and Robert to peruse. The two ladies left a few formal instructions for the men and left them alone. The sight of the cartons brought on deep breaths of anticipation. Sam was finally here after all these years. Now where would he begin? These cartons promised to present some story, some finding, something.

One thing that simmered in the back of Sam's mind after all these years was the Autopsy Report that Judge George McInerney ordered the Suffolk County Coroner to furnish for his attorney from October 21, 1968 (Autopsy Report referenced throughout the book in multiple chapters). That outstanding document should at the very least by today's politically-charged judicial standards bring a contempt charge to Suffolk County. Maybe it grew legs and walked off into Gardiners Bay to forever enjoy the dark abyss. Out of sight, out of mind.

The men divided and conquered at the outset of their dig. Sam guided Robert to announce what he found from his set of boxes. When the first carton tops were popped, the seekers of information found a mix of files and envelopes lodged in disarray. The boxes were somewhat labeled and full of mostly disorganized contents.

Sam's initial set of papers sparked a memory of already possessing copies of items like correspondence letters from the court and his criminal records. He and Robert collected and photocopied other documents related to motions and so on. Tired from their deep dive into paper trail utopia and a long drive, a second wind blew over Sam. He literary fell to one side of a table.

Short of looking like the casualty of a 911 call, Sam could not believe the finding he uncovered. A box paid a dividend from the past at almost the cost of a heart attack. Robert aided Sam in regaining his balance and breath. Sam handed a piece of paper to his son-in-law. It indicated on two different spots that on May 27, 1968…

the grand jury in Suffolk County dismissed jury indictment number 609/68.

The dismissal was before Sam Sommer went to trial for the murder of Irving Silver in 1970. It was time to do something with this stunning discovery. First, Sam needed to determine whether or not he wanted to live or die. Could this be the game-changer in clearing his name for a murder he did not commit? On the other hand, all those wasted years put him in front of unchartered devastation. Railroaded. A cover up.

The bottom line… Sam should have never been arrested much less sent to trial.

***

15.

SHORT OF A WHISPER

"Would the defendant please rise," instructed Judge Pierre Lundberg. In a trance Sam Sommer rose like a lost ghost out of place in the world.

About twenty feet stood between Sam's freedom or several years behind bars as Lundberg prepared to ask the foreman to read the jury's verdict in the *The People of the State of New York vs. Samuel Leonard Sommer* murder trial on December 16, 1970.

The Tenth Judicial District Suffolk County Courthouse in Riverhead, New York, filled again after three days of grand jury deliberation on whether Sam Sommer would pay for the alleged murder of his business partner and relative, Irving Silver. Incidentally, the courtroom was almost wall-to-wall despite the trial getting next-to-nothing in consistent publicity.

On this day, however, a few randomly scattered cameras joined the assembly likely since word got out that the jury reached a verdict. New York print media icon *Newsday* and a smaller island paper, the *Suffolk Sun*, sent reporters.

In Sam and Elaine Sommer's view, at least the clowns could return to the circus, and the three-piece suits and black robes could go back to purgatory. For once, the manufactured wrinkles under their eyes from a two-and-a-half-year grind could close in bloodshot solace—even for just a flash.

After four-plus weeks of exhaustion in a room reserved for justice, this trial felt like it strayed in favor of selective hearing and wink/wink-look-the-other-way glances. Sam and Elaine courageously pushed the frolics aside and converged on being husband and wife again, along with father and mother to seven children. At last these two inseparable gifts of the American Dream had something to hold onto—a verdict and one another.

The couple cautiously believed that a not guilty verdict by way of a heap of reasonable doubt would finally acquit Sam and set his life right again. The very fact that Sam saw a judicial victory overturned and then having to rehash his innocence all over again produced the caution.

Sam's short history in the judicial parade snowballed into more baggage. His journey toward the truth hit another roadblock. On the first day of jury deliberation in the murder trial, a stinger from the bench infected Sam's faith in the "system." He fell short of a whisper after hearing what Lundberg said to the jurors in open court as part of his standard instructions to a jury concerning deliberation procedures (paraphrased and without prejudice):

"Mr. Sommer hit the deceased over the head with a pipe and then ran him over."

Really? Speechless. How could Sam or his team cough up anything verbal following that unethical abuse of power from the bench? Sam looked at his attorney Eugene Lamb, flabbergasted by what just came out of the judge's mouth.

Was Lundberg drinking? Was he stoned? Wishful thinking for a bottle or a joint in place of cruelty. Intentionally or not, the justice just threw instructions at a jury straight from Suffolk County's playbook of "Fuck you, we're in charge."

Now, two days later, everyone waited to see if that dirty spoke on a wheel of jury deliberation considerations would taint the process of virtuously reaching a verdict. The whole Lundberg directive took everyone for a ride to a place they've never been or heard of before (without prejudice, it is unknown if the judge commanded his instructions intentionally or accidently).

"Has the Grand Jury reached a verdict?" asked Judge Lundberg.

"We have, your Honor," proclaimed a middle-aged white businessman. Elaine quivered and covered her face in the first row behind her husband.

"We the Grand Jury in the case of *The People of the State of New York vs. Samuel Leonard Sommer* find the defendant, Samuel L. Sommer,

Guilty... of Murder One."

"NO..., NOT MY HUSBAND!" drilled the courtroom air.

Elaine Sommer took over the courtroom. Even Judge Lundberg refrained a few moments from attempting to restore order.

Sam turned away from the defense table and stretched toward Elaine over a wooden barrier. Two bailiffs and Lamb disallowed that from happening after a couple steps. It took three guys to hold back the smaller, but rugged and muscular Sommer. His years of tussling with hundred-plus pound sides of beef posed a battle.

He fought to hug Elaine and still couldn't emit a whisper from the ongoing astonishment. While he couldn't offer a word, his wife shouted in contrast to his handling of the disbelief. One Sommer froze in a lockjaw state while the other turned ballistic.

Elaine bellowed, "Not my husband" from deep inside a huddle of family and friends around her. Loved ones hovered over her—many of them peered at the jury in disgust. She was then escorted out of the room with repeated screeches of "No" and "Not my husband." Sam remained refrained at gate's edge. Elaine's fight was one side of an epic battle between gasps and gavel.

For a second, Sam was more perturbed at not being able to embrace his wife than he was the verdict. His look at the jury sent a message, "This fight's not over." His mind centered on Elaine and what lied ahead for her survival with seven kids.

"Order!" "Order!" accompanied the pounding of the gavel from the bench now that Mrs. Sommer was outside the room.

Sam's darkest day found him watching the foundation of his life ushered out of a courtroom. From that day forward everything he did was geared toward making up for this one moment in a Suffolk County courtroom.

The gavel stopped and the distant cries from the hallway faded. Pin drop. Lamb hugged Sam and told him that he'll keep fighting. Sam grabbed his lead attorney while Joe Scibilia joined the two men at the defense table.

Chitter chatter still consumed the room. "Order!" followed another round of gavel bangs from the now-standing Lundberg. Most of the jurors' heads were down, unable to look at Sam. Despite his life hanging on the edge, Elaine and the kids inundated Sam's mind. He cared less about giving a statement solicited by Judge Lundberg. In fact, he barely heard the request from the bench.

Sam realized it would make no difference to address the courtroom. A handful of clear-cut reasonable doubt arguments during the trial should have raised ample uncertainty about his guilt. He figured his defense arguments were ignored by deaf ears during the trial anyway, so why bother saying anything now?

Sam stared Lundberg down in what resembled a bout of metaphorical silence. Seething eyes then swung over to the jury. Most of the jurors countered by finding something to fixate on except the defendant while this eye dance played out.

Lundberg continued the proceeding after Lamb finally told him that his defendant didn't desire to comment. The justice followed suit by negating to comment as well. Not needing to flip the courtroom upside down since Elaine already did so, Sam just stood and shook his head. Lundberg then announced a sentencing date of March 16, 1971.

A heavily-marked gavel adjourned the trial. The mood of the departing onlookers in this post-verdict courtroom personified robotic figures. A week from Christmas, there was no holiday mood or even an exuberant celebration of sending a criminal to prison that normally illuminates a courtroom after a guilty murder verdict. A few handshakes at the prosecution table were all that went down after the verdict was read.

Evil around Sam numbed his feelings toward anyone or anything. He managed to look up through the big top called a justice room to his God, Yahweh, in faith of defeating evil—no matter how long it took.

Lamb bought time with the bailiffs before they walked Sam out of the room where he shortly would be transported to jail back at the Fourth Precinct in Smithtown. The bailiffs granted Sam a few moments in thought and prayer—almost feeling for him after about five weeks of observing maybe the best view of a trial that went extraordinarily unnoticed: common sense.

***

After butterflies enjoyed a short ride in Sam's stomach from winning the Huntley Hearing in March of 1969, his elation succumbed to an overturn of the ruling months later. Between the holiday seasons of 1969 and 1970, Sam had a year to prep for the trial of his life. No more amateur arraignments and rigged appellate justices who used to work for Suffolk County. Goodbye to decent judges dedicated to securitizing "beyond a reasonable doubt"' in Gordon Lipetz and George McInerney and hello to a grand jury. Twelve everyday people now held the key to Sam's next unknown passageway.

Any looming murder trial naturally and sadly brings stark reminders of losing of a loved one (or loved ones) and the fate of an accused. In Sam's circumstance, those realizations were oddly overshadowed by sudden, unchecked onslaughts of abusive power coming not from the inner city but a single county. People of influence who wore badges, black robes, and three-piece government suits were monopolizing justice. The figurehead pulling all the shots was Suffolk County.

The Sommer and Rosen extended families grew further apart except for Elaine's parents and her brother's daughter, Naomi. She would always hang around their house and help with the small kids. Naomi just kind of grew close to the Sommers. For Sam, the angst between families caused too much pain, and Naomi's bubbly kindness as a young teenager further moved him to do something in spring of 1970.

Rather than wait passively for a ticking time bomb about a half a year away in the form of his murder trial, Sam and Lamb hired a private investigator named John Darnell. Darnell was young and aggressive, vying to make a name for himself. The way the landscape of Suffolk County was heading into organized crime and its stranglehold, his pickings for business promised to be good, yet dangerous.

The bottom line for Sam was who in the hell killed Irving Silver? He figured he'd have a better chance clearing his name by finding this needle in a haystack than relying on justice in Suffolk County. Darnell came as a referral from Lamb. He was a quick understudy and soon kicked up some dirt on the one man who seemed to not have to answer one question so far in this mess: Harold Goberman or Masterson or whatever his name-of-the-week was.

The informant who was inarguably working for the police based on earlier testimony from both parties across the aisle owned a dubious history. He was a convicted felon out on parole, had befriended both Irving and Ronnie Silver, and was well-known by underworld aces like Sal Spatarella. Who in totality he had been spying on in the streets in New York and on the Island for the police is unknown.

The late Irving Silver used to comment to Sam that his son was hanging around Goberman too much. That was around the same time when Sam honored Silver's request to give the guy a second shot at life by hiring him to do maintenance at the Deli-Queen. It turned out that Goberman later got into a confrontation with Silver over money when Sam was vacationing in Florida. That went down just before Silver was killed and allegedly going to meet Sam to resume carpooling to work together.

Darnell's sleuthing tracked Goberman down in the big city in the summer of 1970. Since Silver's death and Sam's subsequent court proceedings, Goberman wasn't seen much on Long Island, at least at the places he used to frequent according to Sam's vast business connections. Whatever interpersonal charm Darnell carried as an investigator must have heavily offset his perceived youthful naivety.

It was head-turner enough to find Goberman; it was monumental to get him to speak. Goberman's bad-ass reputation and unpredictable personality would make most young private eyes run the other way, especially with his affiliations to the mob. As mentioned earlier in the book, Sam would have written the book on Business 101 back in the day. Darnell, too, in equal notoriety would have rubbed elbows with the likes of fictional legends Columbo, Mannix, and McGarrett. He had a knack, and with one knock on the Sommer family's door, Darnell lowered the boom against the prosecution for Sam's defense.

Sam didn't kill Silver, according to Goberman, and his statement was caught on audio tape.

In the back of his mind, Sam would have wagered against his own empire that Goberman killed Silver. Hearing the proclamation from the horse's mouth through Darnell on reel-to-reel jumpstarted another look at Sam's defense strategy. This development promised to make for a grand oration from Lamb in the forthcoming murder trial. It wasn't sure, however, if such a confession would be admissible in court on an audio tape.

Goberman also told Darnell that because of his parole and role as an informant he couldn't discuss anything about the murder until June of 1968. If he did, back to prison he would go. That timing didn't jive with Sam's arraignments in late May of that year. Obviously, the defense was unaware of the condition, and the prosecutors advantageously and secretly sat on this little golden nugget of truth. It now explains why the arraignment, or in Sam's case two arraignments, were thrown together hurriedly.

Handshake-driven street contracts, like those set up with informants, held as much water as a rubber raft floating on top of a walrus' tusk. Sam learned about this from Spatarella. It all boiled down to who held the upper hand—the mob or the police in any given circumstance. To complicate the matter further, multiple mob families back then were abound, and police agencies did not often work together (like witnessed in the true story of Frank Serpico).

Suffolk County men of honor would just as seen Goberman shut up forever, but that didn't appear to fly for the 32-year-old criminal. Darnell could have had Goberman arrested as a new suspect in the case (Goberman allegedly never told Darnell who killed Silver—just that Sam didn't do it), but because of his previous ties to police, he held off. He did pre-warn Goberman that he would be subpoenaed to testify in November. Goberman made frequent trips to his hometown of Allentown, Pennsylvania, so Darnell kept the faith that he wouldn't wander too far beyond that.

Darnell's success in lassoing Goberman into being a potential star witness for the defense at the upcoming trial gave Sam a shot in the arm. At the same time, strangely, in retrospect Sam and his lawyers collectively wondered why Goberman was never subpoenaed to testify earlier. Not that it would have made a difference in the favorable outcome of the Huntley Hearing, but who knows what he may have put forward confession-wise during the process. Perhaps it could have stonewalled the prosecution's victory.

***

The murder trial of Sam Sommer began on November 17, 1970. For the most part, the majority of this proceeding resembled the Huntley Hearing from almost two years earlier. Much of the testimony from both sides consistently emulated submissions made in each trial. For that reason and due to the murder trial's outcome already divulged in this story, the following eight highlights denote the major eyebrow-raisers from this proceeding.

Ronnie Silver testified for the defendant. In his own brand of expected complexity, he upheld Sam's story about what occurred the morning of May 17, 1968, when his father was supposed to meet Sam for coffee. From there, the two businessmen planned to carpool together to the corporate office in Commack—nothing out of the ordinary.

The only exception to Ronnie's testimony observed Sam's separation from his vacationing family in Florida. He flew home from Florida to deal with a business concern Irving was having while Sam was away. The issue was Goberman and a bounced check (Chapter 4). Ronnie's deposition connected Sam coming home from Florida to respond to a business matter involving Goberman and Silver. One could hypothesize that Sam returned to "deal with the matter" to the nth degree by way of murder.

Here's where Lamb started to show signs of cowardice as Sam's attorney. In the previous hearing there were times Sam felt he could have been more aggressive—particularly during the arraignments. He felt Lamb shined during the Huntley Hearing, so overall until this point Sam was satisfied with his main defense attorney.

With Ronnie on the stand, though, Lamb failed to see where his testimony could dissuade the defense's alibi, coming across as a score for Suffolk County. He could have steered Ronnie better for Sam's defense. Ronnie's disclosures did not reflect anything he did or didn't do maliciously toward Sam; they were the result of poor legal coaching.

Second, if the halls inside the Riverhead courthouse could talk, they'd build a setting for a blockbuster movie. About two-thirds of the way through the trial, Suffolk County Assistant DA Edward Connors approached Lamb in a hallway during a recess. He proposed a verbal plea bargain to Sam's attorney. Connors offered to reduce Sam's time to five years for assault. While that proposition took place, two reports from *Newsday* and the *Suffolk Sun* congratulated Sam in a different hallway for his forthcoming acquittal.

Lamb quickly relayed the plea bargain to his client thinking this was a steal compared to possibly spending twenty-plus in the big house. Sam remembered Lamb saying that he told Connors that he would likely be elated with the agreement. That sent Sam into the stratosphere thinking his lawyer was losing it.

First, a weak navigation of Ronnie Silver on the stand and now an assumption that, if anything, showed guilt from grabbing the first straw out of a stack of blind hope. Lamb's comment to Connors not only suggested guilt, but also weakness. Sam said his lawyer should have walked away to "discuss the matter with his client" rather than come across like a fragile weakling.

Disappointed to put it mildly, Sam charged back at his lawyer, "Take this plea and put it where the sun doesn't shine. Did you forget? I didn't do anything."

That very exchange opened an infection in the relationship between the two men. Tragically, their deteriorating bond happened at a bad time—in court when a man's life was in jeopardy. For a man who named his last child after the very person who had his back, it looked like Lamb was turning his back on Sam and seeking a premature exit.

Third, a mysterious Autopsy Report comes into play (Chapters 7 & 13). In October of 1968, Judge George McInerney, who was part of Sam's Huntley Hearing in matters outside the proceeding, ordered the Suffolk County Medical Examiner's office to furnish a copy of the Autopsy Report on the deceased, Irving Silver, within five days. Here it is late in the year of 1970 and no report yet.

Lamb overlooked filing a contempt charge against the county. Rather, he focused his attention on the Huntley Hearing and murder trial, figuring the report would "show up" if needed. It wasn't a necessary part of the Huntley Hearing. One lesson Sam absorbed with Suffolk County is that there was, and to this day is, no following of the law. The county is its own law. We'll let Sam himself take it from here on this one:

> Dr. Hugh Ashmore was Suffolk County's Deputy Chief Medical Examiner at the time. During the murder trial he testified for our side that the cause of Irving's death as stated in his Medical Examiner's report was the result of multiple and extensive injuries from a 'hit and run.'
>
> In cross-examination, Connors got Ashmore to admit that some of Silver's injuries were caused by the undercarriage of a vehicle, but not all. He then fell under Connors's spell by eventually stating that the deceased could have been hit over head with a pipe or blunt instrument. Detective Gill's prior testimony supported the pipe theory as well.
>
> None of these declarations appeared in any certified findings presented to the court. Ashmore lied to tailor his testimony to confirm with both Gill and Connors' assumptions. Lundberg subpoenaed to see the Autopsy Report. We broke for recess.
>
> The next day the pipe in question was actually presented to court. Ashmore said blood stains from the pipe represented animal blood. Lamb made sure the court knew that Mr. Silver and his defendant were in the meat butcher business.
>
> An Autopsy Report never showed up; instead, Connors said it was included as Identification in a supplemental report that he was putting together because the pipe was bought into court as evidence. In other words, in so many words the DA's office was saying there wasn't an Autopsy Report to be

submitted as an Exhibit—something jurors are entitled to view.

I found out later, much later, that there was and certainly still is an Autopsy Report floating around somewhere. Regardless, to this day per my right as a defendant, I've never seen the Autopsy Report for my own case. Of all the research I've done for many years, crime labs are well known and respected to serve the interests of independent forces, not just police units and prosecutorial forces.

What a cover up.

Fourth, Lundberg's predeliberation instructions to the jury led to more reasonable doubt in the form of a missed directive. Those involved in clearing Mr. Sommer's name didn't know murder was a game of missed calls. If a quarterback isn't tackled from a missed offside call, no harm, no foul, so to speak. If a missed called happens in the courtroom, a person's life hangs in the balance. To Suffolk County, Sam Sommer was just a game—a successful, hardworking Jew that didn't deserve the American Dream when it was easier to steal one's dream.

Fifth, a waitress from Bernie's Diner on Long Island took the stand for the prosecution. Bernie's was a point of contention for the prosecution as a spot where Sam was to meet Irving Silver around 3:30 in the morning on May 17, 1968, right before the alleged time of his death.

Detective Mansel brought this up to Sam repeatedly days prior to he and his entourage "arresting him" as part of their questioning. At trial, Connors slipped when he got the witness to admit knowing Mr. Sommer's identity and that he frequented Bernie's almost daily. That was it. Lamb jumped on the hanging curve ball left over the plate for cross-examination by the assistant DA.

The witness testified that despite seeing Mr. Sommer at the diner as a regular customer, he was not there the morning of May 17, 1968. Under a redirect, a bamboozled Connors hit her with accusations of memory. How could she recall something like this so long ago? She remembered it was a Friday morning and that Mr. Sommer had been in the day before with another person. She also recalled not expecting to see him anyway until the following week because he was excited to be with his family on a trip (paraphrase).

The testimony did not put Mr. Sommer in the restaurant on the morning Mr. Silver was killed. The prosecution wanted the court to see him at Bernie's that morning as a key narrative to their long-formulated story. That story ranged all the way back to when they first questioned the defendant as a suspect, followed by the interrogation.

Lamb was a brilliant attorney, and when he shined he brought out the sunglasses with his intuitiveness. This particular testimony was another example of his effectiveness. If only he could have married his legal savvy with a bit more assertiveness against the machine, the system. Maybe he was part of the establishment in some peculiar way. Sooner or later as we see in politics and the corruption of the FBI, for instance, an establishment can bring anyone down to levels of deceit and dishonesty.

Sixth, several arguments about Sam's mug shot (see Illustrations) dating back to the battles over it at the Huntley Hearing predictably arose at the murder trial. Three different experts testified at trial that Sam's black-and-white mugshot, the one "on record" during his booking, appeared tampered with. Furthermore, since the mug was not in color because the DA said the negative was misplaced, the defense contended that the image was too blurred to make an authentic determination of its validity. A court order from Judge McInerney in 1969 demanding the submission of the photo's negative had yet to be fulfilled by the prosecution.

The People contended that the photo was authentic and showed that the defendant's accounts of being beaten to the extent he wanted the jury to believe were lies. The prosecution showed the mug shot several times to the jury in concert with what the defendant alleged. The DA asserted that his story would have produced unmistaken indications of brutality than what the mug shot submitted as evidence revealed.

The only mugshot showed the defendant with a potentially-closed left eye, which the People said could have been the result of a flinch from a camera flash. The rest of the picture exposed slight darker areas around the facial area, similar to looking at parts of an X-ray where something out of sorts illuminates. Again, without a colored photo, it was too hard to establish 100% of the facts either way here. The DA added any assumed injuries could have resulted from a prior automobile accident the defendant was ostensibly involved in.

In repudiation, the defense contested that Mr. Sommer's physical condition was vastly in contrast to what the submitted mug shot showed. More on these assertions come to life after many years in Chapter 21.

Seventh, the prosecution hung a large portion of its fate on attempting to convince the jury that Sam murdered Mr. Silver over a $50,000 insurance policy the two men set up as business partners. The defense submitted Sam's income records contrasting money as a motive since he was already making a solid living.

In fact, Sam exposed through brochures and real estate papers that he planned to put a down payment on the

Miami estate of Gianni Versace. Sam and Elaine toured the renowned Italian fashion designer's Florida home while on vacation prior to Sam returning to New York ahead of his family when he learned of Silver's death. Lamb also showed the court that Versace's estate was in deed listed for sale when Sam was in Florida, and he even submitted contact information of the realtor who previously met the Sommer couple.

Lastly, enter Harold Goberman. Connors had him lined up to recount the morning of May 17, 1968, when he was a witness to a brutal crime committed by Sam Sommer. Goberman restated a few answers to make sure his confessions matched what the assistant DA wanted them to. Such a tactic contrasted what Lamb didn't do to Ronnie Silver during his time on the stand. He didn't direct his conversations as effectively as Connors did so with Goberman.

Scibilia whispered a few discrepancies to Lamb as the examination between Connors and Goberman played on. One of those points of contention dealt with Goberman standing next to Sam and allegedly watching him kill another human being. Why didn't Goberman stop Sam? This was a big hole in his remarks as a witness. Goberman would later say that he didn't want to be involved either way in what Sommer was doing. It would be interesting to see how Suffolk County defines *involved.*

When Connors concluded his direct on the witness, Lamb was disallowed a chance to cross-examine him. Connors said the witness had to be excused until later the next day due to an urgent business endeavor he must attend to in Pennsylvania that evening.

Lamb objected while Sam poured a deep sigh that would have been heard a block away in stereo. Sam knew the objection would be overruled, and yes, Goberman was granted permission to step down until the following day.

The convicted felon seemed harbored by the law, somewhat coddled in the courtroom. Sam thought that was remarkably extraordinary. Par for the course.

Goberman did reappear in court for his cross-examination the next day. He admitted that he particularly didn't care for either Mr. Sommer or Mr. Silver. Furthermore, Goberman said he resorted to using people he knew to drive cars at his enemies. Lamb had him on a cliff hanging over the edge for his defendant by way of stacking up more reasonable doubt, but Goberman said he wouldn't testify any further unless he was granted immunity. And just like that, he was let off the stand like a teenager leaving the principal's office with a slap on the wrist.

It was speculated that Goberman never went to Pennsylvania the day before. His performance on the stand showed a day-and-night difference from his other stint, less the two aforementioned statements that likely rose from his planet-size arrogance. Goberman was likely coached heavily, so he then patched up whatever flaws were mentioned from his direct examination with Connors.

16.

GAME FACES

I woke in the morning as if nothing happened the day before. It's like sleep washed away a dream, then a nightmare. Whoosh. Gone. So I brushed my teeth and combed my hair without paying any attention to the custom-made sink and shithole or even the coldness from the walls. Then I saw myself in a dinky mirror, and it all changed.

I saw myself without blame. I realized I didn't do anything wrong; the wrongdoing was with Suffolk County, the system. Everything my lawyer said would not happen to me was a lie. Back to a bad dream. I just needed to take a deep breath.

My lungs filled. My shirt tightened. I wanted to breathe and couldn't. Oh, for a breath. Took them for granted I guess over the years. I exhaled to the opening of a loud cell door. A bitter taste found a home in my mouth to a second round of noise. A guard, a hack as I've already heard them be called, rattled his club through the bars.

He told me to strip naked and come out of the cell. For sure I wasn't in a dream anymore. This was a nightmare, standing upright, wide awake. It was hard to stand tall, so to speak. The hack meant business. All I could do was as ordered.

I left my six-by-nine Shangri-La for the outside on the deep inside, buck naked, spread eagle, and squatting as demanded by the hack. Another hack came by. There was no rhyme or reason for doing what I was doing. I hated them. I spit on one of them. He hit back behind my knees with a club. It was only my second day of twenty years to go on living like this.

Sam Sommer, March 18, 1971

The scene was Sing Sing Prison in Ossining—about thirty miles north of New York City on the eastern bank of the Hudson. An infamous landslide in Peru on that same day killed about two hundred. Sam thought of a landslide that his family was sliding on out of control.

In his heart he told himself he would never let Elaine know about the goings on inside the Sing Sing hell hole. Sam would wear a smile whenever he saw his wife and kids during visitation—no matter what he had to endure.

Lovingly and on her own, Elaine secretly made the same pact within her heart. Whatever turmoil that headed her way she would manage to bottle up when it came time to see her husband. No way was he ever going to know what was going on in Commack with the family other than good. They could be on food stamps and yet she'd come across to Sam that they had freezers full of food. Neither one of them knew of the other's protective states for nearly fifty years.

Elaine set her course on survival. To this day she is known by a small yet respected group of people as one of the rare individuals who could literally flip a switch in life. She went from living with finer things to having to stand helpless next to the unexpected.

Her parents and Anna Sommer tried to concentrate on the shorthanded home front in Stony Brook. Dejected and puzzled, the young children couldn't fully grasp what happened to their dad. Elaine decided love was the only option to the family's survival. She could not accept the court's ruling. Wherever her husband and father to her kids went, they were going to follow. That simple. Clear cut as his innocence.

Against the better judgment of her parents and Anna, Elaine started preparing for life with signs of a traveling gypsy show. Although Sing Sing was not too long of a drive from their home compared to the locations of most other prisons in New York, she was unyielding in her thoughts about moving the family to be closer to Sam. She still had to deal with legal bills, a hefty mortgage, and family businesses re-sinking into both debt and doubt.

Sam's stash in his household closet bank depleted to floor level. No more piles. Friends of the family started to increasingly show up at the house to offer support. Some visitors, however, were unfamiliar to Elaine. They tried to trick her by offering to oversee the family's business ventures for a while. It has been theorized to this day that some succeeded in turning that temporary oversight into a permanent overthrow.

Elaine didn't see it all coming at first; she was too caught up in preparing the oldest kids for school each day, taking care of emotions, and day-to-day life. Visitation from people she didn't even know caused unsettled confusion to an already confusing state of life for the young family.

The murder trial was in the books, engraved only in dull pencil in Sam's mind. Every day was going to be appellate season in his mind, ready to erase history from the judicial sketches in Suffolk County. The nights in prison dripped in agony over his family. Before he could get a grip on formulating an appeal, it was time to come to grips at what really happened over the past three years.

Heaps of reasonable doubt. Goberman. Hand-written indictments with crossed-off information. Testimony from a waitress at Bernie's Diner. Bulldogs disguised as cops. Judges who moonlighted as dictators. Only one person of interest even interviewed for a murder. Between all of these remarkable accounts of common sense, something came over Sam under a restless darkness. Lots of time to think at night behind corroded bars.

In prison, Sam realized that he fell under a spell of gullibility during all proceedings. Up until that point in his life at age thirty-four, Sam believed police officers were good, attorneys gave their time to preserving the lives of others, and that judges and jurors could right a wrong based on facts and reasonable doubt. He trusted the system.

Granted, a naive mindset didn't completely taint this street maverick completely. Getting around the inner city and neighboring burbs because of his businesses taught Sam enough to know how to live in panoramic view. He was in the thick of it in New York's commerce scene and sensed a little fishiness in business dealings from time to time. But the police? The judicial system?

Instantaneously, the cop corruption that came into play in the big city was going down at the same time when Sam was railroaded on Long Island. The investigations and media focus on bad police were taking place on the concrete and around tall buildings, however, not so much on the Island—a classic case of "it can't happen here."

The nightmares started immediately in the big house. It was better to stay awake than sleep. A small light from the hall created corner desk space for Sam on the edge of his cot a few inches wide—barely enough room to read. That's all he did at night was read law books until right before daybreak.

Then he would usually crash heavily and catch a couple hours of sleep.

Most of Sam's nightmares found himself getting snatched all over again by Suffolk County detectives. Days in the big house presented their own brand of trouble as well. He needed to fit in. New York prisons were pure segregation back then. Discipline by a beating here or there was commonplace. We're talking about not walking fast enough in line to the water fountain warranted discipline. Looking at a hack wrong could buy an inmate a black-and-blue eye.

Report it? No one cared. Then more beatings would sure enough follow. The hacks were macho control freaks, and to them a beating at times was more enjoyable than throwing someone in the hole. Research suggests prisons during the 1970s favored a "rehabilitative movement" versus previous years where force was the primary measure of discipline that supposedly led to any hope for rehabilitation.[11] Sam didn't witness such a transformation; life adhered to a hard ass uniform convention, day in and day out. The ones mostly left alone were affiliates to the major Mafia families in New York.

Sam witnessed that first hand in 1974 when he was moved to Clinton State Prison in upstate Dannemora near the Canadian border where the winters hold no mercy. In the Clinton prison yard, groups would gather based on race and culture. The groups were frequently referred to as "courts" or a particular "jungle." On one occasion before Sam was part of a court, he was approached by an unknown figure who asked him to take a walk. A walk in the yard meant it was time for a one-on-one stroll between two men over something no one else should hear.

The man would not introduce himself. He kept attempting to jack up Sam's ego by saying he just had to meet him like a celebrity of sorts. Weary of Sam's impatience from overkill patronage, he asked Sam for any knowledge on the 1972 death of the notorious New York gangster Joey Gallo.

Sam fumed over the inquiry, mainly since he'd been locked up since '71 and didn't even personally know of Gallo. How in the bloody name of anything would Sam know about Gallo's death? Already in a fragile state of distrust from his episodes with Suffolk County, Sam grabbed the guy and shoved him. "Stop the bullshit. Who are you?"

The guy immediately left the yard. Visibly upset, Sam was comforted by a small group of incarcerated mobsters. He discovered the guy was a visitor who happened to find his way into the yard against standard protocol. For a while Sam received some royal treatment from the hacks because of his conversing with a gangster court. Whatever the mob wanted on the inside, it received. Walls meant nothing to these people.

The infamous bloody Attica State Prison four-day riot in September of 1971 that saw the death of thirty-three inmates and ten guards would eventually necessitate improvements in food, cell conditions, medical care, treatment from guards, and an end to punitive segregation, among others.[11] It didn't happen overnight, though. The hacks fought the proposed changes for a number of years citing a lack of control from a reduction in the use of force, according to Sam and other inmates.

The guards ruled the joint, and their ties to the outside were tight. Drugs, money, and the invisible amenity—exchange of information, flew around the big house regularly. Lots of mobster connections going down with a slice of racial tension and control. The blacks seem to have it worse, but Sam's Jewish heritage, if discovered, often led to them being an outcast. Jews in the eyes of the inner society weren't typically treated well. People like Sam often searched to find social acceptance within other cultures.

Sam's prison roots in '71 at Sing Sing relied on sports and smarts as weapons to forging relationships. Inmates drew to his hard-nosed athleticism during pick-up games in the yard. Others gravitated to his quick study of the law. Sam figured while he was working on his own appeal by reading criminal law books, he may as well share some of his findings with others who needed counsel.

Within months of his first year in prison, Sam Sommer emerged as a citizen lawman much to the chagrin of control-happy guards. Whenever a prisoner learned to think for himself, it posed a threat to the hacks. Sam was being watched closely.

Right after the tragic Attica riot, all prisons were on high alert. The event created a chance for Sam to take advantage of a bit of leniency at Sing Sing. Guards were busy undergoing revamped security procedures and worrying about the more violent inmates. That situation enabled Sam to be left alone to build his appeal.

Eugene Lamb would visit once in a while to help Sam build an appellate argument, but Sam knew the days with his attorney would soon be numbered. Disappointed by Lamb's lack of aggressiveness toward Suffolk County at the murder trial stunted some trust in him. He also recently learned that Lamb had a falling out with John Darnell over the investigation of Harold Goberman. Sam got the impression from Darnell that the two couldn't reach terms on money over the investigation, therefore thwarting any further consideration of an audio confession Goberman stumbled into making about killing Irving Silver.

Back at home, the strain of raising kids, figuring out what to do with a number of businesses, and living without her husband took its toll on Elaine. She would try to see Sam every weekend with the kids but at times she went alone. Both husband and wife put on their game faces and played positive for the betterment of hiding pain. They had to do what needed to be done without inflicting worry on the other.

***

It's imperative to return to the magnitude of the discovery made in Yaphank in Chapter 14. The document that contains a dismissed grand jury indictment for Sam's arrest was dated April 22, 1971. That date is *after* Sam was sent to prison in March. It was submitted to a police department file as a Supplementary Report completed by Suffolk County Detective Thomas Gill, Badge 335.

The report begs to offer two important contradictions. First, the dismissed grand jury indictment for Sam's arrest was dated May 27, 1968. That date as provided in the report portends a time frame that occurred after Sam's two arraignments. Indictments almost always happen before an arrest and court proceeding. Was this recorded for sake of documentation in an "oops, we-better-put-something-on-paper-kind-of-gesture?"

Why did it take 44 years for someone to find this information and care about its contradictions when a person's life was at stake for so long?

Second, the supplementary report submitted by Gill lists two dismissed grand jury indictments. What's unclear yet suggestive on the report is they're both listed as the same date—May 27, 1968. Recall Sam was kidnapped out of a running car on May 22, five days before the primary date in reference to two bogus indictments. If he was taken under arrest on May 22, 1968, then wouldn't there have been another indictment from a grand jury for that particular arrest to take place?

These two contradictions alone should have tossed out this case through a courtroom window into a back alley dumpster. Has anything like this ever happened in these United States?

The supplementary report to this day provides rock-solid reasonable doubt regarding the authenticity of his arrest. It's the edifice of Sam's case. Not only did it take half a lifetime to find the report, but why was it done in the first place? Why would a detective involved in the alleged arrest of a defendant conduct a report and submit it to some file after the convicted was already sent to serve time?

Imagine: Someone you know and love is in prison not more than five weeks and a supplementary report like described above is nonchalantly filed away while its own verbiage contradicts justice. There it sat for years while your loved one sat wasting away.

***

Referenced earlier in Chapter 4, John McNamara was a real estate tycoon and well-known Buick dealer on Long Island. He and his father, Thomas, hired Harold Goberman to build a new dealership in Port Jefferson. In 1972, the McNamaras were accused of hiring four men to beat and intimidate Goberman in response to a threat he made against the McNamara family. This was all at the same time the dealership was undergoing scrutiny for defrauding General Motors (GM) millions of dollars.

In documented testimony in the United States vs. McNamara, then U.S. Attorney Desmond O'Sullivan cross-examined Gill, who admitted that Goberman was the target of a confidential investigation into a homicide in which Goberman was considered the main perpetrator. Gill continued to say that Goberman was investigated during the Sommer case. He said he couldn't offer any further comment on Goberman because he was still "under investigation."

Other testimony as part of the McNamara trial cited Goberman picking up a steel pick and threatening the car dealer with it. Another accusation surfaced in which Goberman was going to fire bomb one of the McNamara houses. Some argument at the Port Jefferson job site apparently triggered this whole mess. Legalities of the McNamara trial are shady back in 1972 and 1973 due to the lack of available transcriptions, but the McNamara family went through a number of mistrials and appeals concerning the GM component of their fate, spanning years.

***

More importantly in terms of Sam Sommer's conviction, the fact Gill and Goberman resurfaced and that O'Sullivan referred back to the "Sommer Case" propelled Sam to dig his claws into the matter further.

Sam looked to Lamb to find out more about the McNamara trial and how it could play into an appeal for a new proceeding. At the same time while 1972 winded down, so did Sam's time at Sing Sing. At the end of the year he was moved to Auburn Prison in upper mid-state near Syracuse. His bonding with other inmates became enough for the Sing Sing guards.

The move put his family in a precarious situation. They would go from a relatively manageable regular drive from Stony Brook to Sing Sing to now a day trip to see a husband and father. By this time the Sommer businesses were all but gone from takeover by Mafia affiliations, and Elaine's financial troubles ballooned. She could no longer pay the mortgage, so the Stony Brook home became repossessed, and whatever money that was left after feeding and clothing the kids went toward her husband's appeals.

Her father helped financially up to this point, but he suggested that the family downsize and offered help in doing so. No time. The family tree had been uprooted. Her parents and Anna Sommer offered to bring in some of the kids by relocating them to Florida. Nightmares were not just going on inside the joint; Elaine's were 24/7 in a conscious state.

She fastened her chin strap like a football player hitting the field. It was a new game now. Injustice became the playing field, crowded with players who were once friends and business colleagues turned opposition.

The Sommer family stepped into a threshold of homelessness. It split with some kids going to Florida and others going with mom to Auburn. Not even a winter freeze from upstate New York near Lake Ontario could cool the hot tears that fell from her eyes while she said goodbye to the American Dream. To top it off, Sam had no clue what was going on with his family. No news was good news.

He had his own demons to contend with anyway. Guilt. Not over Silver but the lack of green he let slip away. All those years building an American Dream came without planning for one that would have protected his family. He never found enough time to secure his businesses. Now he had all the time in the world to let guilt fester insecurity in his soul.

Elaine packed up the same station wagon that her husband involuntarily abandoned his dog from nearly five years ago and headed north with no plan other than to be near her loved one. Four children went with her without a school to go to or a backyard to come home to.

17.

LIFETIME

"We lived in treehouses and in the back seats of cars to be near our dad!" The cry felt freed, like a bottle opener finally released trapped pain. Sam's daughter, Karen, didn't hold back in her dad's apartment on October 27, 2017, after she made a five-hour drive from upstate New York to the Hudson Valley region to gather with some family members. "Mom stole food and bounced checks, so we could somehow be close to dad while he was locked up. You have no idea the hell we've been put through from this injustice. They took everything."

Sam didn't budge while sitting at the end of his couch after Karen's words flooded the room with tears. He removed his glasses and prepared to grab a tear from his 81-year-old eyes that had almost seen it all. He certainly heard Karen's heart bleed outward from her pent-up hurt and anger of treehouses and shoplifting. Karen's sisters, Jane and Marlene, along with their brother Robert on speaker phone from Florida, joined Sam's co-author in what played out as an extraordinary confession.

It took courage to bear the miraculous survival of Elaine Sommer and her children to all of us in the room that day. On top of hearing Karen's story of enduring hardship, Sam followed it with another comment that came without warning. There was no time to brace the arms on our chairs.

After clearing his throat, he said, "I never knew. I had no idea."

"I'm sorry, dad, but it's time these sons-of-bitches paid for what they did to this family," clamored Karen. "No one knows what we went through as kids with mom."

Sam just looked at his co-author, shook his head, and humbly shrugged. "Wow. I never knew." he said softly.

Days later after sharing Karen's "story within-a-bigger-story" to family members and friends, most responded with, "That's a movie." Some took it further to say, "A *Lifetime* movie for sure." Some of the best stories in the world are those that would take a lifetime to tell because they've been covered up.

***

What looked like a castle for the wicked in the 1970s, Auburn Prison in Auburn, New York, is one of the nation's oldest correctional facilities. Recognized for serving the incarcerated for 200 years in 2018, the institution in Sam's day behind bars lived up to its gloomy living conditions based on the exterior perception of the building. The culture promoted fear and intimidation. Guards were increasingly growing paranoid because of the recent Attica riot.

Sam kept to his unassuming ways working in the library and using sleep time to study criminal law. Just like at Sing Sing, other inmates gravitated to him for his business know how and growing knowledge of the law. He seemed to go through each day by living out parts of it like he was still on the outside running enterprises. Around these productive distractions, he kept dedicated to addressing two goals: getting the hell out of prison and taking care of his family the best he could.

Part of the strategy to overturn his conviction included a foundational argument regarding who killed Irving Silver. Since no one else was ever interviewed concerning the murder, Sam kept pushing the Harold Goberman card and a missing Autopsy Report that was promised to his defense team through a court order almost five years ago.

Eugene Lamb took the recent McNamara trial and Thomas Gill's testimony to reopen reasonable doubt in a new appeal. For whatever reason, Lamb could not get his hands on the Suffolk County Autopsy Report that a judge ordered in fall of 1968. No one knew where it was. Vanished. Still gone to this day as previously mentioned.

What made the disappearance of an all-important (and highly-standard) report was that it would have called out the DA amended arguments related to the cause of Silver's death. In other words, without an Autopsy Report, the DA got away with changing the cause of death as the murder trial unfolded.

For instance, it was first revealed that Irving Silver died from multiple and extensive injuries per the Suffolk County Medical Examiner's Report. The DA expounded on that finding stating Mr. Sommer then ran over the deceased victim with his automobile. After that, the DA offered new evidence of a lead pipe into the equation. The prosecution submitted that the cause of death came from Silver being hit over the head with the length of that type of "blunt instrument" and then run over by his own car.

Incidentally, the obscurity behind how and when grand jury indictments played a role in Sam's conviction have a direct correlation to the missing Autopsy Report. These indictments were supposedly to serve as strong evidence to make an arrest on a suspect based on how the deceased was killed. Neither of these vital papers have been handled ethically, professionally, or in conjunction with courtroom protocol since the day Sam was stripped of his freedom in the parking lot of a donut shop.

To this day, the People (against Samuel L. Sommer) have yet to also address:

> 1. Did the Grand Jury on May 22, 1968, result in finding Indictment number 609-68?
>
> 2. Were the People prior to May 24, 1968, unsuccessful in obtaining Indictment number 609-68?
>
> 3. Were the People's presentation to the Grand Jury for the charge of Murder or Murder Contrary to Penal Law 125.25, subdivision 1?
>
> 4. Why had the back of Indictment number 609-68 on May 23, 1968,
>
> been crossed out to read May 24, 1968?
>
> 5. Why was the defendant secretly indicted for Murder on May 24, 1968, pursuant to Indictment number 609-68?

ON ALL OF THE ABOVE, THE RECORD WAS SILENT THEN. IT IS STILL SILENT TODAY.

More and more findings began to come into the light during the outset of Sam's time in prison. Consequently, his metamorphosis into a citizen lawman also began behind bars. Sam sought relief from the courts, sternly believing he argumentatively established the appeal of a lifetime with Eugene Lamb.

Lamb and John Darnell were engrossed in post murder trial juror interviews. Those findings would hope to boost a comprehensive appeal that included some of the grand jury notations above like obscurities of crossed-out information.

The discovery of dismissed indictments, of course, weren't uncovered yet for decades (as noted in Chapter 14).

***

Elaine Sommer and some of her children lived out of the station wagon for the first few weeks in Auburn before finding a low-income apartment. She wanted to preserve the little bit of cash she had left to get a grip on a more permanent solution for her traveling road show of love toward a husband and father. Elaine kept everything hush-hush from Sam when visiting, and the children looked their best during visits to the big house. Time and little money were working against her and the kids, however, unbeknownst to Sam.

Each time they left visiting at prison survival mode took over. Sam believed they were living strapped but not at one time out of a car and without much cash. He found blind comfort in knowing his in-laws were watching over the younger children. This routine followed in orderly fashion almost every time throughout the 1970s between Elaine and Sam. She hid the burdens on the outside, and he always came across optimistic about life on the inside and the status of his appeals.

Broken-hearted and helpless, Elaine's parents could not pinpoint her location. They took care of the youngest kids in Florida while trying to track her down. Against her better judgment, Sam's mother honored Elaine's desire to keep her troubles under the radar while conversing with her son in prison.

Sam also spent a lot of his time writing letters to family members on Elaine's side to assure them of his innocence. The letter-writing campaign proved harder to push innocence over the goal than it did going up against the power of Suffolk County. He noted today that when a person combines helplessness with loneliness it's like hitting the bottom of darkness. He said there you will find the abyss of life, and it is relentlessness in wanting to take your life. His nightmares were all about hitting rock bottom.

Sam only remained at Auburn for a couple of years. In 1974, he was moved again—this time to Clinton Prison in Dannemora. The facility nearly borders Siberia in retrospect to climate and remoteness, tucked in New York's northeast corner near the Canadian and Vermont borders. Its nickname, "Little Siberia," was coined by surviving inmates from archaic, army-like guards and the coldest nights on the planet. It's been experienced, according to Sam, that you can feel the cold in your bones in July yet after each winter.

Elaine and the kids followed Sam once again. It was early spring and the family had next to nothing. The car was sold for needed cash and an already split-up family delved further into division. Unfortunately, two sets of parents in Florida couldn't find their beloved Sommers, yet the one living behind bars saw them regularly—oblivious to their homeless state and being off the grid to the rest of the world. When time permitted, Elaine would mail her parents a short letter letting them know that she and the kids were okay. The postmarks likely raised their comfort level by connecting dots about the city Sam's current prison resided in.

The lost family needed to eat and find shelter; therefore, there was no time to suffer. Suffering on the street would have likely meant death for someone in this incredible family. Resolute for a husband and dad and not thinking of themselves, Elaine led perhaps one of the largest-scale expeditions of survival ever realized in the United States. Sam said during the writing of this book that he or any another other man could not have overcome what she did.

She used to have it all and humbly embraced her blessings in alignment with once-valued American principles like family, faith, hard work, and community. When the tables flipped because of lawlessness on Long Island, she was forced to flip a switch that most people would not have the audacity to do.

Not only was Sam Sommer the first known victim of an emerging dirty system known as Suffolk County, his wife Elaine and their kids were turning the pages of another story during the start of a corrupt era (one still running unjustly today).

The start of Sam's five-year stint at Clinton Prison came with his family on a mission for blankets, clothes, and food during the day and a place to lay their heads down at night. They moved into a treehouse and an abandon car along the city's edge and slept tightly together to stay warm. During days when they did not visit the prison, Elaine looked for work or the family did the unthinkable: stole from grocery store shelves.

Landing a job turned out to be challenging without a permanent address. To her own demise, Elaine became too prideful to ask for more money from her parents for it would blow the family's cover. She didn't want anyone to know what her family had experienced. Her determination was fueled by what her husband withstood: injustice. She believed the whole prison thing and conviction would be overturned at any moment. Then her superman would be released and their family would be reunited and on the road to normalcy again.

18.

A STICKY NOTE FROM THE SEVENTIES

Sam Sommer's time at Clinton Prison in the mid-to-late 1970s made some lose their hair. Why would an inmate convicted of murder be so damn good to others who wore the same faded pinstripes? It didn't make sense to guards who scratched their heads in confusion over his steady demeanor. Those in power who got to know Sam didn't know whether to make his life miserable or use his influence to their advantage. A relational dilemma was brewing, and the answer for the hacks wasn't highlighted in a troubleshooting manual on how to deal with a prisoner like this one.

According to Sam, the primary problem for the hacks at the time of his residence in Clinton was adjusting to a post-Attica riot culture. Prior to the infamous blood bath and its media barrage exposing inhumane treatment of inmates, major reform proposals were on the table to clean up life on the inside. Such talks, spearheaded by New York Commissioner of Corrections Russell Oswald, halted after Attica. He jumped the fence in open defense of the guards' safety and ceased allowing prison support groups for the time being during Sam's early years in the joint at Dannemora.[12]

Oswald's change of heart, or strategy, autocratically snubbed federal court orders that called for lawyers, medical staff, and the media to enter New York prisons liberally as "watch dogs." These actions also went against a public sentiment that supported the Attica attack (not the killings) as a long-awaited wake-up call to better humanize the treatment of prisoners.[13]

Sam felt compassion toward the guards despite having seen their dark side when billy clubs did the talking for them. He actually understood the complexity of what they went through from having to anticipate reforms and a bunch of change to running the show again. Naturally, a merry-go-round of emotions spoiled an ability to work with clarity. On the bright side for Sam, the confusion led to letting go of worrying about his type of profile in exchange for bigger matters resulting from the aftermath of Attica, like retraining and meetings on procedures, etc.

Newfound freedom for Sam and other prisoners was significant enough to move the needle in their confined lives. Little things like more time in the library or easing downtime restrictions in cells entered into play. It remained unknown, however, how long these changes would last. For Sam, a gaping hole of opportunity stood before him.

Increased library and cell time forged a couple of new projects for Sam while Eugene Lamb applied finishing touches to his appeal. He enrolled in a distance-learning criminal law class through Boston University and began working toward his high school diploma. That's right, a law course with an Ivy League school while adult basic education studies crisscrossed a higher education offering. Unheard of, even today.

While a fresh appeal was in the works largely concentrated on detective Thomas Gill's voice and others regarding Harold Goberman and the McNamara Trial, word came back on the first appellate action to right a wrong. 14 Based on a number of juror interviews from Sam's murder trial, Lamb submitted a solid argument that caught justice tipping the scales toward dishonorable proportions.

In large part, jurors preconceived a guilty verdict resulting from Judge Pierre Lundberg's predeliberative instructions to look at the case from a dirty chalkboard, not a clean slate (as noted in Chapter 15). The intimidated jurors couldn't do anything but receive the judge's instructions as earnest. By stating "how" the defendant allegedly killed the deceased removed looking at the case from the beginning. Lundberg started the deliberations where he wanted them to, not where they were supposed to in the name of justice. Already guilty.

Lamb summarized his interviews this way to Sam: It's like officiating a free throw contest where each participant takes ten shots. During the contest, the official receives instructions from the event's sponsor to award the winner based on his or her last three shots, disregarding the previous seven attempts. Incredibly, in a United States courtroom that's what went down.

Consequently, jurors found Sam guilty. They told Lamb that without Lundberg's bias directive, a verdict of innocent would likely have been rendered due to loads of reasonable doubt. Consider serving time for something you didn't do and then hearing that those responsible for your freedom believe you shouldn't be imprisoned either. That's not all.

The appeal was denied for the reason that an issue concerning the judge's instructions (whether again intentional or accidental) should have been brought on the spot. On a second appeal with a faster turnaround than the first ruling, a final court decision reaffirmed the first appellate rebuke— that insufficient counsel could have served as a stop gate during the trial. One hand rubbed the other in what was brushed off as "would have, should have."

Clinton represented Sam's third prison in as many years. He didn't believe he was moved for reasons related to a rotation system of sorts. Sam deduced that the reason for such quick exits had to do with posing a threat to the guards resulting from good behavior. Bad behavior meant bad things to inmates in an executioner mentality; good behavior meant confusion. No room for confusion with killers, rapists, pedophiles, drug dealers, and so on in one's daily grill. Hard to argue—it's just the way it was.

It took a number of appeals to get a higher court to finally respond to an attempt to overturn Sam's request for a fresh trial. Lots of resubmissions due to lots of no replies from the system. We're talking years. The appeal predicated on the McNamara trial finally spit out a decision: You got it, his request for a new trial was denied.

Were his appeals getting intentionally delayed, ignored, or a combination of the two? The 1970s set the table for what was to be expected for this man's voice on the outside. From the time he went to prison in 1971, it's as if a sticky note was affixed on the wall next to the main phone at the office of Suffolk County with his name on it. He was to be defeated indefinitely even though he already was.

That little sticky note spoke volumes for many years and still does today while it gingerly hangs on the wall. More on that near the end of this story. It's tragic that one person can be on Suffolk County's "'Shit List" for so many years while Long Island does next to nothing about monumental issues like MS-13 and ongoing government corruption.

In 1978, four years of bittersweet life for Sam by prison standards came to an end at Clinton Correctional Facility. During his incarceration there he earned a high school degree, completed a college-level criminal law class, and nurtured many lives with hope. On the outside, however, his voice remained null and void with Suffolk County and the higher courts.

In early 1979, Sam was moved to rural Green Haven Prison in Stormville, close to where he resides today and not far from his first stint behind bars at Sing Sing (today more formally referred to as Ossining Correctional Facility). Compared to Sing Sing, Auburn, and Clinton, Green Haven didn't stigmatize its inmates and visitors with Dracula-like oldness. The facility was only about thirty years old when Sam entered its heavy doors.

This year also saw the parting of ways between Sam and Eugene Lamb after more than a decade of joining arms to fight a legion of injustice on Long Island. Valiant in the beginning and steadfast throughout Sam's defense, Lamb became exhausted and checked out mentally on the Sommer case. Sam's financial situation hit rock bottom. He stopped accepting money from his in-laws years earlier.

The two gentlemen concluded that Suffolk County evolved into its own untouchable kingdom. Powerful and apparently without accountability (until recent years when finally indictments were made against some in power), the system as Sam calls it today removed whatever or whomever was in its way. In the thick of it was one guy whom they continued to hate, leaving Sam determined to blow the whistle on Suffolk County. Lamb walked away from it all viewing the county as *the whistle*.

The capstone of this era was the survival of Elaine and several of the Sommer kids. The children ought to lift their hands and touch retribution in whatever way they want—a free pass to tell the world what perseverance looks like. Sadly, Elaine Sommer passed away in 2017 after pushing the envelope for justice so long and so hard. We'll read more about her passing in the final chapter.

She was not around long enough to bless more individuals with her genuine heart and to tell her story of survival, but her children, led by Karen, recall many instances of destitution that shake nerves. That is to be left for a separate story because the survival deserves its own moments of page turning. The Sommer kids during the 1970s joined their mom on a quest to simply be with the one they loved—a dad and a husband—a simple objective burdened by unyielding circumstances.

Law enforcement was supposedly after Elaine for bouncing checks to buy food. The children stole from grocery store shelves, working as a team in playbook fashion. A couple of the kids would distract employees with various conversations while the others loaded baggy coats with whatever food they could conceal. Cars, an occasional homeless shelter because Elaine was hiding from the law, and abandon garages were called home.

On the rare occasions when the kids were able to go to school for a few days, they did so more for shelter and food than learning. How in the hell can young kids focus on two-plus-two when their parents' lives didn't add up to making any sense? The other main challenge was Social Services. Elaine shrewdly performed every move in chessboard style to avoid having her kids taken away.

No one was injured or seriously ill from four years in the frigid cold for most of the time in upstate New York. If there was a silver lining from going through hell on earth for the Sommer family members, they could "be with" their rock. Sam remained unaware of what was going on outside the walls with his loved ones. He knew it was a tough ride for them, but at the same time he didn't fathom that their quandary was so day-to-day.

Sam pressed Elaine for a while about receiving money from her parents, but she insisted doing nothing of the sort. Even when his mother and in-laws visited him with the younger kids who were living in Florida, Sam made it look like Elaine relocated to another city. She didn't want her parents to find her for a number of years. Sam never even got her address, partly because there wasn't one, but he felt obligated to respect her desire of anonymity. The two continued to believe the conviction would soon be overturned. Soon? Therein lay the word of a lifetime.

In perhaps the best oxymoron of love ever demonstrated, Sam and Elaine kept a constant string of secrets from one another. In what would typically end a marriage, not to mention a twenty-year prison sentence, these two used the withholding of information from one another in the spirit of true love without even knowing it. The latest example of selectively refraining from sharing information for sake of stress management was Sam not telling Elaine about Eugene Lamb.

How smart was Elaine? Consider this: In all of the visits to see Sam, rarely did any of the children ever slip the tongue about their fate. Here was a woman up to her neck in battling homelessness, hunger, guilt, and lost childhoods for the kids; yet, she championed that level of discipline. We need more Elaine Sommers in this world, God rest her soul.

Speaking of her faith, to survive that long was an answered prayer from God. First, moving again to be near her husband came with its own set of challenges, like transportation top of mind. In that case Sam was able to help her from support his mother's sagging monies. Yes, another secret, but Sam knew Elaine and kids would want to be in the same vicinity of his new prison again. Therefore, she accepted the money without prying where it came from.

Anna Sommer lived a hard life, but her gift to Sam and Elaine when it was needed the most came on the wings of a dove. She passed away in 1979 from heart complications while living with her other son, Morris, on Long Island. He tragically would follow in death four years later in Florida from complications related to dementia.

If that wasn't enough within a five-year period, Morris Rosen, longtime mentor to Sam, father, husband, and successful clothier, passed a year after Sam's brother in

Florida as well from cancer. The illness came on fast and consumed his body way too quickly for anyone to see the disease coming. His death would soon cause his wife Sadie to move back to New York to be with family.

Second, almost a year after Sam got acclimated at Green Haven in the first week of 1980, he received a game-changing piece of mail.

19.

CITIZEN LAWMAN

An envelope arrived for Sam Sommer at Green Haven Correctional Facility while a new year and a new decade entered his world as well. The mail came from his former defense attorney Eugene Lamb. Thinking it was a sentimental goodbye or an outstanding invoice with no deadline since Sam was making forty cents an hour in the prison's library, he opened the seal nonchalantly while sitting on his cot. Surprisingly, a check fell in his lap.

Refund from services rendered? No chance; Sam owed big time, but Lamb gave him some leeway due to their relationship. A lost payment from Sam's old business ventures even though they've been basically taken over? Nope. Money from in-laws? Not this time.

Sam lifted the check in unison with his body from the cot to learn of the mysterious remitter. He read it over three or four times while pacing the stone floor. Finally, he stopped to peer outward from his open cell door during free time. Not knowing why, he looked for a guard to call to. He found a couple of them down the hall but refrained from saying anything. He didn't know what he would say anyway. Perplexity overcame him with a tint of newness concerning his case. He desired to talk to someone, anyone.

Dated 12-27-79 from Royal-Globe Insurance Companies in the amount of $5,000, a small notation in the lower right-hand corner of the check read:

Damages resulting from issues occurring on or about 5/222/68 as per stipulation 73-C-1346

Yes, that is a typo in the memo section of the check as it relates to the date (see Illustrations). The infamous May 22, 1968, episode in Sam's life found him kidnapped, beaten, and arrested at the hands of Suffolk County detectives. The check functioned as a settlement from Suffolk County in admission to its unlawful acts against him almost eleven years ago.

Overcome with his legs wanting to run south and a mind heading northward in search of the meaning behind a receipt of the ages, Sam charmed a guard to let him make an urgent call to his attorney. The recently-fired Eugene Lamb affirmed the check and its recognition of Suffolk County putting a decade-long disagreement of police brutality to bed for good—at least in the eyes of those who issued the payment.

Technically speaking, Sam never agreed to a settlement with Suffolk County over anything, much less the manner in which he succumbed to an "arrest." On one hand, the payment and admission of guilt from the same pricks who fabricated his guilt and conviction showered him with a victory against the system. For someone who waited for a victory against the swamp while holding onto a tree branch in a bog of quicksand, it felt pretty good.

On the other hand, the check sent him a message: Take this chump change and shut your trap. Your case is closed. What exactly did that mean? Did a settlement mean exoneration? Recall this was a one-way settlement. With Lamb out of the picture, Sam didn't miss a beat. The Sam Sommer of 1980 was not the same man of 1971 when he said goodbye to the outside world and his family.

He was now a citizen lawman at age forty-three. Nine years in the big house produced one hell of a sharper mind that already spelled innovation from his younger days as a business king. This meant bad news for Suffolk County— not because he could wave a magic wand and overturn his whole conviction in the snap of a finger.

Rather, this new lawman promised one whale of a dog fight that would last as long as he lived against the Suffolk County system. The system would never be able to sleep, drop its guard, or turn the other way as long as the citizen lawman was breathing. He would attack its central nervous system and shut down the very people and power that destroyed not only his life but the lives of many others since his nab job in 1968.

Sam obviously took the settlement check as an open door to appeal his case once again since all other doors had slammed in his face thus far. Strangely, he kind of thought Suffolk County would expect a quick appeal. He knew from his studying the law that the check signified a civil settlement, not one of criminal nature. Knowing that, he jumped over the rigmarole involved in filing an appeal under a civil premise realizing it would further tie his case in knots.

Since he won the Huntley Hearing in 1969 grounded on the same claim of an unlawful arrest that this check conjectured, the higher court's decision to nullify his victory on appeal that same year should now be disregarded. In the scope of his whole case, his murder trial then never occurred so to speak. Therefore, he is innocent of the crime of murder.

He got busy putting the framework together on that judicial argumentative process leading to innocence. At the same time he blueprinted an appeal under a criminal umbrella, Elaine and the kids at last found refuge in a low-income, government housing program. The money Sam gave her from the settlement aided in the family's recovery from a decade of near-damaging misery (again, unaware to Sam).

Elaine was aware of where the money came from and why, and Sam now understood how his wife and kids would live for the time being. No more secrets. The fact that her kids transported an ounce of stability and shelter in their lives after many years gave Elaine a shot in the arm. She was now free to give it her all in helping Sam prove his innocence. The early 1980s rolled on. There was positivity for a change.

The Sommer's turning over of a new leaf blew away in a hasty breeze, however, with the notification of another prison transfer. Sam became overly enamored with putting together an appeal of real promise that his prisoner hat took a back seat. That didn't come across favorably with the guards. To them, he was a prisoner first and a man caught up in assumed freedom second.

Sam found time in the hole more than he ever did prior to Green Haven during his past two years there. That dampened his appeal work a bit, but he stuck to it whenever he could in between bouts with darkness. He finally saw his appeal off to another shot-in-the-dark court for the first time as his own counsel in fall of 1980. It felt liberating to Sam. Another first: He learned that his latest transfer was based on compromising behavior, not for being a good guy. Go figure.

By spring of 1982 when Sam made his new home at Attica State Prison with all its history and notoriety, the Sommer kids were together in their entirety for the first time in ages. The oldest, Marlene and Linda, were now in their early twenties ready to help organize another move, along with the other older kids who have come a long way in growing up fast. The family gelled, but the times were still filled with uncertainty.

Down the road from Buffalo where winter holds no mercy and snow blots out the sky in no time without warning, Attica was a hike from Green Haven. Sam instantly absorbed the institution's eerie air. He could hear pleads for help behind the cold walls. The place breathed from lost souls who stained its operations forever. It was like everyone was on edge. Humans didn't belong there—too much pain owned the place.

In his first week at Attica, Sam listened to a plethora of complaints from inmates, which mostly included labor abuse claims and visitation restrictions. There was no time to get broken in there; his bad boy colleagues made it clear that a sequel to the bloodbath over a decade ago could happen.

20.

1982

In 1982, a revitalized Sommer family set off to reset their lives. Elaine enlisted the help of her oldest children to give the kids something of a life. Work and school with pressure to build a food service empire was the former daily grind and microcosm of an American Dream for the family. Now, a leaner dream was to just attend school and have an honest look at what tomorrow could bring.

One woman had shepherded a bunch of young kids for more than ten years through one near-disastrous turn after another from living on the street. Their sole purpose was overcoming unknowns behind every moment. They wanted to give a father and a husband support, period. One goal, loads of obstacles.

Now a mom, wife, and kids could show that same level of support by getting it together, so to speak, from a little settlement money and their own brand of unmatched maturity. Intuitive, insightful, or simply fearless, it didn't matter what anyone called this milestone for the Sommers. What mattered went by the name of Elaine Sommer.

Without anyone knowing it except her kids, she extraordinarily took whatever came her way and embraced the challenge. Although their rock was about halfway through his sentencing at this stage in the early 1980s, recent developments related to a surprise settlement had everyone's chin up to keep going.

Earlier in the book it was noted that Sam Sommer would have made one hell of a business professor. Elaine, comparably, wrote the book on championing motivation. No podiums, big stages, fancy web sites, or short-lived uplifting messages—nope, she was the real deal.

In critically examining how she led a best kept story of survival, first, let's recap her role in the Huntley Hearing. She took facts and then made them irrefutable by her attention to detail—motivating a judge and a courtroom. Second, managing survival for modern-day nomads after enjoying a comfortable life not only took strength, it necessitated strategy and humility. Such wisdom produced an outcome, albeit painful. The family made it through earthly hell, and even the skills her oldest kids learned and applied by serving as role models to younger siblings is a remarkable testament.

Sam demonstrated his own echelon of fearless stardom on the inside. He got to know the guys, the gangs, and the grunts of frustration that kept Attica simmering like an overfilled time bomb of rebellion. Still obsessed with studying law, he discovered a forthcoming prison reform proposal before it went public that dealt with removing visitation screens in New York's prisons.

The reform, noted as Number 24 in what turned out to be a federal court decision that same year, saw sweeping changes in visitation protocol at prisons. Some of these changes included allowing kissing and touching of children and spouses during visits by removing the physical barrier between families and their incarcerated loved ones. Other components of the reform allowed children access to toys and age-appropriate movies during family visits.[14]

Sam took the information to disgruntled prisoners who wanted to execute a sequel to the Attica riot. Most, if not all of them, were unaware of the pending changes. Sam then met with the warden, who was obviously aware of the forthcoming reforms. His scheme with the warden was more communication-focused; he wanted the warden to know that some tensions eased a bit by informing inmates of forthcoming positive changes.

Regardless of a noticeably favorable mood swing among prisoners, Sam found himself in the hole for doing something that was not approved by administration. After serving time with bugs and blackness, the process of making better visitation experiences at Attica came into the fold.

That fall, perhaps as a gesture of administrative gratitude and maybe guilty consciences, Sam earned a new job working in the prison's health clinic. He enjoyed helping civilian nurses and doctors treat inmates for a variety of conditions, some omitted from this book and kept to the readers' imaginations. Overall, the clinic served legitimate health issues like viral treatments, bacterial infections, cuts, scrapes, and at times issues pertaining to mental illness.

One morning the health care services inside the Attica clinic met its match. Years later in his apartment surrounded by walls of legal documents, Sam recounted an 'unscheduled appointment' that broke from the bellows of wrath:

> **Sam:** *A steel door slammed against a thick mountain of concrete down the corridor. This door was never supposed to slam. Doors slammed every day in the joint, but this round of thunder left a statement. That big steel door gave an indestructible wall a run for its money. I was ready to run but couldn't.*
>
> *We froze—another inmate joined me in freaking out. I don't recall his name; I believe it was Donny or a name that started with the letter D, but you know, they rotated us in and out of there—new*

faces all the time. I do remember this raging scream from the hallway, "I'm gonna get you, bitch!" just a short distance away in the same direction where the door had slammed. My mouth was like cotton. I wanted to remain silent so clearing my throat was not an option.

We were behind one of a few doors that made up a narrow corridor, or hallway, busy preparing exam rooms for the day—mostly cleaning and some inventory, stocking shelves, and so forth. Behind the rooms were special entrances and exits for nurses and physicians with masked access into the prison. A nurse had just arrived through that door. Let's call her Shirley for sake of memory. I do believe that might have been her first name. Not sure (shrugging).

She was an older lady—one heck of nice gal... got to know her a bit that's why her name could be Shirley (laughing and shrugging). Anyway, she showed up right at the time we heard another, "I'm gonna get you!" It was closer now to our room. Our door was closed like all others in that corridor, so we weren't sure if this big wrath knew where he was going for sure. We knew we were all scared.

Instantly I knew where Shirley was gonna go— in the back room. My instinct said this walking monster wanted her. Once inside the clinic, she and other medical staff had to leave with special clearance like they did upon arrival each day. That took time and guards. There were no guards anywhere. Man, that made the ordeal even scarier. Usually we didn't like to see hacks, but now we longed for one damn guard. The only alternative to hide Shirley was in an adjacent room from where we were standing in a main exam room. It was a smaller, more private room for matters requiring added confidentiality between caregiver and patient.

The wrath appeared nonnegotiable. No pack of cigarettes could win this madness over. Shirley looked like she wanted to run, but where to? There supposedly wasn't even a guard outside the door like usual. This monster was probably a few feet away from our door now, grunting and growling and saying "bitch" repeatedly. That term in prison can run the gamut in meaning, but in this case, it meant Shirley. I think we all knew that.

This evil tirade must have been outside the door—we could hear heavy breathing. Don't move, I mean, that was the name of the game. I think the monster was temporarily unsure of what door to crack open. I couldn't take it anymore, though. I grabbed Shirley by the arm and tiptoed her into the smaller room. I knew I'd be potentially reprimanded for grabbing a person of authority but didn't give a shit. She would likely have been grabbed a lot worse in a matter of moments, perhaps in a deathly showdown with the rage outside the door.

Once Shirley was inside the back room, she briskly shut the door without a sound. Under unimaginable duress she gracefully closed the door while I spun my body far enough away from it in the nick of time. I then quietly moved to the center of the room again near Donny.

No sooner than we exchanged glances on what the hell to do next, the once-locked door blasted off its hinges, splattering wood and slivers through the *exam room like bullets flying from a machine gun. We both hit the deck in fear of seeing a door blown up by human hands in our faces. I recall being cut from wood, but that was the least of our worries.*

"Where is she?" permeated the air—almost making the other doors inside the room pop open from just this giant's voice alone. At least six foot, five inches and pressing three-hundred pounds, Big John we'll say stood looking down at the two of us and demanded answers about the nurse's whereabouts.

Unable to answer this raging man because of Shirley's predicament, we slid to the back of the room on our butts, kind of near where I stashed the nurse. Then Big John reached in his pocket. We thought we were goners. Donny and I covered our heads. I noticed through the cracks of my fingers that Big John flaunted something in his mouth— the strangest-looking thing I ever saw.

He stood there with fists clenched. Donny crawled over to the corner of the room like a little puppy scurrying for shelter. I remained on the floor next to the door of Shirley's room. I gathered this bulky guy could put two and two together and guessed she was in that room. Big John ignored Donny and peered at me on the floor with an object of what looked like two matchbox covers in his mouth.

In between the covers was a large razor blade about three or four times the size of a standard beard shaver made for the everyday man to use at home. Shit, what the hell was that? Pure terror. He was a human weapon (shaking head).

He started walking toward me and I yelled "Donny" out of pure distraction, not knowing what I'd do next. Buying time in a place where all you had was time made this event even more of a wild ride. If I could buy a couple of seconds, then I'd live a couple of seconds longer. That's how desperate the situation was.

I didn't want Donny to get hurt, so my distraction needed a next move. Big John looked at Donny, and I got up and grabbed a part of the door and threw it at the invader. He momentarily stumbled off balance and then marched in a beeline toward me like a wound-up toy on steroids. He swung his head back and forth with that razor in his mouth. My flesh already felt the hurt before he made it within striking distance. I never dreamed a person could physically act like this. Stunned (swallowing air).

Donny yelled for help hoping to get some guards in the room. Big John came near me pissed beyond belief. In a flash, I slid to the side just a bit at the same time he reached for me, causing him to stumble over some furniture, landing right in front of Shirley's harbored location. I'm not sure if he fell face first onto his custom-made weapon or not, but he did not get up right away. I grabbed the back of his head and tried to hold him down when I felt two hands clutch the back of my shoulders.

Yup, determined hands on my shoulders all over again. The grasp flashed me back to my kidnapping in Commack. Astonishingly, for an instant I wanted to be with Big John. Some things never leave you, even in times of life or death, mammoth razorblades, massive giants, you know (frowning).

Guards finally arrived. Big John was secured and Donny and I were removed from the room. I tried to tell the guards about Shirley but was told to shut up. I pointed to her room. They found her in there, unharmed.

We were reprimanded of course for the incident like it was our fault. I wasn't punished for grabbing Shirley; she never said anything I guess. More time in the hole, no more clinic duty, and I lost library privileges for the few months left of that year. I heard Shirley was forever grateful—never saw her again. Oh well, just another day at home.

From the get-go interviewing Sam Sommer, that incident has always amplified the type of person he embodies.

The aftermath of the Big John rampage made Sam and Donny instant warriors of respect by some in the joint, including guards. Sam learned that Big John should have never been at Attica. He required greater care in terms of mental illness. The services he needed went beyond standard rehabilitation found in most prisons back in that day.

The year crawled to a finish. Still psychologically recovering from the wrath and unable to concentrate on his case for a while, Sam found himself reading more to relax his mind. One afternoon a guard interrupted his downtime with news of an unexpected visitor.

A well-dressed man met Sam in the newly-upgraded visitation area where the Sommer family frequented. His name was E. Thomas Boyle, a private practicing attorney from Long Island who made the long trek northward for something important to share. He told Sam he had information on his case that would certainly bring it to appellate court and likely overturn the conviction.

Unable to divulge too much detail at the time, Boyle's visit centered more on meeting Sam and gaining his approval to represent him. Quick to jump on a bandwagon of support from the outside after years of judicial suppression, Sam instantly brought Boyle up to speed on his recent appeals, the settlement, and other matters like the Autopsy Report, Goberman, etc.

Boyle was pumped after hearing about Sam's knowledge of the law and his pulse on the case's essential elements. Boyle assured Sam that he would lead a strong new appeal for him and that it shouldn't take long to get back in touch with him on next steps. He left Sam with a sense of justice reserved for his long-aching heart.

Where did Sam begin to recap 1982? A joyous change of scenery for his wife and children, a hopeful new appeal stemming from an out-of-the-blue yet shady settlement, a brush with a madman who used razorblades to slice people from his mouth and was out to rape or kill a nurse, and a surprise visit from a private attorney who knew of Sam's innocence—take your pick from a year that coughed up stories that should have been destined for *60 Minutes*.

A little extra character from these doings steeped an already-legendary atmosphere inside Attica State Prison at the close of 1982.

21.

HOME STRETCH?

In his hey day, Sam Sommer employed earnest folks out to make a go of it in America. Years later while in prison, he figuratively looked after the livelihood of postal workers as well by bombarding them with outgoing mail almost daily. The civilian lawman continuously showered Suffolk County and various state appellate courts with submissions of new evidence, old evidence, and reminders of missing documents like an Autopsy Report.

Sam finds a way today despite a disdain toward the justice system to cast a joke about most of the prisons having designated "Sommer mailrooms" back when he was incarcerated. He read, wrote letters, and appealed his case in between playing peacekeeper and mentor on the inside, and time spent in those capacities meant lots of mail.

Not much came back from his correspondences, though, during the first dozen years behind bars. On rare occasion when he was able to connect with the District Attorney's office at Suffolk County, a rhetorical response almost in tape-recorder-like fashion would say they never received anything. Even in cases of registered mail, the response was often, "No one here seems to know where it is. Sorry."

In fact, his goldmine appeal about the settlement check finally rendered a decision a couple years later from the courts. Basically, a settlement of this nature was not seen as a judgment. Curiously, the settlement check from Suffolk County did project perjury. The act of perjury at the time the People professed that Suffolk County detectives did not use force against Sam Sommer in 1969 and 1970 to this day merits the reopening of the case. A settlement for reasons herein tells a story of "they admitted to lying under oath."

Sorry? These moments made Sam miss Eugene Lamb and Joe Scibilia, but he didn't doubt his own legal skills. He just wondered if the DA or courts took his independent appeals seriously. Sam confidently knew, however, that he didn't need to contemplate too much on whether his perseverance stuck a thorn in the side of Suffolk County. Sam wasn't going away, but based on the way he had been treated in a post-conviction world with Suffolk County, it was evident the DA still wanted him to go away.

Lamb still left a sour taste in Sam's mouth and Scibilia moved on to insurance issues instead of working on criminal cases. It is noted that the love Sam feels to this day for Scibilia is unwavering. In fact, Joe's son, Joe Jr., was instrumental on this project from a legal standpoint. The two gentlemen came into play during the finishing touches of this book when Sam's case hit new plateaus of promise.

Ongoing wrangles with Suffolk County made it difficult for Sam to look ahead to whether or not he would be released after serving his original sentence of twenty years. Up to this point in 1983, he had served sixty percent of that sentence. He would soon be in the home stretch of putting in the time; yet, what would that final road to freedom look like? Would it lean toward a release or a denial from the parole board?

Part of any projection that would provide a clue to answering these questions had to do with how deep a connection existed between parole board members and Suffolk County. To put it bluntly, how much hate for Sam Sommer still infiltrated a collective prejudice toward the man?

A regular date with the hole in solitary punishment never really seemed to curb Sam's confidence on being released on time. Part of the confinement, he believed, was a game with the hacks—especially after he had been serving for a while. When the guards or administrative heads couldn't figure out how to deal with his good behavior or desire to educate himself, they put him in the hole. He figured it was their way to isolate someone they didn't trust. He wasn't the only one treated in this manner, but those who served in solitary confinement that didn't stem from common offenses like physical encounters or verbal abuse were small.

Such occurrences, the ones Sam could live, breathe, and see on a regular basis in prison, didn't bother him. It was Suffolk County and its discreet power that caused turbulence in his head. A recent upswing in relationships with prison personnel aided his outlook; he started to grow fond of some guards, and vice versa.

So there were two sides to an argument about his future parole hearing. One capitulated to the fear of how much pull Suffolk County really had on the inside—the other yielded encouragement from Sam's flourishing relationships with those in authority. Eight more years to go, though, so there wasn't time to fret too much quite yet.

There was time, however, for Sam to put his best foot forward on integrating his positive contributions to the culture of prisons in concert with reform objectives. He tucked an occasional self-rebellious aura toward guards in his back pocket. A life without his family seemed to be slipping down the tracks and out of sight. "If all else fails," he said to himself, "I can't blow my chance at parole when that day of truth comes."

Sam's second year at Attica remarkably went down uneventful—a good thing due to last year's escapades and giving everything he had for a chance to grab freedom thanks to E. Thomas Boyle. A few weeks passed from the attorney's unannounced drop in that floored Sam with a life-changing message. Sam enlisted the help of Elaine to track Boyle down since he hadn't heard from him as a follow up to the visit.

Elaine left messages for Boyle and after a while broke through. He apologized to her on behalf of Sam and said his plate became full and that he'd circle back to Sam's case as soon as he could. More time passed. Not much from Boyle.

Dejected from having someone make a daylong drive to tell you that your ticket to overturning a murder conviction resembled game-changing material, Sam grew increasingly depressed for perhaps the first time in a long time. In fact, this prison term milestone in '83 marked a time when he dropped his façade to Elaine during visitations. No more putting on a front that everything was fine.

For starters, he and Elaine grew closer together even while apart. Together they unveiled a new period of sharing everything together (except the early days when she and the kids lived homeless). Plus, since Elaine was engaged in the Boyle gateway to exoneration, the husband and wife were naturally bound on the same page of one another's doings.

The extended Sommer family remained divided on Sam's innocence. One family member, George Davis, who married Linda Sommer, had enough of the division. A construction contractor, Davis grew increasingly suspicious of Suffolk County and became concerned over the family's division. He wanted to do something about the matter to say "enough is enough," and his gallant skin in the game on his father-in-law's case uncovered yet more hair-raisers.

For almost two years, the once-promising break in the case from Boyle's fading visit to Attica turned south. He never followed through on his promise to Sam. Davis visited Boyle's firm, but the attorney no longer worked there.

Ironically, a published summary of his career reveals an empty space in 1985 when Davis began sleuthing for Sam. That time frame congruently does not list where Boyle was working as an attorney.[15]

Also in '85, Sam got moved to Auburn—the site of his second prison in the early 70s. In a desperate attempt at drawing a storyline correlation here, let's throw it out there anyway since Sam's life is full of exceptional twists that would bump off best-selling fiction narratives. At the same time the heat was turned up on Boyle, Sam is moved to Auburn but only for a year. The Department of Corrections then returned him to Attica a year later and for less than twelve months.

Through the Freedom Of Information Act (FOIA) Sam had been trying to get a copy of a mug shot negative from his arrest for several years. He and his defense team always felt skeptical of the black-and-white photo that represented his arrest file, wondering why there wasn't a higher-resolution version presented in court. The FOIA process to date only landed replies from the Suffolk County DA noting it was misplaced from the get-go in '68. How convenient, once again, and with another sorry.

Shortly after arriving at Auburn, a Robert Freeman got in touch with Sam. Freeman today oversees New York State's Committee on Open Government. In the '80s he was very involved in FOIA. Freeman's own engagement in Sam's repeated requests opened scrutiny toward figuring why there were so many requests. Freeman gave Sam's request a personal endorsement of sorts to help him get to the bottom of the mug shot issue. Rather than push solely for a negative, the FOIA demand asked for all visuals on file from the '68 "arrest."

Brilliant move. Sam said that he learned from the Freeman experience that if you want milk from Suffolk County you'd better ask for the cow, too. It's not like that office is going out of its way to dig something up in the spirit of customer service and humanity.

The outcome of Freeman's special intervention delivered a FOIA-led *colored* photograph from the Suffolk County DA of Sam's booking on May 22, 1968 (see Illustrations). The image clearly shows redness around his facial area and a closed left eye. More significantly, after deeper analysis Sam noticed a dickie under his sport coat.

This trip down Memory Lane triggered a deafening whistle from years of pent up steam. Sam screamed, "Those bastards" in reflection of his mid-80s finding behind bars. "It didn't hit me at the time because of the shady-looking mug photo (see Chapter 12), but the Suffolk County detectives had put new clothing on me for this photo since they'd ripped my t-shirt during hours of abuse in the cell the night I was kidnapped."

He paused. "That's what they did—covered every step." He curled his lips inward in disgust, exhaled, and sat silent for a few minutes with hands folded during this part of our multiple-years of interviews. We've covered more territory with this fifty-year story than any overpaid special counsel could make up in a politically-charged charade. The Sam Sommer interviews are the real deal. They bravely told of collusion between a branch of government and organized crime with no agenda in mind besides exposing evil.

When Sam received the colored photograph, he embarked on yet again another appeal. In doing so, he wondered if this was the piece of evidence that directed Boyle to visit him almost three years earlier. We'll never know. What we do know is that the mug shot discovery drove Davis to jump in the burning furnace of injustice even further for his father-in-law.

Exhausted and emotionally spent from chasing Boyle's shadow, Davis found energy in the newfound photo. It was one thing for him and Sam to get their hands on it via FOIA;

the image sculpted a chance to open a treasure chest in an attic of secrecy known as Suffolk County, then pose the million-dollar question: What gives?

OK, so covering up documents, information, etc., is part of the process of corruption—we likely agree that is assumptive by nature. But to openly lie? The found photograph is fairly big; a negative by contrast is small. Giving the benefit of the doubt to an argument, albeit a constant drumbeat with Suffolk County, that something was lost, a negative—maybe. Covering up a separate photograph in color, though? Fed up, Davis took his pinpoint focus of resolve straight to the DA's office.

He arranged a transcript-documented telephone conversation with Carl Spitznagel, former Assistant DA with Suffolk County during part of Sam's earlier legal proceedings (see Illustrations). Semi-retired in 1985 and practicing law part-time, Spitznagel agreed to the conversation and knowingly accepted that the content of the conversation could be used as part of an appeal by Sam Sommer.

Davis sent Spitznagel a set of questions to help him prepare for the phone conversation, dated August 15, 1985, at 10:15 a.m. as a legal affidavit.

Here is a glimpse of the relevant takeaways from this conversation, presented ADA for Spitznagel and GD for George Davis:

- ADA admitted that the Suffolk County detectives did whatever they wanted... stating, "That's the bullshit you've got all the time in the squad room," expounding on a question on the use of a dictation machine placed in interrogation settings at the Homicide unit (8).

- ADA said, "I don't doubt for a minute there was no oral confession and I don't doubt for a minute they did bounce your father off the wall (9)."

- GD told ADA he had met up with the former manager of Dunkin' Donuts in Commack where Sam was heisted, a Mr. Whitish. For years Whitish bottled up an eye-witness account of Sam being kidnapped. He feared testifying back in the day out of possible repercussions from those in authority on Long Island. GD said that Whitish saw Sam get seized. Whitish went to court on different occasions to give statements in recent years, but they were always postponed. He was never called back. GD deemed that the detectives got the best of him—wore him down so to speak with threats (10).

- ADA offered to GD that if a new mug shot was introduced as evidence and a photo was potentially tampered with, then that is about as good a grounds for a new trial or new hearing (18).

- GD told ADA that Sam filed another appeal based on a criminal action being prepared by Thomas Boyle in 1982 (without knowing what the action entailed—the story of Boyle visiting Sam at Attica with new evidence carried the load). It took three years for a federal court to find the notice of appeal—always claiming they couldn't find it (20).

- GD further informs ADA that the Supreme Court of the United States earlier ruled against an insurance company's deposition that the original mug shot may have been tampered with, indicating that the appeal needed to be filed within three years (the problem here was that there was a court order that was ignored for the negative in the interim) (20).

• Perhaps a kicker, GD told ADA that during the McNamara trial Suffolk County Detective Thomas Gill took the stand and said that (Harold) Goberman committed the murder of Irving Silver—and that unbelievably they couldn't even get a new trial even on that (22)?

• ADA replied to the Gill-Goberman reference by saying, "That's flimsy ground to get a new trial on (22).

• ADA continued to comment on the previous claim by saying you'd have a much better chance at a new trial with the People deliberately tampering with evidence (22).

• ADA then changes the subject to tell GD that the cops don't trust the assistant DAs too much. It is not unusual for any of us to have information withheld by the police department from us because they just don't trust us. I don't think I realized it until three or four years after I left the District Attorney's office and probably later than that, just how bad the situation was in the police department. The cops keep to themselves. Their attitude is shit (23).

• "I have long since learned not to trust the Suffolk County Police Department," divulged ADA.

• ADA stated, "The system goes out of their (pardon the grammar—recorded verbatim) way to protect itself… and the idiot judges we have (26)."

Photographs, truths about bad cops from a former assistant district attorney, detectives taking the stand and saying what they have to in order to protect the system while contradicting innocence and guilt, and the victim of it all moved again from Attica to Shawangunk Correctional Facility in late 1986. Two patterns settled into play when it came to Sam's prison moves. In the '70s they partook from his good behavior; in the '80s his transfers ran parallel to when a lot of outside legal activity and findings about his case were in play.

22.

COURT CRUSADER, CUOMO, AND COMMISSIONER

A country club by prison standards provided what appeared to be the last home for Sam Sommer before he possibly transitioned back into society. The late 1980s cautiously marked the closing in on a long-awaited appearance before a parole board, but it was one day at a time for the growingly-anxious family member. To make matters extra restless, Sam knew that every time he felt like getting settled long term in a prison, the state moved him to another one.

Shawangunk, located not too far from the Hudson River Valley region northwest of Newburgh, recently opened in 1985 as yet another maximum security facility. Its neighboring medium security prison, Wallkill, assumed one side of a dual set up between the two facilities where resources could be shared to save money without traveling far. Shawangunk introduced a new sex offender rehabilitation program at that time and today remains to house infamous serial killer David Berkowitz, better known as the Son of Sam.[16]

The thought of freedom didn't wrench a knot in Sam's stomach, but rather it did in his mind. Basically his entire stint behind bars was in many cases as productive and purposeful as was his time in society. Now in his late forties, there remained enough time for Sam to make a dent in the civilian world again in perhaps five or six more years. Such an ambition, however, came with baggage.

For instance, freedom to Sam meant that the system won. A life of incarceration had been devoted to studying law, preparing appeals, mentoring others, earning a high school credential, saving lives, preventing riots, and in his spare time—trying to stay abreast of the outside. From his humble days at Sing Sing fighting the drip/drip of painstakingly passing time, over the years Sam learned how to fight the torture of the tick by offering himself to others.

On the other hand, freedom meant family. A materializing goal of getting out soon in relative terms superseded all else. Starting over with a clean slate also equated to getting an unrestricted crack at taking on the system with the support of a family devoted to backing his every turn, hands on and head on.

Today, Sam acknowledges that he has never kicked the nightmares altogether and never will. He still shrieks over being confined in tight spaces and in small rooms like he recently endured from two surgeries in his eighties. The nightmares come and go. He just sleeps whenever he can. Trying to follow a regular regime of sleep at night like most people do only welcomes darkness in his mind.

Sam ruffled a few feathers once in a while in the joint, but he also left a legacy while going through arguably the nation's most challenging period of prison reform. He himself *was reform*. A disturbing paradox on the outside was that Suffolk County had yet to go through any kind of reform.

Finally, a break in that bleak and depressing recognition of injustice. At last someone aside from Sam Sommer, the guinea pig of fifty-plus years of steady Suffolk County corruption, exuded boldness to blow a whistle on Long Island. In 1985, Suffolk County Court Judge Stuart Namm initiated action from then-Governor Mario Cuomo by way of a special prosecutor to examine criminal misconduct by the Suffolk County police and DA's office. His commission for an investigation surfaced from the role officers and the DA played in two homicide cases tried before him.[17]

While Sam started to serve what looked like his final four years in prison in 1987, a public safety committee of the Suffolk County Legislature turned up substantial criminal misconduct by the county police department and DA's office thanks to the governor-led enquiry.

At the same time of Cuomo's inspection of Suffolk County lawlessness, a state investigation commission uncovered controversies concerning homicide cases in Suffolk County. Those included perjury by Suffolk County assistant DAs, negligent record-keeping by police, and the overuse of confessions. Suffolk detectives apparently extracted confessions or other oral admissions in ninety-four of their homicide cases (over a set period of time).[17]

Both legal experts and law enforcement personnel compared that statistical finding to other jurisdictions. It showed a remarkably high figure in contrast to other law enforcement agencies when it comes to the use of confessions—provoking major skepticism toward Suffolk County. An educated correlation was drawn by the commission's report that the culture inside Suffolk County's government signified that you "were supposed to do whatever was necessary to arrest and convict." The same report concluded that under DA Patrick Henry the county was mostly concerned about its image in the media.[17]

More accounts of this investigation can be found in Namm's 2014 book, *A Whistleblower's Lament: The Perverted Pursuit of Justice in the State of New York* (Hellgate Press, first published April 13, 2010). Namm served as a justice on Long Island between 1975 and 1992. Similar to Frank Serpico's fight to bring down crooked cops and their supervisors, this court crusader's valor in drawing attention to fraud in Suffolk County delivered some integrity back to the bench.

Namm moved to North Carolina in 1993 after the Democratic Party decided not to nominate him for re-election behind the bench. Speculation arose that the reason behind that decision had to do with the judge's ongoing criticism of Suffolk County. Namm cited in a 2014 *Newsday* article that there have been $30 million in settlements with plaintiffs who claimed police misconduct in Nassau and Suffolk Counties since 2002 alone. Imagine what kind of dirty deeds went down from the time Sam was seized and 2001.

We know this. Since Namm exposed Suffolk County through his book, the following is a small sampling of more recent headlines pertaining to influencers attached to the county (listed verbatim as published):

> Bellone, Spota go head to head with corruption claims in Suffolk[18]
>
> 4 Suffolk detectives transfer out of DA's corruption bureau[19]
>
> Suffolk County District Attorney on Defensive as U.S. Inquiry Expands[20]
>
> Scrutiny for Suffolk County's District Attorney Amid a U.S. Inquiry[21]
>
> The Strange Rise and Violent Fall of Long Island's Dirtiest Police[22]
>
> Bad Cop, Worse Cop: James Burke and the Overwhelming Stench of Corruption in Suffolk County[23]
>
> Column: Charges surface on Suffolk County corruption[24]

In N.Y., A Fight to Reform Police Force Accused of Being 'Rotten'[25]

Ex-Suffolk County Police Chief Pleads Guilty to Beating Up Suspect Who Stole His Sex Toys[26]

Several Suffolk Cops Charged in Burke Beating & Cover-Up Case, Docs Show[27]

These developments stirred Sam's psyche. Elated and floored. Stick it to 'em Namm, he cheered from one sideline, to... on the other hand saying to himself, "Do you believe this shit?" It didn't take Sam long to absorb that *he was the first victim of a tireless string of malicious government activity on Long Island.*

All this time people in positions of power could have thrown the book at Suffolk County from Sam's appeals as simple awareness-raisers by themselves. Even if he has been a lifetime target for whatever host of reasons, why have others suffered or died at the hands of Suffolk County? He ran out of adjectives to describe this part of influential America. Senseless was the last word that stuck in his mind back in the late '80s after learning of Cuomo and Namm's work.

Sam spent the next few months doing what he had always done when new developments about his case entered the scene—appealed them. When his prison time was all said and done, he submitted more than thirty appeals—some with a third-party lawyer and most on his own. His incarceration reached a point where his sights and energy focused on parole. A fight to clear his name would only intensify after release, if that outcome would hold true.

The state investigation into Suffolk County would last a number of years. To an extent, Sam credited the probe's publicity toward building favor for his parole hearing in 1991. Prior to Cuomo's crackdown in the late '80s, Sam enlisted the help of Robert Levy, an up-and-coming judicial all-star and senior staff attorney with the New York Civil Liberties Union.

Levy was warmed by Elaine Sommer carrying boxes into Shawangunk to prove her husband's innocence the first time he met the couple in person. Passion, Levy thought, there is no substitute for passion when it comes to persevering toward something a person believes in. To this day, that memory dwells in Levy's heart.

Currently Levy wears the black robe as a federal magistrate judge for the Eastern District of New York, an appointment he has held since 1995. He was instrumental in preparing for Sam's parole board hearing in 1991. Aware of this book, Levy believes to this day that Sam was innocent of the crime. Years later (see Illustrations) he sent Sam a note with those very sentiments. His hands have been tied to take his beliefs any further for reasons of conflict and his current judgeship.

Part of Levy's pre-parole hearing work for Sam included finding no major resistance from family members of the deceased and the alleged crime, the public at-large, and even Suffolk County with one unusual warning. In spring of 1991, a parole board gathered at Shawangunk for inmate Samuel Leonard Sommer's hearing. Right out of the gate, the same opening question posed to Sam turned out to be one of the most memorable lines in the classic motion picture *Shawshank Redemption* (Castle Rock Entertainment, Stephen King, 1994). "Do you feel you've been rehabilitated?"

"No, because I never committed a crime," Sam replied in a down-to-business tone.

After a short pause from the parole commissioner, the older white-haired gentleman followed with that aforementioned unusual warning. "We were notified by one of the detectives involved in your case that if you come within twenty feet of him he's going to blow your head off."

Gulp. A stunned throat pulsated, not so much in fear, but at the sound of such words. Sam was more taken by the commissioner's statement than anything else. Who in the hell says such a thing at a parole hearing?

Beyond that, the hearing didn't amount to much more in resemblance to a token job interview. The parole board, clearly attuned to Sam's case and Suffolk County's intimate awareness of his sentence, in a seamless manner granted him release from prison, pending a follow-up assessment.

Sam sat with a bigger inside smile than he displayed on the outside after receiving the decision. The parole board told him it could take up to a year to finalize the process, but there had been no current indication that the ruling wouldn't stand. Sam didn't think it would take that long to authenticate a ruling, yet he was in no position to question anything having ventured this far upstream.

Part of the process of validating his parole hearing dealt with undergoing a number of personal interviews with parole committee members. The parole board did this, according to Sam, to determine mental capacity and behavioral traits that could suggest revenge, negativity, and the like. The process also enlisted feedback from family members. According to Sam, among those who did not oppose his release were Ronnie and Barrie Silver.

Once the interviews were completed, an official Parole Report was generated and submitted to the jurisdiction of oversight involving his case—Suffolk County. The county would have a chance to contribute toward the report in favor or against his release on parole. In lay terms, does the parolee pose any dangers to society? Is he a flight risk? They start examining from worst-case possibilities and work backward, so to speak, toward the positives.

Suffolk County Detective Thomas Gill piled arguments against Sam's release on behalf of the homicide division.

He described Sam as 'vicious' and that he killed for profit (see Chapter 15) over a joint insurance policy shared by the deceased while in business together. He noted that the parolee was $187,000 in debt from the time that he was "arrested" to imprisonment.

Through Levy, Sam said he assumed normal business debt from investments and growing ventures, but that the majority of his balances were from paying multiple bails, legal bills, and two mortgages from moving his family to Stony Brook in 1969. He also had exhausted some funds buying a retirement home for his parents and supporting his mother the best he could for years. Levy said on behalf of Sam that the $187,000 total was outlandish—made up from a detective who harbored overwhelming hate toward him.

That claim held water for two reasons. First, what did the debt total's time parameter have to do with a motive to kill Silver? The supposed figure was factored after his death. Second, because the parole commissioner opened his mouth about a detective's threat to blow Sam's head off, it made Gill's opposition to Sam's release personal. Levy did an admirable job of guiding Sam through his parole process.

Once finished, the parole Report was given to Sam for a quick glance. His eyes danced over the following title and prefatory summation and right into the body of the content:

Samuel Leonard Sommer, Case #36471

History of the Offender

Summary of the Indictment: Samuel Leonard Sommer was indicted by the Suffolk County Grand Jury on May 24, 1968, under Indictment #609-68, which charged him with having committed the following crime:

Count 1 Murder Contrary to Penal Law Section 125.25 Subdivision 1

As part of its process of completing the report, the parole board recorded the language "Contrary to Penal Law Section 125.25 Subdivision1." *In penal law legal terms, that denoted MANSLAUGHTER* (see Illustrations). Was Sam not only wrongfully convicted but sentenced of the wrong crime—making his whole legal proceedings erroneous? Yet another shocker. Welcome to digging in like never seen before once released from prison and going after this out-of-the-blue exhibition, something that would take Sam time to see the report for what it was.

At the time Sam didn't detect the meaning of the report's penal law because he only briefly saw the document. In addition, he naturally perused the report to look for anything glaring that could have hindered his release—getting out of prison was top of mind above all else. Furthermore, he was promised a copy of the Parole Report and never received it. It was slipped into the archives and uncovered much later in life. More on that in the last chapter.

Back to the reason for Sam's big inner smile after hearing of his fate at the parole hearing, done out of sarcasm, was that he at least answered his own question about three decades' worth of many unanswered appeals. They must have been received, read, and discussed. How could they not have been when a parole commissioner makes such a bizarre disclosure? Evidently the People were pretty up to speed on Sam's diligence and perseverance for such a bomb to drop like it did.

What was Suffolk County afraid of? Sam going postal? The only thing that went postal at the moment in 1991 or otherwise was a ton of thank you cards heading out in the mail to those who stood behind him for so long while in prison. After a final year of gut turns and restless nights from hanging on the edge in hope of a parole ruling going untampered, Sam was released from prison on lifetime parole on March 3, 1992.

23.

OUTSIDE, IN

A green light for inmates to gather around some cake and soda didn't go on regularity inside New York's prisons. No guard's retirement party this time around either, which did happen once in a blue moon.

A few hugs, handshakes, and a runaway tear here and there characterized this get together at Shawangunk Correction Facility. Some guards put on a going-away splash for Sam Sommer before he set foot on free soil for the first time in twenty-one years in March of 1992. He had not expected this gesture, and it sent him off momentously to begin a parole sentence of ninety-nine years.

Outside Shawangunk a rented limousine awaited with his whole family packed like sardines to welcome a husband and a father home. Sandwiched in between a boatload of loving bodies, the stretched car only traveled a block or two. Sam got out and marched with confidence into a Department of Motor Vehicle Center to take his written driver's test all over again. He passed in one attempt. The family then cruised around for a bit before stopping for a huge meal to celebrate near New Windsor—about fifteen miles from the now big house of distant memory.

Elaine recently rented a duplex in the same city, a bourgeoning suburb of Newburgh by the Hudson River, around an hour-plus drive from New York City. Support from her parents and family members helped make the rental a loving home for the heroic homemaker—assistance in which she gladly accepted after refusing charity all those years. Sadie Rosen sprung for the limo ride, too, figuring the family deserved it after years of nomadic travels.

Elaine's sights were set on a fresh start with her husband. All the kids were on their own, some married, others sought education that once eluded them in place of finding something to eat each day, and a couple of adult children held steady jobs. They all fell on their feet because of a resilient mother.

Daughter Jane hoped to open a chain of hair salons in the greater Orange County region near her parents' residence. She worked with her dad in his latter days at Shawangunk and became an understudy of his business prowess. Now free, Sam didn't miss a beat from his days as a business champion and helped his third-oldest child get the first salon all set up with her husband, Robert.

The business bug had bitten Sam instantaneously upon release from prison, yearning for the bustle again. He was having fun releasing pent up energy by spending time with family after following regimen after regimen for three decades. The pleasure of rediscovering his wife and dabbling in business ideas ceased in their tracks at times, though.

Nightmares returned. They joined painful memories of Long Island. In the back of his mind that chunk of New York was a tempting Sunday drive away. He fought inner demons that wanted him to head in that direction. Sights of what happened to his businesses and chilling reminders of losing a partner and relative rattled his nerves. Too early yet to relive those hits on the heart.

Within a couple of months of getting settled with Elaine, Sam fielded a call from an executive at Hebrew National, longtime New York-based purveyor of kosher beef cuts, hot dogs, and related meats. Cited earlier within the context of a senior-level official from the company referring Sam and Elaine to an adoption opportunity in Greece (Chapter 3), this time the food giant offered Sam a high-level position.

Humbled, Sam declined. Although cash was tight and the job would have restored his family's finances, for some reason money wasn't driving him. He enjoyed a business challenge like Jane's venture, but that was for a family member. "Making it" again on the outside like he experienced in his younger days had not taken center stage.

Undeniably creeping back into his life as a priority was the clearing of his name from the murder charge. Wonderful distractions and pleasures of husbandry and fatherhood combated the eating away of his mind that was under attack regarding Suffolk County. If a trip to Long Island was in the cards, then he'd cleverly play his hand on a particular destination rather than visit old sites of agony. In other words, in and out.

What would a preferred location look like to Sam? Eugene Lamb.

It had been a several years since the Christmas cards stopped between the two gentlemen. Sam planned to call Lamb at his office and arrange a visit at some point; there was an interest in gaining the lawyer's pulse on the latest criminal cases with Suffolk County. In late summer of 1992, Lamb put out the suspense of Sam calling him by getting in touch with the Sommer couple in New Windsor.

Lamb congratulated Sam on his release and then invited him and Elaine to his house to share something important. Stunned and ready to grab the car keys on the spot, Sam and Elaine made the three-hour drive to Sayville in south-central Long Island to meet with Lamb the next day. It was the biggest workout yet for an aged, two-door used car that Elaine's parents were able to provide for them.

In Sayville, after a few hugs and trips together on a time machine into the old days between the couples, Lamb asked Sam to join him in a separate room away from their wives. Sam could see he was troubled. Lamb couldn't get comfortable on a chair, but he insisted that Sam take a seat by pointing at another chair with twitching hands. Trembling, Lamb tried to compose himself but couldn't, so he shot a torpedo off the tongue without a buffer while the two were still in limbo trying to relax.

"Sam, forgive me. I know who killed Silver all these years. It was wrong of me."

He turned his back on Sam and with head down gazed out the window into his backyard. Sam rose and walked next to Lamb and gently put his hand on his former attorney's shoulder. "Gene, what did you say?"

"Sorry. I tried." Head shakes created a breeze in a thoroughfare of small space between the two men.

Clenched fists and a drool of disgust over what was withheld for years overtook Sam. He turned away from Lamb out of anger. Now composed, Sam skipped over an entire spiel on "why" in place of "how." The "why" wasn't as big of a surprise... he had been dealing with that word for an eternity. In the back of his mind, Sam figured Lamb wasn't a hundred percent on the up after being with him for a number of years. Someone, somehow, someway got to him. It was the "how" that curved Sam's ears. Knowing how Lamb knew this could lead to greater discoveries about his case.

"How in the world did you know this, Gene, other than me telling you I never killed him?"

"They [those at Suffolk County] basically pressured me over time—wore me down if you will. It became a whatever-it-took-to-put-you-away mission. The detectives talked all the time about making sure [Harold] Goberman was protected and that he couldn't afford to take the hit."

"Goberman," Sam voiced. "The damn book should have been thrown at him."

"I know, Sam. Please, I'm so sorry," expressed Lamb touching Sam on the arm.

"How did they wear you down, Gene?"

"That's all I can say, Sam. Thanks for coming over. I'm so glad you are out; you and Elaine deserve to be together again."

"You have no idea what this means, do you?" posed Sam.

"I owed it to you," said Lamb.

"You owe me nothing and never have except the damn truth," Sam pointed at Lamb in the direction of the middle of his chest. "You only think you cleared your conscience by having us come all the way out here."

In an instant Sam grabbed Elaine and respectfully said goodbye to the Lamb couple. Elaine figured something was up but went quietly along with her husband's procession out the door. His quick pace retold a trek from the older days when he ran at the speed of industry on parade. This time, however, he had Elaine by his side disturbed by what he was about to tell her.

Knowing his wife would want to set the record for the zaniest U-turn in the history of Long Island and send Eugene Lamb into tomorrow, Sam waited a while to tell her what he said. Any hope of a friendship was certainly gone forever now. What hurt most from the visit and heavy load that befell his heart was that they trusted this man so much. Their youngest son was named after Lamb. Sam suspected that Lamb did what he did to clear his soul, so to speak.

Once the dust settled enough from the Lamb encounter to regain focus on his family, Sam worked for his daughter and spent time with Elaine checking out picturesque Hudson Valley together. Simple things—walks, laughs, sightseeing, etc. soaked up their time together. Sam also picked up a part-time job at a local deli.

A bid to regain Lamb's statement for use in reopening his case didn't fizzle from Sam's mind. He wanted to devise a plan on how to win him over in order to use the thunderous leak in a new fight to clear his name.

Some of the considerations to formulate a successful appeal included a fresh lawyer, seeking some sort of immunity for Lamb, and what to combine the discovery with, if anything, concerning other outstanding appellate arguments. Like a careful artist picking out his or her supplies for brush strokes of a lifetime, Sam gave this possible silver platter some time to put together.

In fall of 1993, one of Jane's employees needed help finding legal counsel for her downtrodden father. The individual lost his job and faced a lawsuit from a former employee for something he claimed he didn't do. The citizen lawman couldn't resist the chance to galvanize his legal mind and volunteer to help the man.

Sam assembled a defense plan for the man to present in a deposition before a judge. Long story, short, the man's suit against him was dismissed. He was even awarded a small settlement for which Sam refused to accept any monies. He did have to accept, however, some street stardom as a consequence from assisting the man whether he liked it or not.

Sam adamantly did not welcome or need any notoriety for his act of kindness. Word got out probably through the gracefulness and jubilee of the defendant that Sam was this new kind of lawyer who could come up with winning cases for anyone from New York to Mars.

A knock on Sam's front door about a month after the legal settlement found himself staring down the barrel of a shotgun called parole officer. Busted. Sam violated his parole by impersonating an attorney. This man's life, even out of prison, kept reaching mind-boggling peaks.

Back to prison on October 27, 1994. This time he would leave Elaine on the outside and head in with soiled memories of a gallant second attempt at joy with his wife. His new sentence saw a stretch of two years—give or take depending on good behavior.

Right across the Hudson River to the northeast, Sam started re-serving at Downstate Correctional Facility in Fishkill. A different attitude accompanied him, knowing this incarceration was on his hands. An adoring force of gravity pulled Elaine right with him; she rented a house with her mom in the neighboring community of Wappingers Falls.

Short-lived at Downstate, Sam made a return visit to Shawangunk before moving to Woodbourne Correctional Facility in late '95. His stint at Shawangunk took shape with a few challenges of bullying from those who recalled his glorious exit a few years earlier. Almost out of jealousy that he was released and then "blew it," some inmates and guards had lost respect for Sam.

Thankfully, he didn't spend much time there and Woodbourne lifted clouds of catastrophe that lingered at the same prison he at one time said goodbye to. Woodbourne, a short drive north from Shawangunk, was the oldest of the Hudson region's plentiful doses of prisons.

While Sam's second go-around of being surrounded by massive walls went on, Elaine and her family tried to reconnect with Lamb. A goal of originating a strong appeal that dovetailed Sam's previously-plotted scheme was in play. No dice. Lamb rolled out of his Sayville residence and could not be found.

Wallkill was Sam's latest rehab stop. He had been transferred four times in two years and could sense there wouldn't be much opportunity to break in friendships long on his second tour of time. His reputation and noted prison behaviors for sure disallowed him for getting too cozy at one joint for long. On December 17, 1996, Sam heard the gate slam shut behind him at Wallkill and he repeatedly reentered society. No limo, just Elaine, a rusty two-door, and a look from her that you better never do this again greeted his steps of freedom.

24.

TURNTABLES

We found in Chapter 14 game-changing proof that grand jury indictments were tossed out not once, but twice, against Sam Sommer's arrest in 1968. We were right there with the seventy-nine year-old in the basement of the Suffolk County Archives in Yaphank, New York, in 2015 when he fell over from finding those documents—covered up for decades.

Many legal experts simply concede that's the whole case. It's the meat off a bone of injustice. No one gets arrested for murder against two grand jury indictments, unless it happens in Suffolk County. And it did. The theft of Sam Sommer instigated a snowball so big over a half a century that corruption on Long Island has woefully morphed into a norm. Why should a battle still be going on to lift his name against a wrongful conviction?

Current Suffolk County District Attorney Timothy Sini has publically pledged to clean up corruption in his neck of the woods. We only can hope that he doesn't succumb to the fallen timbers of temptation along the way that all his predecessors have—beginning with the era of Sam Sommer's kidnapping.

A month after digging up documents in 2015 destined for behind the glass in a museum, the local Freedom of Information Act (FOIA) officer and principal clerk for Suffolk County informed Sam and his son-in-law that there were more cartons to sift through in Riverhead. These two good folks were more than helpful to Sam. What a change of heart on Long Island. Tables were slowly starting to turn.

Riverhead. Lots of bad memories there for Sam. By the grace of God his return visit after about forty-four years came with a breath of newborn confidence. He rode the coattails of Yaphank's regurgitation of crucial evidence heading into what could be another answer behind door number two in Riverhead's archives. Sam was mentally prepared for anything this time around.

How do you top finding out that you should have never stood trial from a piece of paper? In Sam's mind, hopefully you don't. A hefty expectation surrounded his curtain call to the archives, however. Even the smallest findings could complement the evidentiary power behind tossed-out indictments that at the very least should reopen his case.

At Riverhead's police station, yet another punch in the stomach from power-hungry ghosts of yesterday. Will the beating on this man ever stop? The Probation Report introduced in Chapter 22 touched Sam's hands during the scouring of papers. He vaguely recalled that time period and that a copy was never issued. Always one to connect what "should have been" with "what the heck," Sam called Robert DiNezza over to share his encore revelation.

"I told Robert that one word amid the whole report tells the story," Sam recollected. "Contrary." Here is a recap of the parole report's title in which that word carried a ball of injustice over the goal line once again in the case of Samuel Leonard Sommer:

> Count 1 Murder Contrary to Penal Law
> Section 125.25 Subdivision 1

See, when all else failed for Sam by way of Lamb, exhaustive, unanswered appeals, and sore necks from influential people looking the other way over a lifetime, his back pocket held an ace: his wisdom. The word *contrary* above didn't belong there. Besides, the very way it is written denotes the legal interpretative of manslaughter.

It takes one serious string of newfound evidence to surface for fifty years to claim this is the nation's longest and most intriguing fight for justice. Ever. Period. For this many cover ups to be disrobed for this long makes a reasonable person wonder when the injustice will stop. Even marathons have endings.

***

Sam and Elaine converged on opening a deli in New Windsor while he wrapped up his sequel under lock and key. Near the end of Sam serving time at Wallkill, Elaine moved back to New Windsor and rented an apartment. She started working for Jane and saving as much money as she could. The move was the result of losing her mother to heart problems; Sadie had brightened Elaine's world for a few memorable years while the two got a chance to live together.

With Sam out of prison, in 1997 the Sommer couple leased space in a strip mall in New Windsor and opened Family Subs, a small delicatessen that offered sandwiches' and wraps. For a few years they made enough cash flow to live on and pay the lease, but a small business was on the verge of defaulting. The couple had very little collateral to back the loan, which basically provided restaurant furniture and start-up cash for supplies. In 2001, the store closed.

Their brief run at small business ownership collapsed short of a far cry from the old days. Wearing a deli apron with gray hair did benefit the couple, though, in an unseen way. The store may have shut down, but when the doors were open the restaurant functioned as a bridge. Family Subs linked Sam from getting by to getting to an age where he could begin collecting Social Security.

Elaine remained working for Jane and Sam stayed out of trouble by not offering any more legal services to anyone. He got to know his kids and now grandchildren more closely due to that shorter interval out of prison the first time.

The couple then relocated to nearby Liberty to explore a couple of other business opportunities and gain a fresh start after the Family Subs attempt. Those ventures didn't pan out in Liberty. The empty exploration left Sam a bit restless, so at the age of seventy, he decided to put the boxing gloves back on again to clear his name. In late 2006, Sam and Elaine ventured back to New Windsor into a small one-bedroom apartment in which Sam calls home even today.

Personalizing and allocating time with family over the past decade allowed Sam to apprehend how much pain and suffering his kids sustained. Hearing their accounts (in line with Elaine, nothing about homelessness) of stripped childhoods and next-to-no education fired up the now-elder Sommer to get back in the ring with gloves laced. Guilt besieged him. The remedy to rid the guilt was turning the tables on Suffolk County if it was the last thing he ever did.

Robert Levy, a federal magistrate judge at the time of Sam's transformation into a boxer and a judgeship he still holds today, looked into the missing Autopsy Report—one that was ordered by a judge a lifetime ago. Levy tutored Sam in the process of filing a federal lawsuit about the Autopsy Report.

In doing so, a federal judge, John Gleeson, asked Suffolk County officials to hand over the Autopsy Report in question to Mr. Sommer. Gleeson did not order the County to do so perceivably because of the amount of time that surpassed, but in his dissent he indicated that "I cannot fathom the county's persistent failure to provide Mr. Sommer a copy."

In other words, the county should put the issue to bed once and for all and pay whatever consequences it needs to.

Nothing happened—broken record. Sam called it the final nail in the coffin. He knew that Suffolk County was more powerful than the White House. Let's repeat what the heck just transpired...

A federal judge couldn't even get to the bottom of injustice—thousands of days' worth of contempt of court.

Sam lost his wind. Gluing old reports from a medical examiner, a coroner, and a district attorney's office together so that they lawfully tell the same story didn't look promising. Was that too much to ask for in one's life? Did Mr. Silver die from multiple injuries? Did he die from a hit-and-run? Was he killed from being hit over the head with a pipe? Too many theories, too much dishonesty from Suffolk County. If anything, doesn't the family of the deceased have a right to know?

Back in the '90s after helping Sam during his parole hearing preparations, Levy submitted a personal affidavit (see Illustrations) to Suffolk County basically stating that Mr. Sommer didn't received a fair trial and that his conviction was tainted. He continued to rebuke the county for missing documents and court files, in addition asserting serious misconduct by police.

Sam got into doing stuff with his wife, welcoming great-grandchildren into the mix, and celebrating family gatherings. The joys of these simple occasions pledged to rid his illnesses of Suffolk County's modus operandi. The objective commendably took a high road like a man of his character would do; yet, Suffolk County couldn't shake its own shadows.

Maybe if the county had undergone a campaign of public forgiveness and mercy, Sam would have thought of letting go. Not the case. A steady diet of Long Island's ongoing troubles wouldn't subside. Seeing residents of that part of New York stomach such deceit pushed Sam over the edge.

In the summer of 2015, Sam awoke to an epiphany drenched in sweat. His shirt weighed from the saltiness of perspiration—a different kind of sweat that he was used to from waking to nightmares that have never left him. Those were cold sweats. This one saturated his razor-thin body in warmth.

"A book." Those were the first worlds out of his mouth while he sat up in bed. "My story for the betterment of others, so they don't have to go through what I did—that's it. Plus, Suffolk County can't stop a book. Maybe that will be the collateral to open some eyes."

He thought of Eugene Lamb. An old friend said he passed away in the summer of 2012. Lamb moved to Laurel, New York, on the Island's northern easterly tip. He lived under an unpublished address. Oh, what could have been with Lamb's push for justice in these dwindling years. It's also worth mentioning that Harold Goberman passed away in 2015. Sam was unaware of that until just a couple of years ago. Another would have/could have if only rungs on the ladder of lawfulness led to one another in unison.

So a walk around the block began in telling the world about the nation's longest-running fight for exoneration. A few months after starting the book project, Sam and Robert DiNezza made those two unprecedented and unforgotten trips to the Suffolk County archives. After grabbing hold of one of the biggest cover ups to our justice system in proof of tossed out grand jury indictments, Sam proceeded to bring the rip off of humanity to the attention of a federal judge.

> AUTHORS' NOTE: We ascertained to never assume cases of injustice won't spill dark surprises at any time. In putting the finishing touches on this remarkable journey, we noticed that on one of

the copies of the Supplementary Report the letter "a" was not crossed off in the word "Indicated." In other copies of the same report and in a copy of a Disposition Report signed by Gill as well, the letter "a" in the same word was crossed out (see Illustrations). It made us wonder how extensive the manipulation of court documents ran (end of NOTE).

On July 5, 2017, Elaine Sommer passed away suddenly at the age of seventy-nine right after she led her husband through a serious surgery for his age to remove a blood clot in his leg. Devastated to lose his rock, the book admittedly to some family members was the only thing that kept Sam going. He would have rather been with her in a better place, but she wanted him to see the project through for sake of justice and Jewish people.

Two significant developments and another health concern entered the story in 2018. First, a couple of individuals sitting on information about Sam's innocence were found to be alive. Retired Suffolk County Detective Thomas Gill, through his son, believed justice was served and wished Sam well. His son has been notified regularly about the project on behalf of his father, and detective Gill was offered a voice in the story on numerous documented occasions. He declined.

E. Thomas Boyle, the former private practicing attorney-turned Suffolk County Attorney who went out of his way to visit Sam in prison to assist in overturning his conviction, was reached by phone in late August. He said, "I don't want to comment on this matter," click. He was called back and breathed heavily on the other end of the receiver for over a minute apparently afraid to say anything. Both Boyle and Gill live off of Suffolk County pensions. Sam lives off of the truth. Everyone we've come across during this work has always been conditioned to look the other way when the truth stood before them.

Second, God answered another prayer. On an attempted call to a law library in New York City, we misdialed and reached the New York City Bar Justice Center. Upon apologizing and then ready to hang up the phone, a beam of light stopped us. Bar as in legal bar? Why not? We took the opportunity to explain Mr. Sommer's situation and the City Bar Justice Center jumped on the case without hesitation and initiated the process. Current assistance from the Federal Pro Se Legal Assistance Project has begun. The tables are turning.

In fall of 2018, Sam underwent successful hip surgery with Elaine's spirit by his side. He also survived a 911 call right after returning home from rehab dealing with a blood clot. His son, Robert, and his wife, Betty, who were visiting from Florida, were there to see him back on his feet, along with daughters Jane and Marlene. This story was meant to be told.

Once railroaded and then derailed, Sam's refurbished train is full of a new army of supporters. On track again, it has left the station heading in a direction toward justice, not revenge, simple justice. Stay tuned.

Take it away Sam... *Why must I tell my story? That is a question I've asked myself time and time again since leaving prison. Each time the same answer comes back to me.*

Over the years I have received unsolicited messages from family members, friends, and long-time supporters whom I've never met, etc. What is clear is that nothing has changed in Suffolk County with its brand of justice. Only the faces have changed.

I have concluded that nothing will ever change the court system, which encourages the other cheek to preserve corruption in places like Suffolk County. Politics and money are corrupting forces within our system of selecting judges, especially trial judges, who are not in favor of reforms and have no regard for judicial values.

The investigating detectives have woven an illusionary web in which justice became entangled. They did so in order to ensure that trial objectives and common concerns clouded a sense of right and wrong.

Justice demands more from those who are appointed to uphold and enforce the law.

ACKNOWLEDGEMENTS

1.— Chapter 2

   Weichselbaum, Simone (2012-06-26). "Nearly one in four Brooklyn residents are Jews, new study finds." *NY Daily News*. Retrieved 2015-09-23.

2.— Chapter 2

   U.S. Bureau of Labor Statistics

3.— Chapter 3

   Politakis, George. *"The Post-War Reconstruction of Greece: A history of economic stabilization and development."* Palgrave, McMillan, 1944-1952, 2018.

4.— Chapter 3

   Goldstein, Joseph & Rashbaum, William. "Extortion Charges for 29 Tied to Trash-hauling Industry." *New York Times*, January 16, 2013. Extortion Charges for 29 Tied to Trash-Hauling Industry. Will

5.— Chapter 4

   Rehfeld, Barry. "The Crass Menagerie: Phony Alligators, Bogus Gremlins, and Other Fakes." *New York Magazine*, October 15, 1984. .

6.— Chapter 4

    Fritsch, Jane. "G.M. Official Testified in Suspect's Extortion Trial." *New York Times,* April 19, 1992. .

7.— Chapter 5

    Shiva.com and the Sommer family, along with other Jewish descendants.

8.— Chapter 7

    Smith, Andrew. "Thomas Stark, influential Suffolk judge, dies." *Newsday,* April 30, 2014.

9.— Chapter 7

    USLegal.com

10.— Chapter 14

    "Suffolk DA Spota Not Offended FBI is Handling Corruption Investigation." *WLNY CBS,* August 13, 2014.

11.— Chapter 16

    Pollock, Joycelyn M. "The Philosophy and History of Prisons, The Rationale for Imprisonment." *Texas State University–San Marcos*, Sept. 28, 2005 (11).

12.— Chapter 18

    Robbins, Tom; Schwirtz, Michael; Winerip, Michael. "Revisiting Attica Shows How New York State Failed to Fulfill Promises." *New York Times & The Marshall Project,* August 25, 2016.

13.— Chapter 18

    Robbins, Tom; Schwirtz, Michael; Winerip, Michael. "Revisiting Attica Shows How New York State Failed to Fulfill Promises." *New York Times & The Marshall Project,* August 25, 2016.

14.— Chapter 20

> Steel, Lewis M. "Understanding the Legacy of the Attica Prison Uprising: Did the terrible events at Attica lead to a more enlightened prison and penal system? No. The repression, instead, became worse." *The Nation,* September 26, 2016.

15.—Chapter 21

> *Ballotpedia*

16.—Chapter 22

> *Prison Visiting Project, Correctional Association of New York*, July 2009

17.— Chapter 22

> Davis, Peter L. *Newsday*, January 12, 2008.

18.— Chapter 22

> *http://longisland.news12.com/story/34744089/bellone-spota-go-head-to-head-with-corruption-claims-in-suffolk* - (No date provided. Suffolk County DA Spota was asked to resign in 2016. He was arrested on October 25, 2017.)

19.— Chapter 22

> Lopez, Tania. *Newsday*, May 26, 2016.

20.— Chapter 22

> Goldstein, Joseph. *New York Times,* June 2, 2016.

21.— Chapter 22

> Goldstein, Joseph. *New York Times*, February 8, 2016.

22.— Chapter 22

> Hayden, Michael Edison. *Vice*, March 14, 2016.

23.— Chapter 22

    Saul, Joseph. *Newsweek*, January 4, 2016.

24.— Chapter 22

    Grossman, Karl. *Shelter Island Reporter*, June 19, 2016.

25.—Chapter 22

    Lane, Charles. "All Things Considered." *NPR.org*, February 26, 2016.

26.—Chapter 22

    Chung, Jen. *New York Public Radio (Gothamist)*, February 26, 2016.

27.—Chapter 22

    Bolger, Timothy; Twarowski, Christopher. *Long Island Press,* December 22, 2016.

ILLUSTRATIONS AND DOCUMENTS

On the right: This is a copy of the haunting document Mr. Sommer discovered at the age of seventy-nine in the Suffolk County Police Archives, forty-four years after going to prison. The covered-up Supplementary Report completed by a detective who kidnapped him shows that Mr. Sommer should have never stood trial due to the dismissal of grand jury indictments for his arrest. It was conveniently submitted to a carton headed for basement darkness a month after Mr. Sommer went to prison.

after Reinterlungs Ex B & C

POLICE DEPARTMENT
COUNTY OF SUFFOLK
Supplementary Report

53188	6-22-71		214			5-17-68
		2nd	211	28-108		

Murder - 1st Degree
Inv. of Death - Poss. Hit & Run - Ped.   Bennington St. & Rutland La., Melville
IRVING SILVER   79-25 150th Street, Kew Garden Hills,

The undersigned received official notification of the cause of death from the Office of the Medical Examiner, listing same as:

Multiple and Extensive Injuries

Homicide

Negative for ethanol.

M. E. #68-1095

The undersigned also received Court Disposition Report from the Office of the District Attorney, Riverhead, N. Y., listing same as:

Defendant - SAMUEL LEONARD SOMMER

Murder - Art. 125 Sec. 125 Sub. 25

5-23-68 - arraignment

5-24-68 - adj.

5-27-68 - Dismissed Indicated by Grand Jury #609-68

Murder 125.25 - Dismissed Indicated by Grand Jury

Hon. Frank P. DeLuca, 1st Dist. Commack

Presented 5-23-68 Handup 5-24-68

Murder #609-68 DeNovo

5-24-68 Hon. Stark - Not Guilty

11-17-70 and 12-16-70 Hon. Lundberg - Guilty

3-18-71 Hon. Lundberg - Deft. sent. to indefinite term of life imprisonment with minimum of 20 years - deft. remanded.

In view of the above facts and there being no further action to be taken at this time, it is requested by the undersigned that this case be CLOSED.

CERTIFIED
Police Department
County of Suffolk, N.Y.

Det. Thomas Gill #315

Sam Sommer with three of his daughters in 2017 (from left): Jane, Karen, and Marlene

Right: This Police Department, County of Suffolk Court Disposition Report (not deposition) completed on the day Mr. Sommer was kidnapped in 1968 shows a crossed off letter "a" after the word Dismissed. This negates and contradicts a 2017 argument by the Suffolk County DA about a typo (referring to the Supplementary Report that did not contain the crossed off letter).

CERTIFIED
CENTRAL RECORDS SECTION
SUFFOLK COUNTY POLICE DEPARTMENT

68-83188
May 22, 1968
A 3620
214 P.R. 1968

Sumner Samuel Leonard   4 Zinnia Court, Commack, N.Y.
6-7-36

Murder Art. 125 Sec. 125 Sub. 25

May 23, 1968   Frank F. DeLuca
Det. Thomas Gill #335   214

Eugene Lamb - Garde City, N.Y.

CK-CR-2614-68

5/23/68 - arraignment
5/24/68 - adj.
5/27/68 - Dismissed Indicted by Grand Jury. #609-68

Murder 125.25

Dismissed Indicted by Grand Jury

Hon. Frank P. DeLuca, 1st. Dist. Commack   Thomas P. Gill Det-335
Presented 5-23-68 Handup 5-24-68

Murder #609-68 De Novo

5-24-68 Hon. Stark - Not Guilty.

11-17-70 and 12-16-70 Hon. Lundberg - Guilty.

3-18-71 Hon. Lundberg - Deft. sent. to indefinite term of life imprisonment with minimum of 20 years - deft. remanded.
SING - SING

609-68   68-83188

Right: A copy of a check from Suffolk County in 1979 sent to Mr. Sommer in prison further proves his innocence. His arrest was both unlawful and criminal in nature. Seeking another appeal with the check as leverage, an appellate court claimed the money was for damages, not a settlement. Ironically, Mr. Sommer's 1969 victorious Huntley Hearing was based on the same admission, meaning his unlawful arrest superseded any recognition of damages. Further appeals were repeatedly delayed or ignored before his release in 1991.

"EXHIBIT B"

ROYAL-GLOBE INSURANCE COMPANIES

Check No. 31918876
Date: 12/27/79
Amount: $5,000.00
To the order of: Samuel Leonard Sommer
County of Suffolk, Holbrook, N.Y.
Pay: Five Thousand and 00/100 Dollars

In payment of: Damages resulting from accident occurring on or about 1/22/68 as per stipulation 73-C-1346 FSC

All parties named as payees must endorse exactly as drawn. When endorsed by any other person or agent of or for payee proper evidence of authority must accompany draft. Corporation endorsements other than "For Deposit" must be by authorized officer thereof.

Endorsement of this draft by payee or payees is acknowledgment of full settlement, satisfaction, compromise and discharge of claims and demands of every nature and kind for loss, damage, injury or expense as set forth on the face of this draft.

For Workmen's Compensation and Accident & Health only: When properly endorsed, this draft constitutes payment for as set forth on the face of this draft.

Samuel Leonard Sommer

If endorsed by mark, disinterested witness sign below

_____ Witness

_____ Address of witness

Right: This undated document allegedly submitted at some point during or after Mr. Sommer's 1969 Huntley Hearing (although it was not found in the trial transcripts) was prepared by then Suffolk County DA George Aspland. It clearly raises more than enough reasonable doubt that Mr. Sommer did not murder Irving Silver. The accusations against Mr. Sommer were based on an alleged oral admission that followed his kidnapping and beating.

COUNTY COURT : STATE OF NEW YORK
COUNTY OF SUFFOLK
------------------------------------x

THE PEOPLE OF THE STATE OF NEW YORK :

        -against- :   Statement Pursuant
                                      Code of Criminal
SAMUEL L. SOMMER, :   Procedure § 518-

               Defendant. :

------------------------------------x

    The deprivation of the use as evidence of the confession or admission ordered to be suppressed herein has rendered the sum of the proof available to the People with respect to the trial of Indictment Number 609-68, charging defendant with the Crime of Murder so weak in its entirety that any reasonable possibility of prosecuting this charge to conviction has been effectively destroyed.

                                              _____
                                              GEORGE J. ASPLAND
                                              District Attorney
                                              Suffolk County

Right: Note the reference from a judge about an unexplained bruise (in reference to Mr. Sommer) during an interview conducted by Mr. Sommer's son-in-law with a former Suffolk County Assistant DA in 1985. The supposed tampering of Mr. Sommer's mug shot to this day serves as both a contentious and unresolved argument by the defense due to the defendant's physical appearance on the night of his "arrest."

18

trial and appear to show that Sam's claim that he was striped naked and beaten was pure fabrication. We had the mugshot examined by an expert. The expert -- I have got three different paragraphs here, of reasons where the experts says the mugshot was indeed tampered with. If you want to me go through what he says, I have it in front of me.

A   Stop right there. If, in fact, you have got reliable experts that testified the mugshots introduced in evidence were tampered with, that is about as good a grounds for a new trial or new hearing as you are going to get.

Q   You never knew anything about the mugshot?

A   All I remember -- at the moment all I remember about it is the fact we went -- on the first appeal apparently there was a bruise -- there was a bruise on him that could not be explained away. The judge was Lipsitz, saying throughout the confession, saying -- there was an unexplained bruise. Part of it comes back to me. This is one of -- hell, I forgot how many appeals I've handled. I don't completely

Right and Next: An affirmation document authored on August 5, 2006, from United State Magistrate Judge, Eastern District of New York, Robert Levy submits the absence of an Autopsy Report while searching for critical records. Such legal action by the Honorable Levy reveals Mr. Sommer's case would "demonstrate the flaws in the police investigation and serious oversights by trial counsel which, in my view, tainted the trial and his conviction (1)."

UNITED STATES DISTRICT COURT
EASTERN DISTRICT OF NEW YORK
---X
SAMUEL SOMMER,

              Plaintiff

-against-

SUFFOLK COUNTY DEPARTMENT OF
HEALTH SERVICES, et al.,

              Defendant.
---X

AFFIRMATION

01 CV 2201 (ADS)

Robert M. Levy affirms as follows:

1. I am a United States Magistrate Judge in the Eastern District of New York. I make this Affirmation in my individual capacity, at the request of Samuel Sommer, the plaintiff in this action. In so doing, I express no views on the merits of this litigation and have not read the pleadings. I am writing solely because of my responsibility to my former client, Mr. Sommer, whom I represented for several years prior to becoming a judge, in a proceeding pursuant to New York State Criminal Procedure Law 440.20 to set aside his criminal conviction.

2. In the course of my representation of Mr. Sommer, I made Freedom of Information Law requests and attempted to search all available records in an attempt to locate critical documents that I believed would demonstrate the flaws in the police investigation and serious oversights by trial counsel which, in my view, tainted the trial and his conviction.

3. As part of my search for records, I visited the record room at Suffolk County Criminal Court, where the files relating to Mr. Sommer's trial and sentencing were kept. I requested the complete record and personally reviewed every docket entry and the entire contents of the file that was provided to me. To the best of my recollection, the autopsy report

performed on the victim was not in the court file.

4. I also reviewed all the records submitted to the appellate courts prior to the filing of the CPL 440.20 petition. Again, to the best of my recollection, the autopsy report was not among them.

I declare under penalty of perjury that the foregoing is true and correct.

Executed on the 5th day of August, 2006 in Brooklyn, New York.

_____
Robert M. Levy

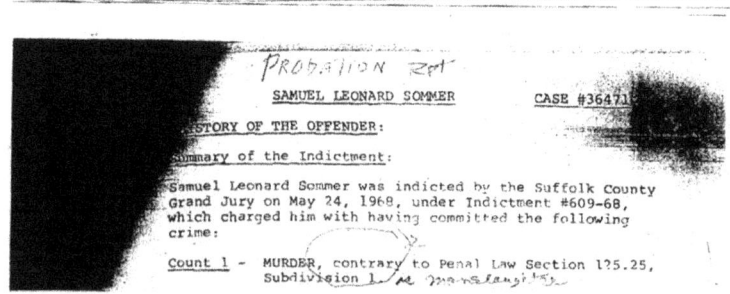

Above: Another unearthed document found by a seventy-nine-year-old Sam Sommer thanks, finally, to the Freedom of Information Act in 2015. This dusty, partial piece of paper somehow came into play during Mr. Sommer's parole hearing in 1991. "Murder, contrary…." not only shows this May 24, 1968, indictment was made up after his kidnapping and beating, but it nullifies his murder conviction all together. Note the handwritten reference to manslaughter.

Right: Samuel Sommer's mugshot on the night of his 1968 "arrest."

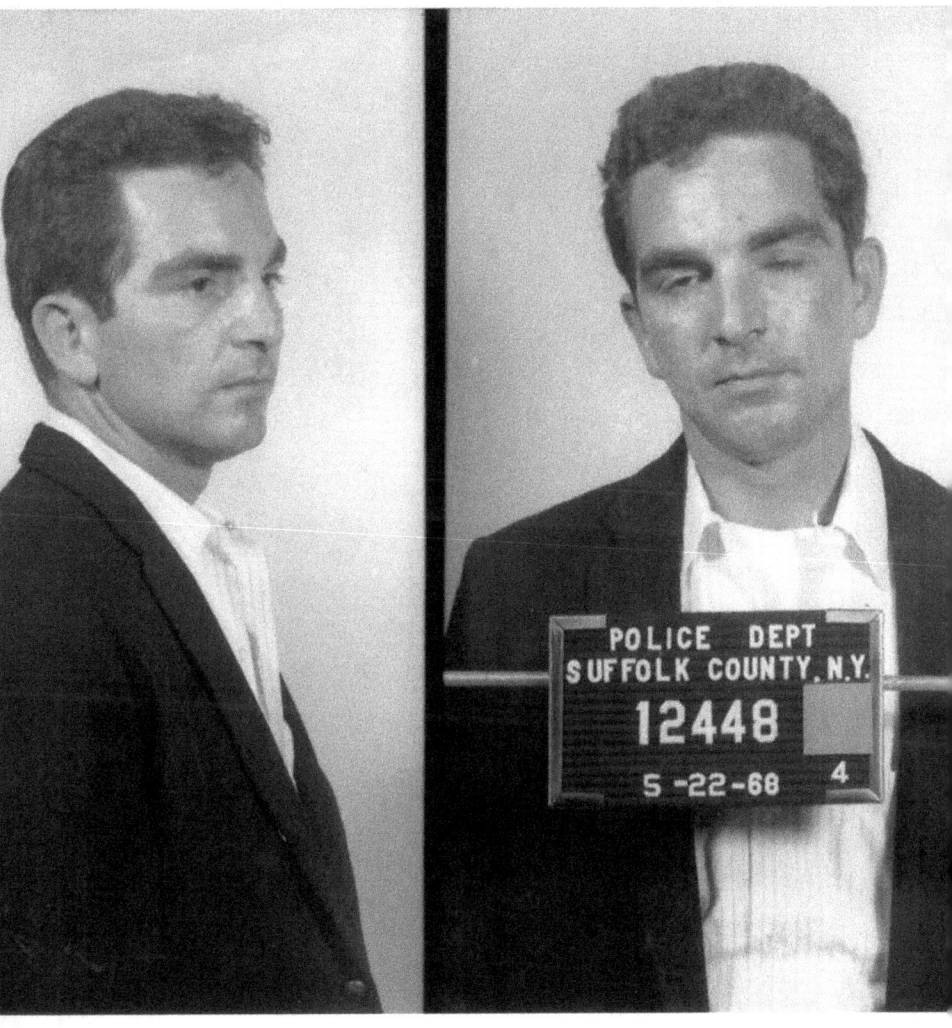

For More News About Samuel L. Sommer and Christopher Jossart, Signup For Our Newsletter:

http://wbp.bz/newsletter

Word-of-mouth is critical to an author's long-term success. If you appreciated this book please leave a review on the Amazon sales page:

http://wbp.bz/railroadeda

AVAILABLE FROM JOHN FERAK AND WILDBLUE PRESS!

WRECKING CREW by JOHN FERAK

"Whatever you thought you believed about this infamous case, get ready to change your mind or be more convinced than ever. ... Fascinating." —**New York Times bestselling author Steve Jackson**

In 2016-17, while working for the USA TODAY NETWORK's Wisconsin Investigative Team, author John Ferak wrote dozens of articles examining the murder case again Steven Avery, who had already beat one wrongful conviction only to be charged with the murder of Teresa

Halbach in 2005. The case became the wildly successful Netflix "Making A Murderer" documentary.

In WRECKING CREW: Demolishing The Case Against Steven Avery, Ferak lays out in exacting detail the post-conviction strategy of Kathleen Zellner, the high-profile, high-octane lawyer, to free Avery. To write this book, Zellner, perhaps America's most successful wrongful conviction attorney, gave Ferak unique access to the exhaustive pro bono efforts she and her small suburban Chicago law firm dedicated for a man she believes to be a victim of an unscrupulous justice system in Manitowoc County.

http://wbp.bz/wca

AVAILABLE FROM ALAN R. WARREN AND WILDBLUE PRESS!

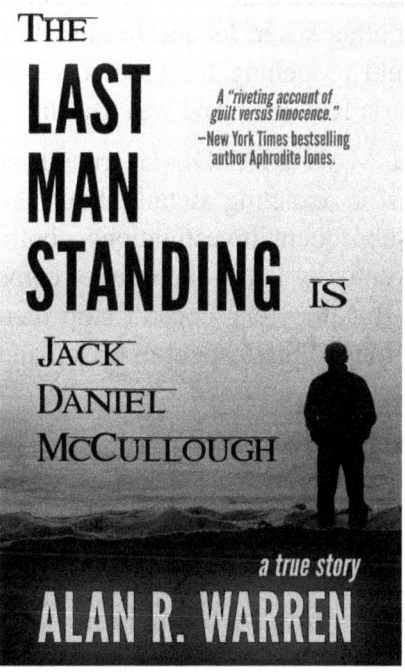

THE LAST MAN STANDING by ALAN R. WARREN

It was a shattering death bed confession by a heartbroken mother. But would it solve the oldest cold case murder case in American jurisprudence?

In January 1994, Eileen Tessier told Jack McCullough's half-sister Janet Tessier that he, her son, kidnapped 7-year-old Maria Ridulph from their neighborhood in Sycamore, Illinois and killed her in December 1957. It was a case that tore the child's family apart, as well as dividing and terrifying the town as the days, then the months, and finally the years passed with no arrest.

In 2008 the Illinois State police reopened the case against Jack after receiving an email from Janet Tessier about their mother's deathbed confession. After the Illinois State police interviewed Janet and learned that Jack had also been accused of raping their other sister, Jeanne Tessier, they reopened the case. But would reopening the case solve the question of who killed Maria Ridulph? And was McCullough the killer?

In THE LAST MAN STANDING, true crime author Alan Warren writes in exacting detail about the kidnapping, murder and subsequent investigations—both in 1957 and 2008—that eventually led to the murder conviction of Jack McCullough. But the story doesn't stop there as it delves into the years McCullough spent in prison and the efforts to have his conviction overturned.

Was McCullough the brutal killer of a little girl? Or was he the last man standing when the justice system decided he needed to pay for the crime? You decide.

http://wbp.bz/lmsa

AVAILABLE FROM HENRY J. CORDES AND WILDBLUE PRESS!

PATHOLOGICAL by HENRY J. CORDES and TODD COOPER

A Brutal Serial Killer Was Stalking Omaha. But Who Could Kill With Such Precision?

Detective Derek Mois wasn't sure what he was dealing with when in March 2008 he walked into a home in an affluent Omaha neighborhood and was confronted with the bodies of an 11-year-old boy and the housekeeper. Both had been murdered with kitchen knives plunged into their throats. Who would do something so vile, and why? Lacking answers, Mois and other detectives working the case were stumped. Five years later, a strikingly similar crime occurred in which two more victims were brutally murdered with knives expertly thrust into their jugular veins. The modus operandi of the murders pointed Mois and a special task force in the direction of looking for a serial killer. But no one could have anticipated that path would lead to the Department of Pathology at Creighton University.

In PATHOLOGICAL: The Murderous Rage Of Dr. Anthony Garcia, authors Henry J. Cordes and Todd Cooper, who covered the story for the Omaha World-Herald, recount the dramatic tale of deep-seated revenge, determined detectives, and the sensational trial of the doctor-turned-serial killer.

http://wbp.bz/pathologicala

See even more at:
http://wbp.bz/tc

More True Crime You'll Love From WildBlue Press

A MURDER IN MY HOMETOWN by Rebecca Morris

Nearly 50 years after the murder of seventeen year old Dick Kitchel, Rebecca Morris returned to her hometown to write about how the murder changed a town, a school, and the lives of his friends.

wbp.bz/hometowna

THE BEAST I LOVED by Robert Davidson

Robert Davidson again demonstrates that he is a master of psychological horror in this riveting and hypnotic story ... I was so enthralled that I finished the book in a single sitting."—James Byron Huggins, International Bestselling Author of The Reckoning

wbp.bz/tbila

BULLIED TO DEATH by Judith A. Yates

On September 5, 2015, in a public park in LaVergne, Tennessee, fourteen-year-old Sherokee Harriman drove a kitchen knife into her stomach as other teens watched in horror. Despite attempts to save her, the girl died, and the coroner ruled it a "suicide." But was it? Or was it a crime perpetuated by other teens who had bullied her?

wbp.bz/btda

SUMMARY EXECUTION by Michael Withey

"An incredible true story that reads like an international crime thriller peopled with assassins, political activists, shady FBI informants, murdered witnesses, a tenacious attorney, and a murderous foreign dictator."—Steve Jackson, New York Times bestselling author of NO STONE UNTURNED

wbp.bz/sea